The Hollywood Curriculum

Studies in Criticality

Shirley R. Steinberg
General Editor

Vol. 495

The Counterpoints series is part of the Peter Lang Education list.
Every volume is peer reviewed and meets
the highest quality standards for content and production.

PETER LANG
New York • Bern • Frankfurt • Berlin
Brussels • Vienna • Oxford • Warsaw

Mary M. Dalton

The Hollywood Curriculum

Teachers in the Movies

THIRD REVISED EDITION

PETER LANG
New York • Bern • Frankfurt • Berlin
Brussels • Vienna • Oxford • Warsaw

Library of Congress Cataloging-in-Publication Data

Names: Dalton, Mary M., author.
Title: The Hollywood curriculum: teachers in the movies / Mary M. Dalton.
Description: Third revised edition. | New York: Peter Lang, 2017.
Series: Counterpoints: studies in criticality; Vol. 495 | ISSN 1058-1634
Includes bibliographical references and index.
Identifiers: LCCN 2016050898 | ISBN 978-1-4331-3085-4 (paperback: alk. paper)
ISBN 978-1-4331-3885-0 (ebook pdf) | ISBN 978-1-4331-3887-4 (epub)
ISBN 978-1-4331-3886-7 (mobi)
Subjects: LCSH: Teachers in motion pictures. | Education in motion pictures.
Classification: LCC PN1995.9.T4 D36 2017 | DDC 791.43/652372—dc23
DOI 10.3726/978-1-4331-3885-0
LC record available at https://lccn.loc.gov/2016050898

Bibliographic information published by **Die Deutsche Nationalbibliothek**.
Die Deutsche Nationalbibliothek lists this publication in the "Deutsche
Nationalbibliografie"; detailed bibliographic data are available
on the Internet at http://dnb.d-nb.de/.

The paper in this book meets the guidelines for permanence and durability
of the Committee on Production Guidelines for Book Longevity
of the Council of Library Resources.

© 2017 Peter Lang Publishing, Inc., New York
29 Broadway, 18th floor, New York, NY 10006
www.peterlang.com

Printed in the United States of America

For my students and my teachers, especially the two who launched me on this course of inquiry, Kathleen Casey and Svi Shapiro.

CONTENTS

PREFACE TO THE FOURTH EDITION

Looking at popular representations of teachers in the movies and linking the depictions to curriculum theory and critical theory was a natural project for me. With an academic background in media studies and a professional background in television and film before I started my doctoral program in cultural studies and education, this research provided a way for me to integrate my love of media, politics, and education. Fortunately, my dissertation committee at the University of North Carolina at Greensboro agreed and provided valuable guidance for the project that ultimately became the first edition of this book over 20 years ago and the foundation for other articles, chapters, lectures, and books. In addition to this one, I co-authored a book with Laura R. Linder in 2008, *Teacher TV: Sixty Years of Teachers on Television*, and Laura and I co-edited a new anthology this year, *Screen Lessons: What We Have Learned from Teachers on Television and in the Movies*.

After three editions (1995, 2007, and 2010) it is time to make some additions and some adjustments to *The Hollywood Curriculum: Teachers in the Movies*, and I find in the process that there are both surprises and disappointments in the current representation of educators in popular culture. First, while I'm pleased by some of the strong revisionist films (like *Half Nelson*, 2006, and *Detachment*, 2011) and complex and compelling television series (like the fourth season of *The Wire*, 2006, and, for its depiction of an administrator, the fourth season of *Friday Night Lights*, 2009–10) that have provided a richer range of educator characters, I'm disappointed that the depiction of the "good" teacher has largely been pushed to the wayside by representations of educators that seem influenced by 15 years of education policy and public discourse that undermine public schools and deprofessionalize teaching.

I don't think No Child Left Behind was a "cultural moment" in the sense that all representations before 2001 were in the mold of the idealized teacher and everything after was negative, but there has been a broad shift in the volume and degree of representation over this period favoring negative representations of educators. There were complex portrayals before 2001 (the movie *Election* was 1999, for example) and heroic depictions after (*Freedom Writers* was released in 2007), but both negative portrayals and complex portrayals have become more common over the last 15 years, and the tropes of incompetence (*Bad Teacher*, 2011), disengagement (*Art School Confidential*, 2006), and even corruption (*Cheaters*, 2000) have become more and more dominant. The situation is even worse on television.[1]

I think about the relationship between media and culture as circular (and intertextual) – media affects culture, and culture affects media. It is difficult to find a linear cause and effect, but broad patterns exist, and there were depictions of "bad" teachers before recent conservative policies gained traction and started undermining public education (which has long faced funding inequalities at local levels because of the mechanism linking budgets to property taxes, creating a sliding scale where rich areas get more money than poorer areas). There are still depictions of "good" teachers in the classical mode I label The Hollywood Model, which is found in both television and the movies, but not so many as before. Seeing the dizzying array of selfish, crass, and incompetent educators – which is the dominant depiction on recent television series such as TV Land's *Teachers* (2016–), TruTV's *Those Who Can't* (2016–), and HBO's *Vice Principals* (2016–) – makes me sad, angry, and concerned about how public perceptions of the field will be influenced if there are not some powerful counter-narratives produced soon and in sufficient numbers.

I am almost astonished by the work that has been published on the depiction of teachers in popular culture and, particularly, in movies over the last two decades. There have been books, anthologies, articles, and many conference papers devoted specifically to this area of inquiry. Perhaps this should not be so surprising. After all, media and schooling are both ubiquitous. Some of the most interesting work published in recent years goes beyond textual analysis of the films and recounts how professors use popular culture texts, especially motion pictures, to prepare pre-service teachers for the classroom. In the article "Culture and Pedagogy in Teacher Education," Ronald Soetaert, Andre Mottart, and Ive Verdoodt discuss exercises they use in a teacher education program to help reveal "literacy myths" in popular texts. Others, including Dierdre Glenn Paul and James Trier, have written about their choices to use popular teacher films in teacher education programs for similar reasons, and the range of texts considered and exercises Trier has developed and written about is robust. Others uncover truths about teachers in the movies related to particular disciplines, such as Jacqueline Bach's work on the cinematic approaches to teaching Shakespeare. And, still others provide a curriculum for teachers who want to integrate films into their classrooms. One of the better of these resources is *Celluloid Blackboard: Teaching History with Film*, edited by Alan S. Marcus, but there are a number of other guides and filmographies available to classroom teachers who want to integrate film into the curriculum.

There are also scholars who take a discipline-specific look at education and popular culture, such as sociologist Robert C. Bulman's *Hollywood Goes to High School: Cinema, Schools, and American Culture*, which provides perspective on high schools according to the social class of the students. Some of the more recent books take a broader survey to look at movies, television, and music, such as *Education in Popular Culture: Telling Tales on Teachers and Learners*, by Roy Fisher, Ann Harris, and Christine Jarvis, *Dial M for Mentor: Reflections on Mentoring in Film, Television and Literature* by Jonathan Gravells and Susan Wallace, and *How "The Teacher" is Presented in Literature, History, Religion, and the Arts*, edited by Raymond McCluskey and Stephen J. McKinney. The discussions in these works are vigorous and useful, and I have not scratched the surface but, instead, have tried to provide a broad sweep of some of the strands of discourse in the conversation about education and the movies. One brand new book makes an especially important contribution to the literature. Jacqueline Bach's much-needed examination of non-fiction media, *Reel Education: Documentaries, Biopics and Reality*, takes a critical look at the truth claims related to media texts about education that are constructed around "real life" and how these texts should be evaluated and taught.

Aside from the conventions of the good teacher movies, a great deal has changed since I began this work over 20 years ago. My first work on the topic, begun as a paper for Kathleen Casey's curriculum theory course, looked at twenty-six films, and I viewed them on VHS. Sometimes even finding the films was a challenge. Now, I can find a number of the films I want to review

XII THE HOLLYWOOD CURRICULUM

on-demand online, or I can have a DVD delivered to my mailbox in a day or at most two. I am aware that this sounds a bit like telling a child I walked twelve miles through the snow to get to school because it's so much easier now than it used to be, but the truth of the matter is that I will never again have to spend money to buy a terrible movie like *The Teacher* (1974) just so I can take a look. I am grateful for that dramatically improved access to films – many things are so much easier than they used to be with regard to this project and other critical media studies work that engages me.

What is next? Will films continue to exert the cultural power that they have for decades? I wish I knew the answer to that. I believe the dominance of the print culture has been supplanted by the moving image, but that means so much more than it used to – it's no longer just film and television. Actually, I'm not sure exactly what it means. My now 24-year-old son has grown up in a non-linear, digital age, and he engages media differently from the way I do. We still watch movies together sometimes and talk about them, especially the "classics." In the preface to the previous edition, I wrote, "I don't think motion pictures, in the conventional sense, hold the same power over him that they do over me. He has always known a control over these narratives that is still new to me." Now, I see clearly that I was wrong then because he is as engaged with moving images as I am and enjoys a full range of viewing plea-sures from the television series *Justified* (2010–15) (which we are currently watching together when he comes by for a visit) to classic films from all cin-ematic traditions.

When I was a young teenager and saw part of Jean Cocteau's *La Belle et La Bête* (1946) on a public television station, I knew I was witnessing something special even though I had missed the beginning and feared not only that I could never see the film again but that I couldn't even learn what it was. As a three-year-old, my son would tell me to start *The Mask* (1994) at chapter seven because that's when Jim Carrey would put on the mask, and the action would start. He could choose to skip the exposition because he had the power to "cut to the chase." In a way, he could produce the media he engaged almost from the very beginning. It is the same for our students, all of whom have their own experiences and preferences and ideas about media and the world. The only way we can learn from them is to listen, and learning is essential to teaching. Sometimes movies can bridge the gap or, at the very least, help us notice things about ourselves as individuals and as a culture that we might not find so accessible otherwise.

Note

1. I have become quite troubled by these representations and how the dominance of these narrative patterns will affect perceptions of teachers and public education for years to come. See Bethonie Butler's article "Does Television Have a Teacher Problem?" in *The Washington Post*, published July 16, 2016.

ACKNOWLEDGMENTS

The idea for this book originated in conversation with Kathleen Casey. I owe an enormous debt to her and to Svi Shapiro, both of whom followed this work in the first edition page by page, contributing countless useful comments and challenging me to interrogate my own assumptions about the movies and culture. Likewise, Fritz Mengert and Hephzi Roskelly generously provided their own insights and suggestions about the *Hollywood Curriculum*. On this most recent edition, Chad E. Harris and Laura R. Linder were immeasurably helpful. A special thanks goes to my friends and colleagues at Wake Forest University and to David Solomon, whose daily encouragement coached me through the revision process.

For their more directed contributions through engaging conversation, with technical support, or by suggesting a book or movie title, I would like to thank the following people: Karen Anijar, Jackie Bach, Brooke Barnett, Pearl Berlin, Danny Borrell, Susan Borwick, Terry Bowers, Anne Boyle, John Bruns, Mark Burger, Carrie Buse, Linda Cabiness, Dawne Clark, Naeemah Clark, Rebecca Clark, Matt Clarke, Pam Cook, Elizabeth Currin, Steve Dalton, Eddy Daniel, Mary DeShazer, Ryan Eanes, Emily Edwards, Kirsten Fatzinger, Susan Faust, Denise Franklin, Adam Friedman, Candice Funderburk, Mary Gerardy, Ellen "Lennie" Gerber, Mary Ellis Gibson, Rebecca Goodrich, Ellen Hendrix, Woody Hood, Michael Hyde, Brett Ingram, Jennifer Jackson, Renata Jackson,

Steve Jarrett, Nick Johnson, Robert Johnson, Sherwood Jones, Mark Joyner, Melanie Joyner, Susan Joyner, Bill Kane, Karen Kantziper, Molly Keener, Carol Keesee, Doug Kellner, Brenda Knox, Candyce Leonard, Allan Louden, Jack Lucido, Sarah Magness, Martha Mason, Annemarie McAllister, Raymond McCluskey, Erin McInnis, Lauren McInnis, Stephen McKinney, Kathryn Milam, Maggie Mileski, Lisa Napoli, Jody Natalle, Stokes Piercy, DeeDe Pinckney, Dale Pollock, David Purpel, Ben Ramsey, George Reasner, Mary Reeves, Randy Rogan, Spencer Ross, Kaitlyn Ruhf, Katie Scarvey, Marshall Shaffer, Dalton Smoot, Ronald Soetaert, Lynn Sutton, Edwin G. Wilson, Emily Herring Wilson, Hu Womack, Bob Workmon, and Christopher Zydowicz.

Earlier versions of some material in Chapters 2 and 3 appeared in the article "The Hollywood Curriculum: Who is the Good Teacher?" published in *Curriculum Studies* 3(1):2–44 (1995). Earlier versions of the sections on *High School High* and *Elephant* in Chapter 8 appeared in "The Hollywood View: Protecting the Status Quo in Schools Onscreen" in Mirror Images: Popular Culture and Education, eds. Diana Silberman Keller, Zvi Bekerman, Henry A. Giroux, and Nicholas C. Burbules. Peter Lang: New York, 2008, pp. 9–22. I gratefully acknowledge permission to reprint from my earlier work.

Finally, I would like to acknowledge the role each of the contributors to *Screen Lessons: What We Have Learned from Teachers on Television and in the Movies* for the ways their wonderful essays re-ignited my enthusiasm for this project and informed some of the elements of the new edition of *The Hollywood Curriculum*: Jarrod Atchison, Jacqueline Bach, Steve Benton, Robert C. Bulman, Dennis Conway, Erin Currin, Jennifer S. Dean, Adam Dovico, Emily D. Edwards, Alexa Erb, Christian Z. Goering, Chad E. Harris, Abigail Kindelsperger, Seung-Hyun Lee, Christine Mallozzi, Erin L. McInnis, Walter C. Metz, Raúl Alberto Mora, Rosemary Nyaole-Kowuor, Rob Phillips, Suzanne Regan, Sharon Marie Ross, Lara Searcy, Stephanie Schroeder, Shelly L. Shaffer, Roslin Smith, Stephen Tropiano, John Peter Watts, Susan D. Weinstein, Wendy R. Williams, Shelbie Witte, and – again – my co-editor, Laura R. Linder.

· 1 ·

INTRODUCTION

It seems as though I have always been interested in popular culture, particularly television and the movies. Increasingly, what originated as a personal interest in the aesthetic dimensions of these particular mediums has become more centrally situated in theories linking mass culture and political struggle under the rubric of cultural studies. The literature of cultural studies has emerged with amazing rapidity. One unifying thread running through much of this research is the idea that scholars writing from this perspective, using their own diverse methodologies, openly state their point of view and take the further step of directly advocating change.[1] It is in this context that I began to think about the way popular culture constructs its own curriculum in the movies through the on-screen relationship between teacher and student. The social curriculum of Hollywood implicit in popular films is based on individual rather than collective action and relies on that carefully plotted action rather than meaningful struggle to ensure the ultimate outcome, leaving educational institutions, which represent the larger cultural status quo, intact and in power.

It is my plan here to use that research, in concert with a discussion of Dwayne Huebner's five frameworks for valuing curriculum, other critical lenses, and my own interpretations of a number of films, primarily commercial movies, as the basis for a discussion of the meaning of popular culture and its importance in a democratic vision for education. Essentially, I will view these films through various sets of interpretive lenses: viewing the "good" teacher through three of Huebner's value frameworks; viewing the "bad" teacher through Huebner's two remaining value frameworks; viewing the "gendered" teacher through the lens of feminist literature; viewing the "gay" teacher through the lens of queer theory; viewing teachers who engage in physical relationships with students through the lenses of sexuality and power; viewing race, ethnicity, and social class through various critical lenses; viewing the various depictions of administrators in the films considered and placing their roles in a larger political landscape; and, finally, viewing students and schools through the lens of critical pedagogy.

Students, parents, and everyone else (except perhaps those adults who are able to observe teachers in various schools) have a very limited frame of reference for evaluating curriculum as it is played out in the classroom. Knowledge of this type tends to be based on personal experiences or on anecdotal conversations with others about their respective personal experiences. I do believe, however, that general knowledge about the relationships between teachers and students, knowledge beyond the scope of the personal or anecdotal, is created by constructs of popular culture played out in the mass media. In "Working-Class Identity and Celluloid Fantasies in the Electronic Age," Stanley Aronowitz writes that individual and collective identities are constructed on three sites: "1. the biologically given characteristics which we bring to every social interaction; 2. givens that are often covered over by social relations, family, school; and 3. the technological sensorium that we call mass or popular culture" (197). Aronowitz maintains that "electronically mediated cultural forms" are the strongest components in the formation of cultural identities (205). Michael Ryan and Douglas Kellner argue that film is a particularly potent form for establishing and reinforcing these social constructions:

> Films transcode the discourses (the forms, figures, and representations) of social life into cinematic narrative. Rather than reflect a reality external to the film medium, films execute a transfer from one discursive field to another. As a result, films themselves become part of that broader cultural system of representations that construct social reality. That construction occurs in part through the internalization of representations. (12–13)

In short, we borrow from the stories of the films we see to help us create ourselves as characters and organize the plotlines of our daily lives.

This type of knowledge is far removed from the intentionally abstract musings frequently collected by professional theorists with a traditional bent and packaged into convoluted manuscripts destined for arcane periodicals. Yet, the same theorists often write about these "electronically mediated cultural forms" and the mass audiences that enjoy them with unveiled contempt and a critical distance that implies their unfamiliarity with their subjects. Except for a few passing references to competing works, this book starts with the assumption that popular culture is an important and often overlooked source of social knowledge. In a later section, "An Overview of Curriculum Theories," I introduce a discussion of the value systems and curricular language employed by Huebner in "Curricular Language and Classroom Meanings." My purpose in combining Huebner's specific metaphors for curriculum with the larger discussion of meanings and popular culture is to explore the tension between static meaning solidified in most educational discourse and the dynamic way of viewing popular constructions in the context of on-going struggle.

This book reconciles the theoretical and the everyday by finding ways to ground the theoretical in the everyday. Or, as Henry A. Giroux and Paulo Freire write in their foreword to *Popular Culture, Schooling, and Everyday Life*, the book argues for

> ... a theory of popular culture that embodies a language of both critique and possibility, a language that not only frees educators from certain ways of defining public philosophy, leadership, and pedagogy but that also sheds light on some of the most pressing problems confronting schools and society, while simultaneously providing a vision capable of animating a democratic and popular public culture. (viii)

The larger purpose of this work is to uncover several layers of meaning embedded in popular texts and reveal to teacher and student alike that even commercial Hollywood films are at once polysemic and complex.

While I may think about connections between the viewer and the film text in abstraction, I also live those connections in my day-to-day life and know that my relationship to the movies I watch is dynamic rather than static. I believe that films not only support multiple interpretations but also that those meanings seen by the viewer will change over time. According to postmodern theories, meaning is not fixed; the "grand narrative has lost its credibility" (Lyotard 37), and boundaries we have long accepted between "life" and "art," between "high art" and "low art," between socially constructed male and female roles, and between academic disciplines have proved inadequate with the categories collapsing under our critical gaze.

At the same time, film and literary criticism have frequently focused on finding *the* meaning from a particular text. Working from various theoretical models, scholars (and popular reviewers) have set out to convince readers that scholarly (and other published) interpretation represents the "true" meaning of the text. They frequently imply that this "true" meaning is inherent in the text and merely awaits their expert analysis. While the content and context of the text may set boundaries for possible interpretations, it is incorrect to say that those meanings reside in the vision and voice of the author or intrinsically in the text itself. Meaning resides in the space between the text and the reader where the images evoked by the first become inextricably linked to the context provided by the second. As John Fiske writes on Stuart Hall's theory of articulation:

> To articulate has two meanings-one is to speak or utter (the text-centered meaning) and the other is to form a flexible link with, to be hinged with (the reader-centered meaning in which the text is flexibly linked with the reader's social situation). What a text "utters" determines, limits, and influences the links that can be made between it and its readers, but it cannot make them or control them. Only readers can do that. For a text to be popular, it must "utter" what its readers wish to say, and must allow those readers to participate in their choice of its utterances (for texts must offer multiple utterances) as they construct and discover its points of pertinence in their social situation. (1989, 146)

While the interpretations of some readers will undoubtedly be more persuasive than the interpretations of others, all interpretations should be treated as equally valid, if not equally persuasive, responses to the text. The responses of informed readers,[2] the meanings they find in the text, will probably be more compelling and quite possibly more enduring than the responses of uninformed readers, but the ease with which the reader engages the text does not influence the validity of the individual reader's interpretation.

I agree with Wolfgang Iser's argument that "the message travels two ways; the reader of the text 'receives' it by composing it" (21). Only by finding ways to describe the transaction between text and reader can we learn about the effects of the work. Yet, I don't wish to imply that every reader engages every text with the same intensity. Just as some readers – informed readers – will arrive at more compelling interpretations of a given text than others, some texts offer a richer array of possible meanings. For readers to arrive at compelling interpretations of a film text, the film must engage the reader with material that inspires intense interrogation, and the reader must approach the text with an aesthetic stance. Two central ideas related to the elevation of the reader should be reiterated here: the "reader" of the text is ultimately another "author," and the meaning of the text resides between the text and the reader.

Charles Eidsvik writes, "The film maker and viewer begin in the same place. They construct speculative-narrative worlds using the everyday languages of perceived reality as a base" (26). Think about that statement. The filmmaker and the viewer begin in the very same place, and both interrogate the text using their respective experiences as readers. The relationship between readers and text is dynamic – it is a dialectic – and it is in the process of interrogating the text that readers find its meanings. Louise Rosenblatt says that the general resistance to elevating the role of the reader is related to the fear of "brash literary egalitarianism" (105). Learning to think about the reader as author and the author as reader also creates a precedent for collapsing the boundary between teacher and student so that teachers allow themselves to become students in their own classrooms at the same time that students gain the authority to share their own knowledge with teachers and other students.

Critical Theory and the Popular

The cultural studies explosion in academic institutions and among intellectuals writing internationally over the last couple of decades is certainly not a spontaneous occurrence. While influences on the movement are many, I will consider two of them briefly here along with a few words about cultural studies as a locus for considering popular artifacts of public culture. In *Critical Theory, Marxism, and Modernity*, Douglas Kellner writes about Critical Theory as one of the most enduring products of the Institute for Social Research, a German research institute with a Marxist orientation often referred to as the Frankfurt School (1989, 1). According to Kellner, the work of the "Critical Theorists" is "distinguished by the close connection between social theory and cultural critique and by their ability to contextualize culture within social developments" (1989, 121). It was not until the 1930s, when members of the Institute were in exile in the United States, that they solidified their theories on mass culture. Kellner writes:

> Adorno and Horkheimer adopted the term "culture industry", as opposed to concepts like "popular culture" or "mass culture", because they wanted to resist notions that products of mass culture emanated from the masses or the people. They saw the culture industry as involving administered culture, imposed from above, as an instrument of indoctrination and social control. The term "culture industry" thus contains a dialectical irony typical of the style of Critical Theory: culture, as traditionally valorized, is supposed to be opposed to industry and expressive of individual creativity while providing a repository of humanizing values. In the culture industries, by

contrast, culture has come to function as a mode of ideological domination, rather than of humanization or emancipation. (130–31)

The Critical Theorists conceptualized the culture industries against a cultural backdrop that included the rise of Nazism and America's massive World War II propaganda campaigns. It is not surprising that manipulation is central to their theories, and it is important to note that theories of audience manipulation have subsequently been granted their own academic corner in the communication discipline under the heading "persuasion."[3]

Cultural studies today is in many ways a legacy of British cultural studies, especially from work undertaken at the Centre for Contemporary Cultural Studies at Birmingham in the 1960s and 1970s. Describing just what cultural studies means is difficult even when one restricts the discussion to one time period and location. Stuart Hall writes that the theoretical work of the Centre is more appropriately called "theoretical noise" because even the members of the collective working there did not always agree.[4] After commenting on the disagreement, anger, and silence that punctuated exchanges among colleagues at the Centre, Hall attempts to address areas of agreement about the nature of cultural studies:

> Now, does it follow that cultural studies is not a policed disciplinary area? That it is whatever people do, if they choose to call or locate themselves within the project and practice of cultural studies? I am not happy with that formulation either. Although cultural studies as a project is open-ended, it can't be simply pluralist in that way. Yes, it refuses to be a master discourse or a meta-discourse of any kind. Yes, it is a project that is always open to that which it doesn't yet know, to that which it can't yet name. But it does have some will to connect; it does have some stake in the choices it makes. It does matter whether cultural studies is this or that. It can't be just any old thing which chooses to march under a particular banner. It is a serious enterprise, or project and that is inscribed in what is sometimes called the "political" aspect of cultural studies. Not that there's any one politics already inscribed in it. But there is something *at stake* [sic] in cultural studies, in a way that I think, and hope, is not exactly true of many other very important intellectual and critical practices. Here one registers the tension between a refusal to close the field, to police it and, at the same time, a determination to stake out some positions within it and argue for them. (278)

The Centre is important to my work and is included here for several reasons other than its influence on international (and American) cultural studies. The Centre pushed studies of popular culture, particularly television and film, to the forefront and also addressed narrative research and questions about the nature of power through perspectives attentive to feminism and racial identity.

Finally, I turn to the burgeoning enterprise that we call cultural studies. *Cultural Studies*, the anthology put together from the international conference "Cultural Studies Now and in the Future" held April 4–9, 1990, at the University of Illinois at Urbana-Champaign, became sort of a handbook for students of cultural studies, and one of its editors, Lawrence Grossberg, became an intellectual cheerleader for the validation of the popular. In the introduction to their book, Grossberg et al. argue that cultural studies is "anti-disciplinary" and certain to reside uncomfortably with other academic disciplines. They write:

> The choice of research practices depends upon the questions that are asked, and the questions depend on their context. It is problematic for cultural studies simply to adopt, uncritically, any of the formalized disciplinary practices of the academy, for those practices, as much as the distinction they inscribe, carry with them a heritage of disciplinary investments and exclusions and a history of social effects that cultural studies would often be inclined to repudiate. (2)

Grossberg et al. write about the complexity and contentiousness of cultural studies. Because it is dependent on context for analysis, cultural studies cannot become entrenched; it must change its meanings and its uses to remain relevant.[5] But, one consistency in cultural studies is its participants' commitment to openly subjective argument. Yet, in virtually all traditions of cultural studies, its practitioners see cultural studies not simply as a chronicle of cultural change but as an intervention in it and see themselves not simply as scholars providing an account but as politically engaged participants (5). Grossberg et al. argue that cultural studies is more than a theoretical enterprise, that it bridges theory and material culture (6). The absence of prescribed methodology and disciplinary boundaries in cultural studies offers me the opportunity to undertake this research in a way that consciously exposes my own perspective instead of hiding my positions and my politics beneath a cloak of false objectivity. My intention is to ground the theoretical in the everyday and, hopefully, to find ways to let teachers and students make meaning in their own lives as they claim ownership (and sometimes "authorship") of their own experiences. Popular film, rich in meanings both fluid and diverse, offers an intersection for the theoretical and the everyday.

Struggle, Consent, and Intertextuality

For the Critical Theorists, the dialectics of culture – "the ways in which culture could be both a force of social conformity and one of opposition" – were a major concern of theorists writing about the culture industries (Kellner 1989, 122). From the Critical Theorists of the Institute for Social Research to more recent devotees of cultural studies, the metaphor of struggle has been central to understanding the interaction between mass culture and its consumers. In offering suggestions for practitioners of contemporary cultural criticism, Kellner recommends a stronger commitment to critique of that dialectic. He recommends something much closer to what Hall terms "wrestling with the angels" as a metaphor for theoretical work (1989, 280).[6] Kellner writes:

> Rather than seeing its artifacts simply as expressions of hegemonic ideology and ruling class interests, it is preferable to view popular entertainment as a complex product that contains contradictory moments of desire and its displacement, articulations of hopes and their repression. In this view, popular culture provides access to a society's dreams and nightmares, and contains both ideological celebrations of the status quo and utopian moments of transcendence, moments of opposition and rebellion and its attempted containment. Recent studies of popular culture also show how social struggles and conflicts enter into works of popular entertainment, and see culture as a contested terrain, rather than a field of one dimensional manipulation and illusion. (1989, 141)

Kellner's recognition of the complexity of any process designed to determine the meaning(s) of artifacts of popular culture and his use of "diagnostic critique" to engage a "dialectic of text and context ... to situate and interpret key films" (2010, 34–35) opens up a space for discussing the consensual relationship between the consumer of popular culture and the product that is consumed and, by extension, the relationship between consent, pleasure, and the popular.

Giroux and Simon construct a theory of popular culture based on three features. First, the concept of hegemony explains how the terrain of daily life can become a site of "struggle over and accommodation to the culture of subordinate groups." Second, the terrain of daily life is also a pedagogical process with structuring principles that are political and arise from the production of subjectivity. Third, hegemony is informed by consent, which specifies the limits and possibilities "of the pedagogical principles at work within cultural forms that serve in contradictory ways to empower and disempower various groups" (10). Giroux and Simon continue their discussion of popular culture and consent by exploring the dialectic of ideology and pleasure through a category they label "the persuasive." Generally, the persuasive refers to the hegemonic function of pedagogical processes to preserve dominant interests in tandem with the opportunity for resistance (14).

John Fiske introduces several interesting ideas that are worth discussing here before moving on to applications for the study of popular culture. First, there is the very notion of "the popular." What constitutes a popular text, or cultural artifact? Fiske is only one of many to point out that the postmodern world proscribes the separation between art and life, between "high" and "low" culture (1992, 154–55). The collapse of the constructed distinction between these categories opens up a wide range of cultural artifacts for interrogation. In *Understanding Popular Culture* Fiske says that popular culture is "made at the interface between the cultural resources provided by capitalism and everyday life." He maintains that "popular discrimination," or the choices people make among the products of the culture industry, is related to issues of function rather than quality because it is "concerned with the potential uses of the text in everyday life. Three main criteria underlie this selection process: relevance, semiotic productivity, and the flexibility of the mode of consumption" (129). The popular text must be "producerly." By this, Fiske means that popular texts exhibit the dialectic, or struggle, discussed previously by Kellner and Giroux and Simon. "Producerly" texts, those that offer themselves for ready public consumption, reluctantly expose the weaknesses of their preferred meanings while trying unsuccessfully to repress or contradict meanings other than the preferred (104). Fiske writes:

> The commodities produced and distributed by the culture industries that are made into popular culture are those that get out of control, that become undisciplined … their indiscipline is the indiscipline of everyday life, it is familiar because it is an inescapable element of popular experience in a hierarchal power-structured society. (1992, 104)

To analyze popular texts, Fiske argues, requires a "double focus." One must "focus on the deep structure of the text in the ways that ideological, psycho-analytic analyses and structural or semiotic analyses have proved so effective and incisive in recent scholarship" while also focusing "upon how people cope with the system, how they read its texts, how they make popular culture out of its resources" (1992, 105).

Finally, let's consider Fiske's notion of intertextuality as an eloquent complement to Grossberg et al.'s call for cultural studies to remain "anti-disciplinary,"[7] to Kellner's plea for dialecticism in critical studies of culture, and to Hall's infusion of the personal into the study of the popular. Texts never exist separate from context. When a reader engages, or interrogates, a text, the act is never separated from that reader's own lived experience or from the other (and possibly competing) texts that reader has engaged. The text is incorporated into the reader's everyday life at the same time the reader's everyday life becomes part of the construction of the text. Fiske writes:

> Because of their incompleteness, all popular texts have leaky boundaries; they flow into each other, they flow into everyday life. Distinctions among texts are as invalid as the distinctions between text and life. Popular culture can be studied only intertextually, for it exists only in this intertextual circulation. The interrelationships between primary and secondary texts cross all boundaries between them; equally, those between tertiary and other texts cross the boundaries between text and life. (1992, 126)

Similarly, I will attempt to dissolve the boundary constructed between theory and everyday life in the service of a critical pedagogy charged with infusing schools with democratic vision and making them cultural sites for promoting social justice.

An Overview of Curriculum Theories

Curriculum theorists run the gamut from pragmatists like Ralph W. Tyler, whose four-step system takes the curriculum planner from selecting objectives to evaluation of their achievement, to Henry A. Giroux and Paulo Freire, who see curriculum grounded in an exploration of one's relationship to the world. These poles of theory range from an examination of ways to improve the efficiency of our present society, with key beneficiaries being those currently in positions of power, to an alternative view that explores the dynamics of power relationships as a means to create a more just society. Research by scholars like Jean Anyon has documented that in many cases curriculum is used to perpetuate the stratifications of represented classes.[8] Many others have also written about the aptly labeled "hidden curriculum."

Because the stakes are high – in fundamental ways the stakes are our very way of life – the public discourse and debate over curriculum is often fierce even though the debated topic is frequently defined as something quite separate from curriculum. As Elliot W. Eisner and Elizabeth Vallance put it:

> Controversy in educational discourse most often reflects a basic conflict in priorities concerning the form and content of curriculum and the goals toward which schools should strive; the intensity of the conflict and the apparent difficulty in resolving it can most often be traced to a failure to recognize conflicting conceptions of curriculum. (1–2)

Those who speak the language of public education frequently do not bother to examine its conceptional underpinnings. Sometimes the culprit is our inability to recognize the different meanings we attach to our common language, and other times it is a more fundamental difference in philosophy. Throughout it all, theorists tend to ignore the validity of the personal in favor of establishing universal models. Hollywood, it appears, has its own model of curriculum theory, a model that exalts personal experience in a broad aesthetic-ethical-political sweep, making curriculum and teaching one.

Throughout this text, I talk about curriculum in a language that comes from Dwayne Huebner's work in *Curriculum Theorizing: The Reconceptualists*, edited by William Pinar, specifically from definitions found in "Curricular Language and Classroom Meanings" (217–35). Huebner identifies five "value frameworks" of curricular thought: technical, scientific, (a)esthetic, political, and ethical. In the present book, Chapters 2 and 3 are organized around the three value frameworks that are consistent with "good" teachers in the movies, (a)esthetic values, political values, and ethical values. Huebner says that if educational activity were valued (a)esthetically, it "would be viewed as having symbolic and esthetic meanings" and might fall into at least three categories: in the first category it is "removed from the world of use"; the second category is focused on wholeness and design; and the third category involves symbolic meaning (226–27). Huebner says that "ethical valuing demands that the human situation existing between student and teacher must be uppermost, and that content must be seen as an arena of that human confrontation" (229). He adds that educational activity must not be seen as existing only between people but should instead include activity between students and other beings in the world. Huebner identifies political valuing in the context of power dynamics in the classroom and cautions that "if power and prestige are sought as ends, rather than as means for responsible and creative influence, evil and immorality may be produced. Yet dreams and visions are not realized without personal or professional power" (224–25). Chapter 2 looks at characteristics of "good" teachers in the movies and how those traits combine to create a stock character who fits into the Hollywood model.

Overview of Subsequent Chapters

I have grounded the discussion in this chapter in the emerging field of cultural studies and developed ties to Huebner's value frameworks of curriculum. Looking at commercial Hollywood films, I find a generic representation of the "good" teacher in the movies that is presented as a radical model. In fact, the Hollywood version of the good teacher merely tugs a little at the cornerstone of the institutional hierarchy. There are equally vivid representations of the bad teacher and the gendered teacher in these films. Nevertheless, we are all consumers of this popular culture model of the radical teacher and undoubtedly construct our own notions about what it means to be a teacher, and what it means to be politically active, under the influence of this Hollywood ideal. For some of us that influence is predominant while for others it is slight, but the influence of popular culture is inescapable. Certainly, there are alternate discourses about teachers and teaching, but I have selected Huebner's five value frameworks for curriculum as one way of looking at the role teachers and teaching play in the films discussed here. The contrast between metaphors for teaching delineated in Huebner's models and the more fluid meanings found from approaching these film texts as artifacts of popular culture exposes the tension inherent in these competing modes of inquiry and, additionally, the tension that exists within the latter mode when popular culture is viewed as a terrain of struggle. The purpose of this first chapter is to present central questions about the role popular culture plays in our everyday lives and, more particularly, questions about how we can use the intersection between the popular and the personal as a place to create new meaning so we can openly challenge the popular culture construction of curriculum and radical teaching.

Subsequent chapters contain an overview of the themes found in the films used to analyze teachers and teaching in the movies. Over 230 movies inform this analysis. Most are films that have had a theatrical release in the United States. Most are American films. I have decided to focus on these movies because their general release in American theaters, accessibility for rental, online viewing, and telecasts have made them part of this country's popular culture. These movies, which are listed in the filmography at the end of the book, reflect over 85 years of film history and cover established genres that include drama, comedy, musical, horror, science fiction, and action-adventure. While it is ultimately up to the viewer to make connections among films (and other texts) and decode them as similar – or not – I believe a number of the films considered here, certainly many of the films most important to this research, might be set aside in a category of their own: the genre of good teacher movies. Although there is not clear consensus among scholars about whether or not genres actually exist let alone what constitutes them, I believe good teacher movies exhibit distinct and identifiable characteristics, or conventions, and these patterns are significant because they are replicated over time and seen by audiences repeatedly. Not all of the films discussed in this book fit the narrower grouping of good teacher movies – some are hybrid forms that include good teachers and bad teachers as the terms are laid out in subsequent chapters – but I am interested in the question of genre as a matter of context and am looking for connections among this group of films and larger cultural and political concerns.

Figure 1.1. Sidney Poitier as Gregory W. Miller and Glenn Ford as Richard Dadier in *Blackboard Jungle*, 1955. In this scene, Miller shares a moment with Mr. Dadier in the classroom. Just 12 years later, Poitier would go from playing a tough student to an iconic good teacher in *To Sir, with Love.*

This familiar form, established in such movies as *Goodbye, Mr. Chips* (1939) and *The Corn is Green* (1945), is canonized across the decades in films like *Blackboard Jungle* (1955), *To Sir, With Love* (1967), *Conrack* (1974), *Dead Poets Society* (1989), and *Freedom Writers* (2007). The genre seems to have reached a level of such maturity by the 1990s that teacher movies have developed into texts that comment on one another with a range that extends from silliness to sophistication. The genre has become firmly established with conventions that are so widely recognizable (and surprisingly consistent) that there are now examples of the form that must be identified as parodic, *High School High* (1996),[9] and revisionist, *Election* (1999), *Half Nelson* (2006), and *Detachment* (2011).[10] Clearly, parody and revisionism cannot exist unless it is conceded that a basic form exists. With the release of these films, the cycle of good teacher movies as a genre is complete. In Chapter 2, I construct what I term The Hollywood Model to outline the shared characteristics of the stock character presented in the movies as the good teacher. Who is the exalted teacher on the silver screen? Typically, he or she is an outsider who is usually not well-liked by other teachers, who are typically bored by students, afraid of students, or eager to dominate students. The good teacher gets involved with students on a personal level, learns from those students, and does not usually fare very well with administrators. Sometimes these good teachers have a ready sense of humor. They also frequently personalize the curriculum to meet everyday needs in their students' lives.

Figure 1.2. Anne Bancroft as Annie Sullivan and Patty Duke as Helen Keller in *The Miracle Worker*, 1962. Bancroft won the Best Actress Oscar for this role, and Duke won the Academy Award for Best Supporting Actress.

Chapters 3 and 4 explore connections between Dwayne Huebner's value frameworks of curriculum and the Hollywood curriculum. Throughout these chapters, I talk about curriculum in a language that arises from Dwayne Huebner's work on aesthetic, ethical, and political value frameworks for curriculum. Chapter 3 recalls the characteristics of good teachers in the movies and demonstrates how teachers in the movies respond to curricular issues, ways that correspond to the three value frameworks described earlier. The chapter explores the value frameworks in sections titled "The Aesthetic Classroom,"

"The Ethical Relationship," and "The Political Language." Alongside this analysis of the films in the context of Huebner's metaphors, I offer competing readings of the various film texts. It is important to note that when Huebner's other two frameworks, technical and scientific, appear in these films, it is generally in a negative context associated either with a particular bad teacher or with school administration. In Chapter 4, I look at the role of the bad teacher in the movies and incorporate Huebner's value frameworks into that analysis. Huebner describes the technical system as having a "means-ends rationality that approaches an economic model. End states, end products, or objectives are specified as carefully and as accurately as possible, hopefully in behavioral terms. Activities are designed which become the means to these ends or objectives" (223). He writes that "scientific activity may be broadly designated as that activity which produces new knowledge with an empirical basis. Hence, educational activity may be valued for the knowledge that it produces about that activity" (225). Again, as in Chapter 3, these films are also discussed as artifacts of popular culture, and competing interpretations of the film texts are explored.

In Chapter 5, I examine the role gender plays in movies about teachers. Here I look more deeply into these films than Huebner's model permits, particularly into the films that star women as the central character, and see the difference that the gender of the teacher character appears to make in the development of these film narratives. In subsequent sections, this chapter discusses the role of nurture, the historic and contemporary constraints placed on women teachers, the teachers' acts of resistance in the contexts of dealing with administration and of political action and, finally, the divided lives that teachers have been forced to lead in our neighborhoods (historically) as well as on our local movie screens (even today). The work of feminist scholars has opened our eyes to the lived experience of women teachers. Their research has made a valuable contribution toward helping us understand the role gender construction and power relationships play in the personal and professional lives of women teachers. At the junctures of private and public, of self and culture, it becomes critical to look at the other forces that influence the way we think about women teachers. Certainly, one of these forces is popular culture. Commercial films not only tell women teachers how other people construct them and rearticulate them as characters on the movie screen, these films also shape the way students and parents respond to teachers and the way women teachers respond to public opinion in the construction of their own lives.

Chapter 6 explores a group of films that gives us new possibilities for constructing the good teacher. This is a small but influential group of films released in the late 1990s that feature a gay man in the central role as a good teacher, *In & Out* (1997), *The Object of My Affection* (1998), and *The Opposite of Sex* (1998). What is fascinating about these films, especially the first two examples, is the way their teacher characters rigidly conform to The Hollywood Model of the good teacher outlined in Chapter 2 in every respect except their homosexuality. It will be interesting, and very telling, to see how portrayals of gay teachers develop in future releases. At present, this seems like an attempt by the Hollywood establishment to use gay teachers to provide a new element, or edge, to an undeniably familiar form. Interestingly, Hollywood continues its reluctance to give women teachers, whether lesbian or straight, stories in which they can act out their sexuality without being punished, a topic taken up in Chapter 5 and explored further in this chapter.

In the first of two chapters that are entirely new to this edition of the book, I examine the difficult issue of sexual relationships between teachers and their students. Although I reference a number of films in Chapter 7, the primary focus will be on two recent films: *Palo Alto* (2013) in which the "class virgin" is torn between her interest in a classmate and a flirtation with her soccer coach; and, *The Skeleton Twins* (2014) in which a man who has recently attempted suicide returns to his hometown and resurrects an affair with one of his high school teachers. The surprising thing about the films when compared with most of the news coverage of actual relationships between students and teachers is how nuanced the films tend to be. These teachers in the movies are not cut from a single cloth and neither are the students who become involved with them. There is almost universal agreement that romantic and/or sexual relationships occurring between teachers and students are wrong, yet most communities deal with such inappropriate relationships on a regular basis. And, those are just the relationships that are discovered and reported. How many more of them are undetected? What can the movies, one of our major engines for the cultural transmission, tell us about this type of relationship and how such relationships reflect our values and sense of humanity?

The second of the new chapters focuses on race, ethnicity, and social class and explores how mainstream, commercial films tend to minimize difference, which makes sense as a business decision because movies that appeal to the broadest possible audience make more money at the box office. The approach to storytelling situating conflict around a protagonist and antagonist, rather than creating a collective social space, is a continuation of the classical narrative paradigm. This structure is representative of good teacher movies, but it is a pattern found in the majority of movies that deal with schooling because of Hollywood's bias toward individualism. Chapter 8 uses the parody *High School High*, which is superficial and even silly at first look, as a mechanism for revealing hidden truths about teachers, students, schools, and the larger culture. It is essential to recognize difference, the intersectionality of identity, and the institutional oppression directed at people because of those identities before we can find a way forward to locate common ground. Our future as a culture depends on our ability to do this and to use schools to their fullest potential as sites for preparing students to be self-actualized and engaged citizens.

Chapter 9 looks at the role administrators play in schools in the movies. While there are only two films considered here that feature school principals as protagonists, *The Principal* (1987) and *Lean on Me* (1989), principals and assorted administrators play important supporting roles in many of the films about teachers and schools. Sometimes those supporting roles are, actually, supportive, but more often school administrators are one-dimensional representatives of the school as a societal institution. From the perspective of good teachers, these stuffy and authoritarian administrators are usually more concerned with maintaining order, raising test scores, or staying under budget than they are with the welfare of the students. From the perspective of the students, they are hopelessly out of touch. In either scenario, administrators represent the system, and there are profound political implications in these representations.

Chapter 10, which is the concluding chapter, moves from looking at the film texts' primary representations of educators to asking even more pointed questions about schools and the movies while making connections between images projected in these motion pictures and the notion of critical pedagogy. Here it becomes important to listen to student voices in films. Just what does it mean to be responsive at the social and personal levels? While teachers in the movies do serve as mediators who prepare students to meet the world that exists beyond the classroom or as buffers that enable students to grow stronger before meeting that larger world, they are not effective in working with students to create lasting change in the world, at least not as the world is represented in these movies by hierarchical administrative and institutional structures. There is an opportunity for movies to do more than project an idealized model of teacher-student relationships; there is an opportunity to create a new Hollywood curriculum, one that engages in liberatory praxis.

Teachers in the movies wade into these waters, but, as a group, they do not jump in and swim. Many of the Hollywood teachers jeopardize their jobs by tossing aside, if not openly flouting, school policies. Most try to transform their school's stated curriculum into a curriculum that better meets the needs of their students. Many take risks of one sort or another to try to connect with students on a personal level. Still, these Hollywood teachers are working on easing transitions for their students between school and the world outside classroom walls instead of participating in transformations that could radically re-create schools and other societal institutions as agencies invested in creating justice. Time and time again as we watch individual teachers do battle with the hierarchy, we have the satisfaction (as an audience) of an implied win on some small front while the collective organizations remain largely intact. Thus, the individual figure Hollywood loves to glorify, the "little man," remains alone without the force of a collective to take truly transformative action, and the institutions remain unchanged. Are we likely to see many of the teachers projected on the big screen at the local cinema or transmitted to the smaller screens in our own homes engage in praxis? No. Just as real teachers feel the tug of their personal compassion for and obligation to students being countered by the need to maintain their positions of authority in the school hierarchy, real movie writers and directors are torn between realizing their artistic or political vision and producing a "product" that studios know how to market and audiences find familiar enough to buy. That's precisely why the persistent incarnation of Hollywood's good teacher is a staple in films of all genres and time periods – the teacher in the movies is idealized enough to inspire viewers and manageable enough to leave the status quo intact.

Notes

1. Writing in the Introduction to *Cultural Studies*, editors Lawrence Grossberg et al. see participants in cultural studies research as "politically engaged participants" rather than chroniclers of cultural change (5), and see the role of cultural studies as "continuously undermining canonical histories even as it reconstructs them for its own purposes" (10). In *Understanding Popular Culture* John Fiske writes that the study of popular culture has recently begun to focus on popular culture as a "site of struggle" (1989, 20).
2. The term "informed reader" is used here to describe a thoughtful viewer of the film text who considers thematic alternatives to the literal depictions on the screen. This is a viewer who consciously weaves his or her own experiences into the events of the film to create a series of concrete and abstract meanings for the film. The term is not used in the same sense as in Stanley Fish's (1970, 145).

3. In many academic institutions today departments dedicated to the study of communication, as it is generally called, have a comparatively recent history. Their traditions date back to rhetorical practices and theories of Ancient Greece, but more recently many scholars have aligned themselves unapologetically with the practices of contemporary social scientists, forsaking traditional methods of proof with the starkly positivist. I feel the need to include here a rather lengthy excerpt from Lowenthal's essay "Historical Perspectives of Popular Culture" that Kellner labels a "sharp polemic" attacking "modern social science."

> Empirical social science has become a kind of applied asceticism. It stands clear of any entanglements with foreign powers and thrives in an atmosphere of rigidly enforced neutrality. It refuses to enter the sphere of meaning. A study of television, for instance, will go to great heights in analyzing data on the influence of television on family life, but it will leave to poets and dreamers the question of actual human values of this new institution. Social research takes the phenomena of modern life, including the mass media, at face value. It rejects the task of placing them in a historical and moral context. In the beginning of the modern era, social theory had theology as its model, but today the natural sciences have replaced theology. This change in models has far-reaching implications. Theology aims at salvation, natural science at manipulation; the one leads to heaven and hell, the other to technology and machinery. Social science is today defined as an analysis of painstakingly circumscribed, more or less artificially isolated, social sectors. It imagines that such horizontal segments constitute its research laboratory, and it seems to forget that the only social research laboratories that are properly admissible are historical situations. (52)

   This excerpt is taken from the anthology, *Mass Culture*, that was published in the United States in 1957 and included critiques of mass culture by Institute theorists.

4. All of the material attributed to Stuart Hall in this section is taken from "Cultural Studies and its Theoretical Legacies" in *Cultural Studies*, Lawrence Grossberg et al., eds.

5. Certainly there are many, many people writing about the meaning of cultural studies and, relatedly, about the meaning of popular culture. There does seem to be a consensus, however, about the difficulty of defining those concepts very specifically. In the first chapter of *Popular Culture, Schooling, and Everyday Life*, for example, Giroux and Simon write:

> ... the concept of popular culture cannot be defined around a set of ideological meanings permanently inscribed in particular cultural forms. On the contrary, because of their location within and as part of the dynamics of consent, the meaning of cultural forms can only be ascertained through their articulation into a practice and set of historically specific contextual relations which determine their political meaning and ideological interests. (9)

6. Similarly, in *Popular Culture, Schooling, and Everyday Life* Giroux and Simon write that "radical educators have attempted to analyze the terrain of schooling as a struggle of particular ways of life" (1).

7. See footnote 1.

8. In "Social Class and the Hidden Curriculum of Work," for example, Anyon studies five elementary schools in contrasting social class communities. She identifies two "Working-class Schools," a "Middle-class School," an "Affluent Professional School," and an "Executive Elite School." She finds that the school work assigned in the various schools seems to develop the skills the students will need as adults to work in jobs their parents currently hold, thus replicating and perpetuating the current stratification of social class. See the bibliography for a complete citation of this article.

9. For more on *High School High*, see Chapter 8 and Dalton (2008, 9–22).

10. For more on *Half Nelson*, see Dalton (2006, 29–34) and "The Only Constant is Change: *Half Nelson* as an Act of Critical Pedagogy" by John Peter Watts in *Screen Lessons: What We Have Learned from Teachers on Television and in the Movies*.

· 2 ·

THE HOLLYWOOD MODEL

Who Is the Good Teacher?

- teacher learns from students

- personalized curriculum

Introduction

In the process of considering over 230 films with teachers as either primary or important secondary characters, it quickly became evident to me that Hollywood dichotomizes teachers and teaching into the "good" and the "bad." In the case of good teachers, these characters are almost always written to conform to a pat standard I have chosen to label The Hollywood Model. In roughly half of the films I have watched, the teacher is a main character that is presented as a good force in the movies, painted against a backdrop of institutional and societal woe, and positioned as markedly different from most of the other teachers and virtually all of the administrators in their respective films. While there are differences and distinctions among them, I think these characters have important, even defining, similarities that create an identifiable pattern of representation across time.

Other people have written about these Hollywood teachers from different perspectives. In an article titled "Teacher in the Movies," Rob Edelman looks at teachers as they have been negatively stereotyped in some movies and characterized as positive role models in others. He sees "idealized" educators portrayed in two types of films: "... sentimental valentines to the careers of single-mindedly devoted teachers, anonymous human beings who over the years touch the lives of thousands; and [films about] instructors in tough, urban schools whose colleagues are cynical, defeated by an educational bureaucracy and the antics of hostile students, yet who persist despite frustration and heartbreak" (28). Edelman cites a lot of examples, but pays too little attention to the types of relationships these teachers have with students. His article focuses mainly on summarizing film plots and categorizing the featured teachers by gender and film genre rather than digging beneath the celluloid surface. By searching for archetypal Hollywood teachers in distinctive film genres instead of looking at curricular issues, he underplays the overarching themes that connect many films that seem, on the surface, to have little in common. He does uncover the dramatic tensions between good teachers and bad teachers and between male teachers and female teachers, but there are also political tensions in these films between the forces of social conformity and opposition, compelling tensions beneath the celluloid surface representing the poles cited by the Critical Theorists as "dialectics of culture."

In "Chalk It Up To Experience: The Sacrificial Image of the Teacher in Popular Media, 1945–1959," Patrick A. Ryan identifies a teacher archetype I had not considered before reading his work. After World War II, exemplary teachers represented in mass media moved ever closer to martyrdom, and "the self-sacrificing, morally upright teacher served to model ethics that further contained the underlying problems and challenges of the Cold War era" (101). He looks at television and radio broadcasts in addition to the films *The Corn in Green* (1945); *Bright Road* (1953); *Good Morning, Miss Dove* (1955); *Blackboard Jungle* (1955); *The King and I* (1956); *High School Confidential!* (1958); and, *Monster on Campus* (1958). Ryan writes that these teachers advocated for people who had been "victimized by racism and prejudice" in service of "educational equity," but that this image of the teacher "largely served a socially conservative function of preserving middle-class norms and the status quo without transforming the economic and racial structures in the United States" (101). Ryan's chapter offers useful insights into the media texts he explores and relevant cultural links.

William Ayers offers a more compelling analysis in "A Teacher Ain't Nothin' But a Hero: Teachers and Teaching in Film." Still, Ayers writes about only five films (*Blackboard Jungle, Conrack* [1974], *Teachers* [1984], *Lean on Me* [1989], and *Stand and Deliver* 1988]), three of which are biopics,[1] and his analysis focuses on viewing the featured teachers as saviors of students. His reading of these films is both highly personal and strongly political. He writes that these movies put teachers and schools in the position of saving children from drugs, violence, their families, and even themselves (147).

> The problem is that most teachers are simply not up to the challenge. They are slugs: cynical, inept, backward, naive, hopeless. The occasional good teacher is a saint – he is anointed. His job – and it's always *his* job because the saint-teachers and most every other teacher in the movies is a man – is straightforward: he must separate the salvageable students from the others to be saved before it's too late, before the chosen few are sucked irredeemably back into the sewers of their own circumstances. Giving up on some kids is OK, according to the movies, but the bad teachers have already given up on *all* kids. That's their sin. (147–48)

This analysis is interesting and instructive, but it is clearly only one critical interpretation of these films. In particular, I disagree with Ayers's reading of the relationships portrayed on screen between the teachers and students. Taken as a whole, these films are not saying that good teachers "give up" on the kids who are deemed unsalvageable. To the contrary, good teachers are deemed successful in most of these motion pictures precisely because they are able to "connect" with the most "difficult" students. The medium of film operates under many constraints, including time. The typical feature film runs somewhere between 90 and 120 minutes. It is a common narrative device in movies to use composite characters to represent entire populations. One might argue that the difficult student in these films actually represents an entire group of students. After all, in many of these films we may hear bells ring – signaling class change – and may see snippets of action in other classes, but

Figure 2.1. Jon Voight as Pat Conroy in *Conrack*, 1974. This film is based on Pat Conroy's memoir *The Water is Wide*.

the primary activity on-screen features the central good teacher and one class with several identifiable students. These constraints and narrative devices are not limited to movies about schools but, in fact, are commonplace in movies about hospitals and athletic teams and courtrooms, to name a few examples.

Ayers also maintains that these films project a particular stance on teaching, which "includes the wisdom that teaching can occur only after discipline is established, that teaching proceeds in states: first, get order; then, deliver the curriculum. The curriculum is assumed to be stable and good – it is immutable and unproblematic; it consists of disconnected (but important) bits and pieces of information" (155). While bits and pieces of this analysis are played out on-screen in some teacher movies, I would not make these final assessments on viewing the five films discussed by Ayers, even outside the larger context of the other films considered in this chapter. Hollywood's good teachers are generally not presented as part of the institutionalized curriculum – that's precisely what makes them good – but neither are they able to escape that dominant system. I think it is necessary to look at the deep structures in these films and to recognize that good teachers in the movies are often presented as radicals who challenge the system while they are, in fact, not in the least bit radical and win only the occasional symbolic victory while effectively changing nothing about the corrupt infrastructures of the educational institutions depicted in these films.

These films are constructed with recognizable patterns, but there are competing interpretations to what Fiske terms the "preferred meanings" of each of these film texts (104). As I discuss The Hollywood Model throughout this chapter, I will also call attention to the tension between the way motion pictures construct the good teacher, ultimately, as a tool of social conformity while positioning these teachers on the surface as representing opposition in the form of resistance to the system. Clearly, there are several elements that are found over and over again in these films, elements that serve to define the good teachers while also drawing the inevitable contrast between these characters and the bad teachers in the movies. Just who is the exalted teacher on the silver screen? Typically, he or she is an outsider who is usually not well-liked by other teachers while the bad teachers are typically bored by students, afraid of students, or eager to dominate students. The good teacher gets involved with students on a personal level, learns from those students, and does not usually fare very well with administrators. Sometimes these good teachers have a ready sense of humor. They also frequently personalize the curriculum to meet everyday needs in their students' lives.

In my analysis of how Hollywood constructs the good teacher, I have used as examples films that have a teacher as one of the primary characters and that include a number of scenes showing that teacher in the classroom with students. I have also selected films that are widely available to general audiences. I have decided to include only those movies here because their general release in American theaters, accessibility for purchase, rental or online viewing, and broadcasts on television have made them part of this country's popular culture. No distinction has been made between private and public schools or between grade levels, because any of those distinctions would be artificial in the face of the overarching similarities among these motion pictures in terms of the established Hollywood model. The films I have watched span over 85 years of film history and represent diverse film genres. Despite their great breadth, these films tell essentially one story about teachers – good teachers are projected on the screen as bright lights in schools of darkness. I do not attempt to completely reconcile the images these films project with the daily activities in school classrooms, but I do attempt to give some definition to the constructed reality that is the particularly Hollywood version of the good teacher and argue that the "leaky boundaries" of these popular film texts allow them to influence our lives intertextually inside and outside the classroom in ways that are undeniable if not precisely measurable.

Teacher as Outsider

That these teachers are portrayed as renegades of a sort situated outside the mainstream should not come as a surprise. After all, Hollywood has built its fortunes on rugged cowboys, the detectives of film noir, and underdogs or antiheroes tugging at the cornerstone of the establishment. The movies have traditionally championed individualism so long as that rugged individual presented as the focal point of countless film narratives remains a loner without the power of a collective force. This construction allows movie heroes to inspire us with their resistance without letting them mount a serious challenge to the dominant ideology of our cultural institutions.[2] A quick survey supports this thesis. In *To Sir, with Love* (1967), Sidney Poitier plays Mark Thackeray, an engineer who is teaching because he has been unable to find a job in his field. In *Mr. Holland's Opus* (1995), the title character views teaching as a temporary gig. Mr. Holland (Richard Dreyfuss) sees himself as a musician and composer although he will ultimately spend 30 years as a high school music teacher. His first day on the job, Holland tells the school principal that his teaching certificate is something to "fall back on." Similarly, Meryl Streep's depiction of Roberta Guaspari in the Hollywood biopic *Music Of The Heart* (1999) evokes a woman who turns to teaching violin in several inner-city schools after her marriage falls apart and she needs to both find an outlet for her time and a way to support her two sons. Her dream was never to teach in the public schools but to stand on a concert stage and perform. Bette Davis plays Miss Moffat in *The Corn Is Green* (1945); she is a woman with an Oxford education in 1895 who moves to Wales to pull young boys out of the coal mines and put them in school.

Many of these outsider teachers are depicted in "true story" films. Jaime Escalante, played by Edward James Olmos, has given up a lucrative job in industry to teach barrio kids in *Stand and Deliver*. LouAnne Johnson's book about her teaching experiences has come to the screen as *Dangerous Minds* (1995), a film starring Michelle Pfeiffer. In this film, Pfeiffer plays Johnson, an ex-Marine hired to teach English in a special program for bright but "difficult" kids before she has actually earned her teaching certification. In *Conrack*, based on Pat Conroy's memoir *The Water is Wide,* Jon Voight stars as a white, liberal teacher sent to fill-in at a poor, all-black school on an island off the coast of South Carolina. In yet another biopic, *The Miracle Worker* (1962), Anne Bancroft plays Annie Sullivan, a nearly blind woman hired to teach Helen Keller. *Freedom Writers* (2007) is the story of Erin Gruwell (Hilary Swank), an enthusiastic teacher from Newport Beach who wears pearls to her interview for a job teaching English in Long Beach, an area known for gang activity.

Sometimes fictive teachers are outsiders in obvious ways, like Whoopi Goldberg's character in *Sister Act* (1992) where she plays a lounge singer who observes a crime then is placed in witness protection disguised as a nun. Naturally, she ends up converting the choir from stodgy to hip, which puts her in a teaching role. One of the more entertaining of these characters, and also musically inclined, is Jack Black's Dewey Finn, a fired rock musician who assumes his roommate's identity as a substitute teacher in *School Of Rock* (2003).[3] In *Teachers*, Nick Nolte plays Alex Jurrell, a disgruntled pseudo-hippie, near-alcoholic, who won't play ball with the administration or with the teachers' union. In *Pay It Forward* (2000), Kevin Spacey plays a seventh grade social studies teacher, Mr. Simonet, whose emotional scars run deeper than those on his body and make it difficult for him to make connections with others. In *The King and I* (1956), as in the versions of this story that preceded and followed it on screen, Deborah Kerr's Anna is a foreigner. In *Summer School* (1987), Mark Harmon plays Freddie Shoupe, a P.E. teacher coerced into teaching remedial English. In *The Substitute* (1996), Tom Berenger plays Shale, a battle-scarred mercenary who goes undercover in a Miami high school to punish students who have roughed up his girlfriend, a "real" teacher.[4] In *Renaissance Man* (1994), Bill Rago (Danny DeVito) is an unemployed advertising executive who ends up teaching Army recruits how to "comprehend," and Damon Wayans makes the reverse trip in *Major Payne* (1995) when he is discharged from the marines and takes over a JROTC program where live grenades and bullets become tools to help students achieve. Finally, in *Kindergarten Cop* (1990), Arnold Schwarzenegger's Detective Joe Kimball is an undercover cop who decides to become a teacher after posing as one. The list goes on, cutting across film genres to clearly cast good teachers (and teachers who become good over the course of the film narrative) in the role of outsider, disliked by other teachers and administrators who perceive them as threats to the status quo. Or, in a few cases, these teachers are relegated to the role of outsider because they are seen as "other" in terms of sexuality, gender, or another perceived difference.

While Hollywood ostensibly positions these teachers as outsiders, they are, in fact, characters that usually operate from positions of relative privilege. Consider for a moment that all of these characters are well-educated. If their primary field is not always education, one cannot argue that Mark Thackeray has a degree in engineering, LouAnne Johnson and Bill Rago have degrees in literature, and Jaime Escalante is trained in both math and computers. All of these characters are also members of a ubiquitous middle class that seems to envelop all of the depicted teachers while, in some cases, putting what should be a sharp division between them and students from working-class, inner-city or, occasionally, even elite student populations. Rather than challenging notions about social class, Jaime Escalante, LouAnne Johnson, and others are determined to deliver their students to the next rung of the meritocracy's proverbial ladder of success, as if helping students fit into the system (and thereby legitimize it) is preferable to changing it. There is a bit of a shift in *Learning to Drive* (2014) when Wendy (Patricia Clarkson), a writer living in Manhattan, takes driving lessons from Darwan (Ben Kingsley), a well-educated Sikh, who has more in common with her than the woman with whom he has an arranged marriage. Wendy is taking driving lessons to increase her independence after her husband leaves her. In this pairing, the teacher is marginalized by class, religion, and race in contrast to the race and class privilege possessed by his student.

Robert C. Bulman argues in *Hollywood Goes to High School: Cinema, Schools, and American Culture* that the dominant theme explored in high school films is a common "ethic of individualism" that is variously displayed in urban public schools, suburban public schools, and private schools (19). Overall, his work is useful as a sociological tool, but Bulman views the films in a way I find a bit reductive because he fails to address the competing messages within and among the films he surveys and overlooks the overarching theme that the institutional structures featured in the majority of these films do not change despite the efforts of teachers and students and regardless of the predominant race, ethnicity, and social class of the student body. In short, there are broad patterns depicted in these films that minimize the categories of social class in terms of how teachers and schooling are presented generally, but there are competing messages within the individual texts and films in the revisionist camp that merit additional attention. We will return to this topic in the Chapter 8.[5] Finally, there are a number of examples of white teachers working with classes in which students of color are the majority. When this is the case, the issue of privilege by virtue of skin color is never directly addressed. Consider the film *To Sir, with Love*. Mark Thackeray is a black man teaching mostly white students in a public school in London during the 1960s, but he has come to them from British Guiana (now Guyana), where blacks are the majority, and he is both better-educated and more financially secure than most of his students and their families. There are plenty of examples of teachers trying to move "under-privileged" students into the "mainstream" but almost no examples of "over-privileged" teachers offering critique, or even serious acknowledgment, of their own relative privilege by virtue of their ethnicity, social class, or education.[6] At least, this is the case in so-called serious films. We will look at the very revealing racial politics of the parodic film *High School High* (1996) in Chapter 8.

Personally Involved with Students

Good teachers in the movies are frequently more closely aligned with their students than with other adults in the school. The teacher–student relationships as portrayed in films vary in their degree of intimacy but often involve some sort of "breaking the rules." To play this behavior out on a continuum from relatively benign to quite dangerous, let's start with *Stand and Deliver*. In this film, Escalante provides a bright student, who is also a gang member, with three sets of books – one for his locker, one for his class, and one for his home – so that his friends won't see him carrying books and tease him.

Chalk (2006) is a compelling film that uses a mock documentary approach to highlight several teachers and a vice principal during a single school year. There is a level of ambiguity about teachers and teaching in this film that is seldom seen onscreen. One teacher is particularly conflicted. Mr. Lowrey (Troy Schremmer) is a first-year teacher who is incredibly uneasy and rigid in his history classroom until he participates in a "spelling hornet" in which teachers compete to spell slang words used by the students. When the students start to prepare him for the competition, he loosens up and begins to form a connection with them then, when he actually wins the hornet, Mr. Lowrey looks happy and relaxed for the first time in the film. It's a nice moment, but the film ends with him trying to decide whether or not to sign a contract to teach another year. The audience is left to wonder whether his tenuous connection with students will be enough to draw him back to a job he is not sure that he likes very much.

In *Looking for Mr. Goodbar* (1977), Diane Keaton plays Theresa Dunn, a teacher of deaf children. Dunn convinces a social worker to bend a few rules to help one of her young students get her own hearing aid. In *Cheaters* (2001), another film based on a true story, Jeff Daniels plays Gerry Plecki, a teacher who encourages the brightest students from his working-class school to cheat in an Academic Decathalon then lie about it when questions are raised about their performance. His justification is that other Chicago area schools have an advantage because of their privilege, and his students should use a "found" test to their own advantage. Is he a good teacher? He's certainly considered one until the cheat is revealed. Robin Williams plays John Keating in *Dead Poets Society* (1989), a teacher at a prestigious, Northeastern prep school. When one of his students wants to try out for a production of *A Midsummer Night's Dream* despite his father's disapproval, Keating's challenge to "seize the day!" outweighs paternal admonitions with dire consequences.

Teachers in *October Sky* (1999), *Powder* (1995), *Akellah and the Bee* (2006), and *Phoebe in Wonderland* (2008) encourage students with special gifts. In *Kindergarten Cop*, Detective Kimball gets involved in a domestic situation after a child in his class (and the boy's mother) are beaten by the child's father. Kimball goes so far as to beat up the father. In *Teachers*, Alex Jurrell returns a Driver's Education car that is stolen by one of his students for joyriding, covers for the same student who "misappropriated" a camera for a class project, and takes a female student to have an abortion – she was impregnated by another teacher. And, in *Sarafina!* (1992), Whoopi Goldberg's character, Mary Masembuko, asks a student to dispose of a gun hidden in her home when the teacher is taken away by soldiers for "questioning" during a State of Emergency declared by the South African government. The students, many of whom are soon to face such "questioning" themselves, never see their teacher again. Most are tortured; some are murdered.

In these movies, it is frequently a measure of the teacher's success that he or she must break through to reach a very difficult or withdrawn student. That process invariably involves a complicated dance with steps forward off-set by steps backward. The breakthrough can come only when the student and teacher develop sufficient trust – when the student realizes that the teacher really cares about the student. In the vast majority of cases, that student is male. This aspect of the cinematically constructed relationship between teachers and students is disturbingly reminiscent of the widely publicized 1992 report by the American Association of University Women (AAUW) entitled "How Schools Shortchange Girls." Several of the movie classrooms contain only male students.[7]

These films clearly articulate a tension that teachers face between responding to the needs of their students and advancing the agendas of their administrators and other school officials. While these films present almost all of the relationships between good teachers and their students as risky because they fall outside the express advancement of the stated curriculum, there is actually very little that is subversive about these encounters and activities. With the very notable exception of *Sarafina!*, there is not much in the way of serious consequences in these films beyond minor policy infractions. Conroy means well in *Conrack*, for example, when he takes his black students trick-or-treating on the white mainland against the superintendent's orders, but the gesture is mostly symbolic. The teacher's righteous indignation and court-supported dismissal is ultimately little more than a minor blip on the already changing social landscape of his hometown. The stakes are somewhat higher in *American History X* (1998) when Avery Brooks, as Bob Sweeney, encourages a former student to gather information on the white supremacist group of which he was once a member. More often, the risks are personal. In *Finding Forrester* (2000), Sean Connery plays William Forrester, a writer who turned recluse after publishing one highly regarded novel. He comes out of hiding to defend the integrity of a 16-year-old neighbor he has been tutoring. In *The Rookie* (2002), based on the true story of major league pitcher Jimmy Morris, Dennis Quaid plays a high school science teacher and baseball coach in rural Texas who faces possible embarrassment to keep a promise to his team and try out for some major league baseball scouts years after his minor league career was cut short by injury.

By the nature of what they do, coaches are teachers – they certainly fit this paradigm – and are personally involved with students. In other films based on true stories, such *We Are Marshall* in 2006 (Matthew McConaughey as Jack Lengyel), *Miracle* in 2004 (Kurt Russell as Herb Brooks), *Friday Night Lights* in 2004 (Billy Bob Thornton as Cary Gaines), *McFarland, USA* in 2015 (Kevin Costner as Jim White), *Glory Road* in 2006 (Josh Lucas as Don Haskins), and *Remember The Titans* in 2000 (Denzel Washington as Herman Boone), coaches inspire teams to overcome the odds and, in the latter three films, to overcome racism.[8] Fictional coaches have a dramatic influence, too. Al Pacino plays Tony D'Amato in *Any Given Sunday* (1999) and drives his team to victory with powerful speeches. Self-awareness – for the student, coach, or everyone involved – is another common and related theme. Jonathan Rhys Meyers plays a soccer coach who helps a young woman grow beyond her cultural restraints (despite their romantic attachment) in *Bend It Like Beckham* (2002), Kevin Costner's Crash Davis helps Tim Robbins's Nuke on and off the field in *Bull Durham* (1988), Samuel L. Jackson's Ken Carter teaches his team there is more to life than basketball in *Coach Carter* (2005), Emilio Estevez's Gordon Bombay learns how to be a kid again in *The Mighty Ducks* (1992), Will Smith's Bagger Vance is a caddie providing life lessons in *The Legend of Bagger Vance* (2000), and Burt Reynolds's Paul Crewe teaches prisoners as much

Figure 2.2. Denzel Washington as Coach Herman Boone in *Remember the Titans*, 2000. This film is based the true story of Coach Boone launching a racially diverse high school football team in Alexandria, Virginia, in 1971.

about self-respect as about football in *The Longest Yard* (1974, and a remake in 2005). A father and son set of characters get into the coaching act when Will Ferrell's Phil Weston and Robert Duvall's Buck Weston are opposing soccer coaches who learn the true meaning of sport in *Kicking and Screaming* (2005).

In the sports classic *Knute Rockne All American* (1940), Knute Rockne (Pat O'Brien) teaches character on and off the football field. Inspired by actual events, *Radio* (2003) is the story of Coach Jones (Ed Harris), who takes a developmentally disabled man under his wing after some football players harass him. Radio, a nickname for the character played by Cuba Gooding, Jr., starts helping out with practices and, after the usual complications, the relationship between the coach and Radio inspires the team and the community. Mr. Miyagi (Pat Morita) teaches his pupil to believe in himself in *The Karate Kid* (1984 and *The Karate Kid, Part II* [1986] and *The Karate Kid, Part III* [1989]). There are many coach-as-teacher movies, but I would be remiss not to mention this fine one: *Million Dollar Baby* (2004). Frankie Dunn (Clint Eastwood) is an indelible character matched perfectly by boxer Maggie Fitzgerald (Hilary Swank in an Oscar-winning performance). The life lessons learned here are hard ones, the learning is reciprocal, and this story does not end happily.

Sometimes coaches break the rules. This is the case for Nick Nolte's Pete Bell in *Blue Chips* (1994). Sometimes they offer a model for how their players should *not* act. Think of Morris Buttermaker (Walter Matthau) in both versions of *The Bad News Bears* (1976, 2005). These are exceptions, however, because coaches as teachers in the movies usually have more at stake than winning a game, and the lessons are often those that complement The Hollywood Model of the good teacher. In any case, the short-term success or failure of a particular teacher (or coach) is not the point in these movies. The point is that good teachers take risks, even risks related to relatively unimportant events, to prove that they care about their students. These movies are glutted with symbolic gestures on behalf of students in place of collective action linking teachers and students. That linkage would demonstrate a very different sort of caring for students, but the mainstream audience is not yet ready for that storyline as a mainstay.

Teachers Learning from Students

Teachers in the movies usually end up learning valuable lessons from their students, or from a particular student. As a parting shot in *Blackboard Jungle*, Gregory W. Miller (a young Sidney Poitier) tells his teacher Rick Dadier

(Glenn Ford), "I guess everyone learns something in school-even teachers." Sometimes the lessons are simple niceties that make everyday life more pleasant, such as the lesson of friendship that his boys teach Mr. Chipping (Robert Donat) in *Goodbye, Mr. Chips* (1939). Sometimes the lesson is that teachers make a difference. Certainly, this is one message from *Hamlet 2* (2008) when students who took drama because they had no other elective become invested in the creative process. A lesson that causes Mr. Shoupe to believe in himself in the inane comedy *Summer School*, causes Miss Honey (Embeth Davidtz) to transform the school and adopt Matilda from the Wormwoods in *Matilda* (1996), causes Kimball to become a real teacher in the formulaic action-adventure-comedy *Kindergarten Cop*, and causes the teachers in *Educating Rita* (1983), *Little Man Tate* (1991), and *The Man Without a Face* (1993) to find the meaning they need to live richer lives than they lived before special students came into their lives.

Unfortunately, the lessons these teachers learn are usually little more than bromides that might have appeared in elementary primers over a hundred years ago. I am reminded of my favorite intertitle from the Charlie Chaplin film *Modern Times*. In the closing scene of the movie, in which the Little Tramp looks over at Paulette Goddard's character winningly, a card comes up that proclaims "Buck up – never say die. We'll get along!" These teachers repeatedly learn that by caring enough (whatever that means) and never giving up on the most difficult students, they can truly make a difference. This storyline has become so clichéd that it is one of the central themes exploited in the parody *High School High*, and it is explored more fully in *Half Nelson* where a teacher who understands critical pedagogy and wants to transform his students must instead rely on a student from his class to keep his addiction a secret. Only in the film *Precious* (2009) does a good teacher – in concert with a social worker and a nurse – present an image that is fleshed out, realistic, and life-changing in ways that transcend what has come before. When Ms. Rain (Paula Patton) asks the at-risk teenagers in her class why they are there, she gets a variety of answers, and when one of them asks her the same question, she tells the class, "I'm here because I love teaching." The moment feels authentic partly because it is understated and partly because she knows many of her students will not make it in the conventional sense, but the teacher is steadfast.[9] Ms. Rain's unflappability is exceptional, however. Maybe she is allowed to be so strong because she is a supporting player in this film, or maybe this film is simply atypical in many ways.

The world of teaching in the movies is filled with pretty platitudes that keep teachers isolated in the classroom toiling against a system that doesn't

care and against students who don't come around until the final reel.[10] By
that time, the teacher is ready to quit, despite that implicit dictum, "Quit-
ters never win, and winners never quit." Good teacher movies are built on a
narrative structure that pushes the protagonist to the brink. The revisionist
film *Detachment* (2011) is exceptional and challenging in many ways. Henry
Barthes (Adrien Brody) plays a roaming substitute who appears to like the
arrangement, which lets him going into classroom after classroom, witness
the pain that students feel, and try to support them with his presence without
staying around long enough to become personally attached. He is able to see
the students' pain because he, too, is broken, and he is often able to give them
the advice and acceptance they need. His own issues keep him from giving
anything of himself or connecting too deeply with students (or colleagues),
however, until the suicide of a student he tries to help opens him up to the
consequences and the impossibility, ultimately, of detachment. The threat of
losing the teacher, or sometimes actually losing the teacher against his or her
will, mobilizes the students in many of these films so that they can finally
deliver their own lesson to the teacher. Theirs is an inspiring but intrinsically
hollow claim that "if at first you don't succeed, try, try again" is the ticket
after all. The students proclaim that their good teacher has reached them
and helped them to "be all they can be." It is a proclamation that celluloid
teachers accept without question. It is a simple lesson that pleases an audience
and assuages lingering public fears that, perhaps, inadequate (and inequitably
distributed) resources and an (often) irrelevant curriculum are problems that
even the most dedicated individual teachers cannot overcome alone in their
own classrooms.

Tension Between the Teacher and Administrators

The very best example of the antagonistic relationship between Hollywood
teachers and administrators probably comes from another biopic, *Lean on Me*.
In this film, Morgan Freeman plays "Crazy" Joe Clark, the highly publicized
principal with a bullhorn and baseball bat brought in to establish order at
Eastside High School in Paterson, New Jersey. What casual viewers of the film
may easily overlook is the first sequence of the movie. Twenty years before
he became principal of Eastside, Joe Clark was a teacher at the same school.
But, was it really the same school? The film opens with Clark teaching a class
full of white students. He has an afro, wears a dashiki, and uses games to
encourage the students in the classroom to learn history. He is energetic in the

classroom, but his hands, empty of the bullhorn and baseball bat to be seen later, are used to issue nurturing touches of encouragement to the students. Clark is called from his classroom by another black teacher to crash a meeting between the teachers' union and school officials where Clark is being sold-out, transferred because he's a troublemaker. He walks down a long, immaculate hallway in outrage, leaving the school for 20 years.

The film resumes with letters spelling "Twenty Years Later" on the lower half of the frame. The immaculate hallway dissolves into a littered passage filled with all types of graffiti. When the new image has completely replaced the old one, silence is interrupted by a heavy-metal song that starts off with these words, "Welcome to the jungle." Students spill out into the hallway, and the contrast is complete. These students are almost all people of color. When Joe Clark comes back into the picture at Eastside, he is the principal, an auto-cratic nightmare who blames the teachers at the school for low test scores and poor control over students while issuing dictatorial platitudes in place of partnership. His single mission is to raise test scores so that the state does not take over the school from the municipality. Here's one example of the rhet-oric he employs at his first faculty meeting at Eastside: "This is an institution of learning, ladies and gentlemen. If you can't control it, how can you teach? Discipline is not the enemy of enthusiasm … My word is law. There's only one boss in this place, and it's me, the HNIC." When a white teacher mouths the letters HNIC with a quizzical expression, a black colleague informs him that that particular acronym stands for "head nigger in charge."

Clark leaves no doubt just who is in charge. At his first assembly at the school, he ceremoniously calls 300 of the "worst" students to the stage and tells them to leave school. When his security force has escorted the "losers" off the stage, Clark warns the remaining 2,700 students to shape up, or "next time it may be you." It should come as no surprise that Clark has been some-thing of a darling to conservatives who want to blame anything or anyone except the system for "failures" in education. Clark tells the students that his program isn't just about test scores; it's about achieving the American Dream. He says, "If you do not succeed in life, I don't want you to blame your parents. I don't want you to blame the white man. I want you to blame yourselves. The responsibility is yours." Perhaps the most telling episode in the film is the way Clark fires the music teacher who does not interrupt her class quickly enough and scurry to the door when the principal appears.[11] She is not cordial to Clark. She is agitated by the interruption in class time because, as she explains to him, she is preparing the chorus for their annual concert at Lincoln Center. He fires her in the hallway for "rank insubordination" after canceling the trip because it did not have his prior approval. Later he glosses over the incident saying, "What good is Mozart going to do for a bunch of kids who can't get a job?" without ever realizing that Mozart and the thrill of performing at Lincoln Center once a year may be the lifeline that keeps some of those kids in school and may provide the only taste of success they will ever know.

Most of the teachers in the movies have conflict with administrators over unorthodox teaching methods and their reluctance to come under their stodgy supervisor's control. A significant number of the teachers in the films I watched lose, or come close to losing, their jobs. Others, like the venerable Mr. Chips, are routinely passed over for promotion. I have chosen Joe Clark as the primary example here because teacher Joe Clark would have never tolerated the brutality of principal Joe Clark, and principal Joe Clark would never have tolerated the free spirit of teacher Joe Clark. The starkness of the contrast makes this an exceptional example. As dramatic, and sometimes melodramatic, as the encounters between good teachers and bad administrators in the movies may be, there is really little substantive about the conflict, and there is never any positive change that comes out of it. Most often these teachers enter the fray on behalf of a particular student or a group of students and take a position seen by administrators as counterproductive to the measurable outcomes they seek: good discipline and improved standardized test scores. The goals of these teachers and administrators are so completely different that they engage in their own respective diatribes without ever conveying one to the other what they really mean. Some of their monologues are eloquently phrased and some are backed by inspiring musical scores, but even when two characters are onscreen at the same time, their lines are presented as monologue rather than dialogue because neither side chooses to listen to the other. It is a construction that benefits the powerful administrators by preserving for them the entrenched support of their bureaucracies while casting the well-meaning teacher back into the classroom with students who are presented as equally powerless.

A Personalized Curriculum

In The Hollywood Model, teachers frequently use everyday events to personalize the curriculum for their students. In some cases, it is a teaching methodology that reveals a teacher's underlying curricular philosophy. Often this occurs in tandem with humor as a teaching technique. In Stand and Deliver, Jaime Escalante enters class the second day wearing an apron and a hat of the type

Figure 2.3. Edward James Olmos as Jaime Escalante *Stand and Deliver*, 1988. In this popular biopic, Escalante works with working-class, Latino students in East LA to help them excel in math and prepare for the AP calculus exam.

worn by short-order cooks. He uses a large cleaver to chop apples and makes wisecracks to interest his students in percentages. He also tries to give his students, all of whom are Latino, a sense of ownership of the subject by telling them that their ancestors, the Mayans, developed the concept of zero, not the Greeks or Romans. He tells them that math is in their blood. In *To Sir, with Love*, Mark Thackeray ceremoniously dumps his copies of the textbooks in the garbage can when he realizes that his students are about to graduate and know nothing that will have an impact on their adult lives. Thackeray sets up a less hierarchical classroom structure built on mutual respect and conversation. When a student asks what they are going to talk about, Thackeray replies, "About life, survival, love, death, sex, marriage, rebellion, anything you want." He tells them it is their duty to change the world and cites their hairstyles, clothes, and music as examples of their rebellion. He shares pertinent pieces of his own life with the students to let them know him as a human being instead of hiding behind the position of teacher. "I teach you truths. My truths. It is kind of scary dealing with the truth. Scary and dangerous." It comes as no surprise that, by the end of the movie, Thackeray has decided to turn down an engineering job and continue to be a teacher in a working-class London neighborhood.

There are many, many other examples. Some of them tend to focus more overtly on a teacher's teaching method. In *Children of a Lesser God* (1986), for example, William Hurt plays James Leeds, a teacher in a special school for the deaf. He uses rock music to convince the students to dance and sing as he leads them. For Leeds, this teaching method is a tool for furthering communication between himself and the students to develop a trusting relationship that can provide a foundation for addressing other issues. Other examples are more directly curricular. In *The Blackboard Jungle*, Dadier brings in a cartoon version of *Jack and the Beanstalk* for thematic analysis, and the resulting conversation is the first productive class period we have seen on the screen. Jurrell repairs the radiator in his classroom while reminding his students that "learning is limitless" in *Teachers*. In *Summer School*, Shoupe bargains with the students, agreeing to perform personal favors for them in return for their attention in class and time out of class spent studying. Perhaps the most poignant example comes from *Conrack*. Conroy bucks the system to take his students to the mainland for trick-or-treating on Halloween. Not only have these children never heard of Halloween, they have never before left their island home. When they reach the superintendent's door, he greets them with a smile and gives the children fists- full of chocolate kisses. The next day he sends Conroy a telegram with news of his dismissal as a teacher.

It is this element (personalizing the curriculum) of The Hollywood Model that contributes most directly to the construction of the good teacher as a radical. In all of these cases, good teachers discard or modify the approved curriculum to try to find a social curriculum that is more relevant to their students' lives. While this effort may make these teachers radical in the eyes of the administrators who employ them and the larger public audience for Hollywood films, there is actually nothing very radical, or even progressive, about what these teachers do in their classrooms. They are, with few exceptions, nonpolitical and are less concerned about social justice than about trying to help their particular students get their own slice of the capitalist pie. Representations of subverting the standard or "approved" curriculum to reach then teach students (which is brilliantly satirized in *High School High*) takes on a new salience in the wake of No Child Left Behind and ongoing debates about Common Core.

Conclusion

The men and women who are good teachers in the movies are not perfect, but if you were to ask the students they teach what makes them different they would probably tell you that these teachers really care about their students and are willing to do right by them at great personal cost. For Escalante, that cost is the wages lost when he leaves a lucrative job in the computer industry to teach in the Los Angeles public schools. For Conroy, that cost is the loss of his job. For others, it is the threat of losing their jobs. And, for Masembuko the cost of teaching her students the truth about their history and themselves is her very life. But, Masembuko is the exception. In her classroom, the lectures become overtly political as she finds ways to make lessons on the dominant ideologies of other cultures throughout history illuminate the oppression her students suffer under apartheid. For the other teachers, having a point of view seems out of the question. It is permissible for these good teachers to care about students and even to advocate for them on a limited basis, but their connections must stay personal and never enter the realm of the overtly political. Hollywood's good teacher is a mediator, or perhaps a buffer, but never a successful organizer. They help their students make difficult transitions into the mainstream of the dominant culture and even validate the meritocracy by helping some of their students make it. Hollywood, like our educational bureaucracy, finds it acceptable for Jaime Escalante to challenge officials representing ETS, a company offering a standardized test in calculus, when those officials accuse Escalante's students of cheating, but it never seems remotely possible that Escalante might challenge the validity of the test itself and the legitimacy of an educational system that assigns human worth on the basis of these scores. When one teacher does challenge the inequity of a system that equips public schools in wealthy areas like elite, private academies while letting poor schools languish, Gerry Plecki's own unethical conduct overshadows and undermines his argument.

The elements of The Hollywood Model that define the good teacher are constructed in the movies in ways that are intended to symbolize the radical or progressive teacher on-screen, but these elements may also be read as constraints that lock these same teachers into the role of fostering social conformity instead of organizing opposition. Remember, the good teacher is typically an outsider among teachers and also has an antagonistic relationship with school officials. By pitting the individual good teacher against the institutions of education in symbolic rather than meaningful action, the imbalance of power makes it impossible for the teacher, even with the tentative or limited help of students, to win. Making the teacher an outsider precludes involving the educator in collective action with other teachers and also eliminates the possibility of dialogue between the good teacher and the representatives of educational bureaucracy. No matter how sympathetic we find the good teacher on-screen, the power imbalance between this individual hero

Notes

1. Biopic is a term commonly used for films based (often quite loosely) on biographical material.
2. Ron Clark (Matthew Perry) is an exception; this biopic tells the story of dynamic teacher who turned around classes of poor students in North Carolina and New York City before opening his own academy in Atlanta, which can be read as a repudiation of the system. Adam Dovico, who taught at Clark's academy, has written about the film and his experience working with Clark in "Ron Clark: The Real 'Good' Teacher."
3. Roy Fisher et al. offer a persuasive critique of School of Rock in Education in Popular Culture: Telling Tales on Teachers and Learners:

> The message of School of Rock is quite ambiguous; on the one hand, rock music is presented as radical and anarchic, an articulation of young people's anger and alienation. On the other, it is perceived as a way of developing transferable skills, and as an after-school activity paid for by wealthy parents. However, a third reading might suggest that the idea of rich and privileged kids being

politicized by the sound and lyrics of rock music represents in itself an intrinsically subversive message. In the end, however, maybe it is the exuberant Dewey who learns the most when he recognizes that teaching is as heroic and radical as playing in a band because both are fundamentally about conveying messages that matter and carrying hope to the next generation. (31–32)

4. He is an outsider and – while he fits the Hollywood model of the good teacher – this substitute clearly pushes the boundaries. In "Representations of Substitute Teachers and the Paradoxes of Professionalism," Lisa Weems finds that most depictions of substitute teachers in popular culture are presented in three basic modes: the incompetent, unqualified teacher; the deviant outsider; and the guerilla superhero. In the three films that constitute *The Substitute* series, it's not difficult to locate Shale as a guerilla superhero!

5. The tendency to minimize the effects of race and social class for teachers, students, and schools has been pervasive on television. For more on this, see *Teacher TV: Sixty Years of Teachers on Television*.

6. *Half Nelson* (2006) is a notable exception.

7. Three interesting exceptions are films in which the female students are gifted in literary studies and writing and are attracted to their male teachers. In the first, *My Girl* (1991), the 11-year-old student has a crush on an inspiring teacher, and he is unaware of her feelings until later in the film. In the second, *Never Been Kissed* (1999), the "student" is a 25-year-old newspaper reporter posing as a high school student who falls in love with her teacher, and he tries to fight his feelings for this particular student. (In its own way, *Never Been Kissed* replays the plot of the 1958 film *Teacher's Pet*, but this time the roles are reversed with Doris Day playing teacher Erica Stone and Clark Gable playing the undercover reporter Jim Gannon, who pretends to be her student then falls for the teacher.) A third exception, *Blue Car* (2002), does not fit the conventional paradigm. This film features an English teacher who encourages one of his students to work with him on her poetry then exploits her vulnerability to force a sexual relationship.

8. Jim White must also overcome some of his own preconceptions when he moves his family cross country to California where he will end up coaching a team of Latino runners in McFarland, California.

9. One of the most authentic teacher characters I have seen is on the television series *The Wire* (2002–08). For an analysis of the series and the police detective turned middle school math teacher Roland "Prez" Pryzbylewski, see the final chapter of *Teacher TV: Sixty Years of Teachers on Television*.

10. *The Emperor's Club* (2002) offers a striking contradiction to the other films. In this movie, Kevin Kline plays Sedgewick Bell, an uptight classics professor at an elite, all-male prep school. He improves a student's grade by one point to encourage a troubled boy and allow him to compete against two other students in a school academic competition. Bell is shocked when the student cheats during the competition and dismayed at his own role in making it possible and eliminating the rightful competitor from participating in the competition. Unfortunately, the film starts with an intriguing premise but never develops into a compelling film because Bell's character is underwritten and the relationships he has with his students – and that they share among themselves – are largely superficial.

11. Ironically, this same actor plays Carla Nichols, an unsympathetic assistant principal at Parkmont High School who hires LouAnne Johnson as a teacher in *Dangerous Minds*.

· 3 ·

THE AESTHETIC-ETHICAL-POLITICAL VALUE FRAMEWORKS OF GOOD TEACHERS IN THE MOVIES

Introduction

In Chapter 1, I described the Hollywood curriculum in Huebner's terms as broadly aesthetic-ethical-political, and in Chapter 2, I established The Hollywood Model as a standard construction of good teachers in the movies. In this chapter, good teachers are analyzed in the context of Huebner's applicable value frameworks with special attention accorded to the way Huebner's clearly delineated metaphors can be employed in reading these film texts alternately as narratives of social conformity or narratives of opposition. It is the "leaky boundaries" (Fiske 1989, 126) of these popular texts, coupled with the absence of boundaries between our lives and the viewing of these texts, that make such intertextual interpretation not only possible but also necessary for making connections between ideas and experiences that allow us access to the richest interpretations of these texts. Teachers and students in the movies move around onscreen before us in a social context that is identifiable as neither modernist nor postmodernist, despite the fact that these films play a pivotal role in creating our collective cultural subjective.[1] In these movies there is usually a social vacuum outside the schools and an ambiguous (though not specifically postmodern) social context inside the schools. The movies I am writing about are mostly mainstream, Hollywood fare as opposed to European art films, independent productions, documentaries, or experimental films. Their narrative structures are generally linear and hero-centered. Their explicit signifiers (some of which were explored or alluded to in the previous chapter) are recognizable features in other films representing many different genres.

Yet, there is more to be uncovered. It is the coupling of the explicit signifiers and themes with what I find implicit in these film texts that leads me to explore the aesthetic classroom, the ethical relationship (between teachers and students), and the limited political language (of teachers) in the movies. As discussed in the previous chapter, Hollywood films about teachers and teaching are neither simply cooptative nor resistant; they function at a level of complexity in which they are both at once. The dramatic tension heightened in commercial films with traditional narrative devices and various production elements is much more obvious than the deeply embedded, but still very real, tensions beneath the celluloid surface that forms the basis for what the Critical Theorists term "dialectics of culture." Just as individual films may present elements affirming both social conformity and opposition, these films also present a multiplicity of meanings that may be interpreted aesthetically, ethically, or politically. While some films appear to lend themselves more directly to interpretation from the perspective of a particular value framework, there is a great deal of overlap.

The Aesthetic Classroom

In "The Art of Being Present: Educating for Aesthetic Encounters," Maxine Greene challenges the superiority of the technical-scientific discourse of curriculum and affirms human consciousness as it is nurtured in the classrooms of the movies.

> We need to think about the creation of situations in which preferences are released, uncertainties confronted, desires given voice. Feeling and perceiving and imagining must, at least on occasion, be given play. Perhaps most important of all: students must be brought to understand the importance of perspective, of vantage point, when it comes to interpreting their lived worlds. The idea of interpretations seems to me to be crucial, that and the realization that "reality" – if it means anything – means interpreted experience. (123)

Giving students the tools to interpret their lives and the world outside them is central to the aesthetic classroom, a curricular framework that is found in all types of films, including one that might best be described as science fiction. In *The Giver* (2014), a community has been structured around avoiding pain, choice, or conflict of any type following a historical calamity that is forgotten by everyone except the Receiver of Memory. When a boy is chosen to become the next Receiver of Memory, his teacher provides holograms with experiences that one after another flood his drab existence with colors and textures and sounds and feelings to change his world forever. Many of the teenage dystopia films that have become popular in recent years have similar themes, but they are staples in traditional good teacher movies, too.

In *Conrack* (1974), Pat Conroy (Jon Voight) takes his students to the woods away from the schoolhouse to teach them the names of flowers they have seen their entire lives but not known. He teaches the students to swim in a project that starts out as political – to empower them to meet the river that has claimed the life of someone from nearly every family – and turns into a transcendent time of play in the water beneath the blue sky and burning sun. During a summer school session, Conroy introduces the class, comprising fifth through eighth graders, to classical music using an old record player and an assortment of record albums. The children are unable to say Beethoven and call him "Bay-cloven," just as their mouths say "Conrack" when they try to say Conroy. Even so, they latch on to the image of death knocking at the door when their teacher plays the Fifth Symphony. Their awareness inspires Conroy, who, with a sheen of perspiration clinging to his pale skin, looks across at their dark faces with pride and says: "Bay-cloven'd be proud of you. Willie Mays'd be proud of you, and from now on, we're going to be proud of ourselves. We're going up the hill, gang. A foot may slip here or there, but nobody's gonna fall."

Later on, when Conroy tells his superintendent that he plans to take the same children trick-or-treating, the older man fails to see the value of such an excursion. "A trip like that isn't worth a pound of cow dung. Those kids don't need trips. They need fundamentals. They need drill and more drill." As Anyon has pointed out, whether these students need "drill and more drill" is not the point.[2] Society has adopted a system in which children who are poor and whose parents are largely uneducated are being trained in school for adult lives spent at repetitive factory and textile jobs. If school is unmeaningful, or even unpleasant, that is appropriate training for their working lives. At least it is appropriate training for those kids who grow up to find work. To teachers in the movies, however, trips and other aesthetic experiences are the fundamentals for all children. In *Conrack*, Conroy pays with his job for taking his class trick-or-treating. The superintendent has him fired. At the end of the movie, as Conroy's boat is leaving the dock, the students play Beethoven's Fifth Symphony, grieving his loss as they would a death. The film, apart from the aesthetic values propagated by Conroy, offers competing messages of oppressive social conformity and opposition to that oppression. Conroy is clearly heroic in his efforts to challenge the institutional hierarchy that dictates blatantly unequal educational practice in his community. Simultaneously, that hierarchy is presented as stable, and even comfortable, to most of the community it serves.

Sometimes aesthetic experiences are grounded in the everyday. Annie Sullivan (Anne Bancroft) uses the tactile features of water and grass and dolls to draw a response from Helen Keller (Patty Duke) in *The Miracle Worker* (1962). Other times, aesthetic experiences are grounded in various disciplines. Pierre Dulaine (Antonio Banderas) uses dance as a way to teach larger life lessons in *Take The Lead* (2006). History teacher Michael "Mr. D" DeAngelo (Ryan Reynolds) makes sitting in a circle, telling stories, and reenacting battles outside part of his every class session in *School of Life* (2005) because, as he tells the students who do not know about his terminal illness, they do not have a lot of time. In *Dead Poets Society* (1989), John Keating's (Robin Williams) teaching comes from his own passionate love of poetry. He urges his students to "seize the day!" On the first day of class, Keating has his students rip the introduction out of their poetry books, an introduction that instructed students to evaluate poems by graphing them mathematically. At first the boys are reluctant, but soon they are ripping pages with abandon. Coming across

Figure 3.1. Robin Williams as John Keating in *Dead Poets Society*, 1989. Mr. Keating's motto to inspire his students is carpe diem, which means "seize the day."

on screen as the embodiment of raw energy, Keating jumps on his desk at the front of the class and proclaims:

Keating: I stand upon my desk to remind myself that we must constantly look at things in a different way. See, the world looks very different from up here. You don't believe me? Come, see for yourselves. Come on. Come on. Just when you think you know something you have to look at it in another way. Even though it might seem silly or wrong, you must try. Now, when you read, don't just consider what the author thinks. Consider what you think. Boys, you must strive to find your own voice because the longer you wait to begin, the less likely you are to find it at all. Thoreau said, "Most men lead lives of quiet desperation." Don't be resigned to that.

Reluctantly at first, then vigorously, the students walk to the front of the class and take turns standing on their teacher's desk.

Keating's infectious spirit gives the students the courage to audition for plays, to call girls for dates on the telephone, and to write poetry. Mr. Nolan (Norman Lloyd), the Headmaster at Welton Academy and a former English teacher, calls Keating down for some of his unorthodox teaching methods in the following exchange:

Nolan: But, John, the curriculum here is set. It's proven. It works. If you question it, what's to prevent them from doing the same?
Keating: I always thought the idea of education was to learn to think for yourself.
Nolan: At these boys' age? Not on your life. Tradition, John. Discipline. Prepare them for college, and the rest will take care of itself.

The irreconcilable dichotomy between the aesthetic curriculum and the rigidly technical curriculum is played out in a symbolic battle over one student in this film, Neil Perry (Robert Sean Leonard). Neil's father, a man of relatively modest means, is constantly pushing his son to excel academically. His measure for that success is good grades and acceptance to an Ivy League college followed by admission to a prestigious medical school. Although Neil does get good grades, his father continually pushes for more. He enrolls Neil in summer science courses. He forbids his son to work on the school yearbook or take on additional extracurricular activities. Neil sees a flier announcing auditions for A Midsummer Night's Dream at a nearby school. He wins the role of Puck and proceeds with rehearsals without telling his father. Neil decides he wants to study acting rather than medicine. When Neil discusses the problem with

Keating, the teacher encourages his enthusiasm but cautions him to discuss the situation with his father and make Mr. Perry see how very important this is to Neil—something the student is unable to do.

Opening night Neil gives a rich performance. His father appears in the audience, but Neil continues as if the magic he is creating on stage could dissuade Mr. Perry's determination to control his son's life. Mr. Perry pulls his son from the stage after the final curtain and takes him home, telling him on the way that he has been withdrawn from Welton Academy and will be going to a military academy. That night, as his parents sleep, Neil stands naked before an open window wearing his headdress from the play and whispers in the cold moonlight, "I was good." Later he creeps downstairs and shoots himself with his father's gun. For Neil, being forced away from the things that gave his life meaning was to have no life at all. Perhaps the only way Neil can exert his right to self-determination in his particular situation is to make this final choice. It is the contradictions inherent in these film texts that allow for polysemic readings. In this case, Neil's death may be read as a final, defiant act of resistance or as an acknowledgment that the societal forces of conformity are too great and powerful to resist. In any case, Mr. Keating's days at the staid institution are numbered from this point forward.

Figure 3.2. *Dead Poets Society*, 1989. At the end of the film Mr. Keating is relieved of his duties, and some of the students mark his departure by standing on their desks in tribute as the music swells and the teacher's eyes fill with tears. What we don't generally recollect is that over half the students stay in their desks with their backs turned to the young teacher.

The Ethical Relationship

In almost all of these films there is a strongly ethical component to the relationship between teacher and student. As the term is used here, an ethically valued curriculum functions in the sense identified by Huebner as "an encounter between human beings" (227). Far from the metaphors of education that denote the student as a thing to be acted upon, such as those described by Herbert Kliebard,[3] the relationship itself is the curriculum. As Kathleen Casey points out in her work with the narratives of women teachers, "nurture is necessary, but it is not sufficient" (1993, 318). Teachers also need authority, but legitimate authority can come only from students and must spring from the relationship between teacher and students.

Mr. Chips (Robert Donat) comes to mind immediately as a teacher who recognizes the importance of personal relationships with students grounded in love and friendship in *Goodbye, Mr. Chips* (1939). That recognition has come over the years by having the boys over for Sunday afternoon tea in his home, visiting with their families, and so on. During a scene early in the film, Chips is recalling the difficulty he had controlling his class as a young teacher. In a flashback sequence, Chips punishes an unruly class by keeping them in late the afternoon of an important cricket match with a rival school. Their team loses, and Chips, admitting he was wrong, says to the boys, "If I've lost your friendship, there's little left that I value." Similarly, Bill Ragos (Danny DeVito) forms attachments with his students, the "squeakers," who overflow the traditional boundaries of the classroom in *Renaissance Man* (1994). His students are a bunch of Army recruits who have been labeled the "Double D's" for "dumb as dogshit." Ragos' task is to teach them to "comprehend," an ambiguous goal never defined in the movie. Ragos is a former advertising executive who is on the job to appease the unemployment clerk and scrape together enough money to buy his daughter a telescope and to send her to Mexico to see an eclipse. He does not want to be in the classroom any more than his students do, but the master's degree he earned from Princeton years before ostensibly qualifies him to be there. In a very unconvincing scene, Ragos begins to reach his students by reading *Hamlet* aloud then having them supply parallel examples of similes, metaphors, and oxymorons from their respective vernacular. Despite the intermittent one-liners and amusing situations, it is quite a stretch for the audience to believe that this collection of inner-city and rural "squeakers" develop such a quick and complete appreciation for the works of Shakespeare. Still, Ragos does develop an on-screen rapport with his students and devises ways to help them overcome personal obstacles and establish a sense of personal worth. All of this is achieved through the interpersonal relationship of teacher and students.

In *Teachers* (1984), Alex Jurrell (Nick Nolte) speaks a strongly ethical language, and we see this philosophy played out in his relationship with a student named Eddie Pilikian (Ralph Macchio). The school is being sued by a student who was graduated without learning to read or write, and one of Jurrell's former students is the lawyer handling the case. Jurrell has been working very hard to convince Eddie to take a remedial English class over until he really learns to read and becomes interested in school. Eddie begins to warm to Jurrell, but there are other factors at play. Eddie is a pawn being maneuvered by his parents who are in the midst of a nasty divorce. In a discussion during social studies class, Jurrell asks students what school does. Students answer that the things they learn in school have nothing to do with their lives. Eddie says, "C'mon, this place is a joke. Why're you being sued by some kid because you didn't teach him nothin'?" Jurrell asks the students to communicate on that topic using any means they want, and Eddie brings in a series of slides that show teachers sleeping during class, security guards frisking a student, female students smoking in the bathroom, and so on. When it turns out that Eddie has taken the camera without permission, Jurrell covers for him, placing his relationship with Eddie above school regulations. The assistant principal, Roger Rubell (Judd Hirsch) is skeptical. "Don't pull some of that Mr. Chips crap with me," says Rubell. "Your job is to get them through this school and keep them out of trouble. That's it!"

Later on, when Eddie's parents come into school furious because their son is taking the remedial reading course again, Jurrell argues the student's case with the assistant principal who tells Jurrell to see that Eddie changes classes. This exchange follows:

Jurrell:	What are we going to do?
Rubell:	You heard me. Drop it.
Jurrell:	He can't read.
Rubell:	He can read enough.
Jurrell:	Enough? What the hell's that supposed to mean?
Rubell:	Goddamn it, Alex. What the hell you want me to do? I am not wasting what little time and money I've got on one kid. For every Eddie Pilikian there are fifty, a hundred kids who learn here-and learn well. Now, we're not here to worry about one kid. We're here to get as many of those kids through the system with what we've got. Now that's reality, and you know it.

Jurrell:	You can't see it, Rog, you can't.
Rubell:	See what?
Jurrell:	This is the same thing we're being sued about.
Rubell:	Don't talk to me about being sued, Alex. I don't want to hear it.
Jurrell:	This is the reason Lisa Hammond is down the hall taking depositions. We're not teaching these kids.
Rubell:	I can't hear you, Alex.
Jurrell:	We're not teaching these kids.
Rubell:	I can't hear you.
Jurrell:	We're doing it again!
Rubell:	I can't hear you.

With that final statement, Rubell turns and walks out the door.

The school board finally settles the case rather than handle the bad publicity that would accompany a trial. That same board tries to frame Jurrell by implying that he has gotten a student pregnant because they are afraid that, should another suit against the school arise, he would be a loose cannon that might damage their case. At first Jurrell acts as if he will leave teaching. When the students in his class and his former student, the lawyer Lisa Hammond (JoBeth Williams), rally around him, Jurrell decides to stay even if he has to sue the school board to keep his position. In the excitement, a fire alarm is pulled. Outside Jurrell confronts Rubell and the school board representative, Dr. Donna Burke (Lee Grant).

Jurrell:	The damn school wasn't built for us, Roger. It wasn't built for your unions, your lawyers, or all your other institutions. It was built for the kids. They're not here for us. We're here for them. That's what it's about. Kids.
Rubell:	Alex, half of them aren't even coming back after the alarm.
Jurrell:	But half will. I think they're worth it.
Burke:	Jurrell, you're crazy. You know that?
Jurrell:	What can I say? I'm a teacher ... I'm a teacher.

With that final statement and swelling music, the film ends. Just how does Jurrell define teacher? Through the friendship and reciprocal personal responsibility he shares with his students. What Jurrell and the students value is not recognized as important to the other, bad teachers or to other characters who represent the teachers' union, the school administration, or the school board. By having Jurrell personally concern himself with students and develop reciprocal relationships with them, the movie effectively isolates and occupies him in such a way that precludes his mustering any serious threat to his bosses' institutional hierarchy. Still, the notion that Jurrell, as a character with the potential for self-determination in a cinematic democracy, *could* mount that resistance fuels the tension in the film text and provides pleasure to the audience.

Many recent films reflect a complexity that is less common in the earlier films, but they still hold true to the general pattern. *An Education* (2009) is based on a memoir by journalist Lynn Barber, and it is ostensibly the story of a talented student in the outskirts of London in the early 1960s who is seduced by a con man of 30 into giving up school for the sort of worldly education he can provide. Although the case for formal education is not made by the head-mistress (played with dourness by Emma Thompson), the girl's encouraging English teacher, Miss Stubbs (Olivia Williams), is there to pick up the pieces, show Jenny (Carey Mulligan) the value of the life of the mind by example, and help the girl prepare for her university entrance exams. Throughout the film, Miss Stubbs has been a voice of reason, and after taking a look at her apartment and independent lifestyle, Jenny finally has a model for a life without her parents and without depending on a man who is much less than he first appears. In *Happy-Go-Lucky* (2009), Sally Hawkins plays a "third year" teacher who is optimistic to a fault. Even her name is perky: Poppy. Her colorful classroom and energetic interactions with the students are matched by her empathy. When she sees one boy acting violently toward a classmate, she pulls him aside, learns about his situation, and enlists the help of a social worker. She is an engaging teacher but also an advocate for her young students. For teachers like these, the "encounter between human beings" is a central component of their teaching.

The Political Language

The language of curriculum theory, much like the language of Hollywood, tends to intermingle components of the ethical and the political. Eisner and Vallance label one description of political values in curriculum[4] as "self-actualization, or curriculum as consummatory experience." Their definition follows:

> Strongly and deliberately value saturated, this approach refers to personal purpose and to the need for personal integration, and it views the function of the curriculum as providing personally satisfying consummatory experiences for each individual learner. It is child centered, autonomy and growth oriented, and education is seen as an enabling process that would provide the means to personal liberation and development. (9)

What is the political project of teachers in the movies? It varies from film to film, but the project is typically one of the factors that motivates the teacher to teach.

In *The Corn Is Green* (1945), Miss Moffat (Bette Davis) is an extraordinary woman who has an Oxford education and a bit of inherited wealth. Early in the film she says, "When I was quite a young girl, I looked the world in the eye and decided I didn't like it. I saw poverty and disease, ignorance and injustice, and in a small way I've always done what I could to fight them." The film is set in Wales in 1895. Moffat's political project is to bring young boys up out of the coal mines and keep them in school until they reach the age of sixteen. Social class, she thinks, shouldn't keep the "nippers" from learning. She uses her inheritance to start the school. The story centers on Moffat's efforts to help one particularly gifted local boy. Theirs is a complicated relationship, but the boy settles down eventually and decides to dedicate himself to his studies. After this star pupil, Morgan Evans (John Dall), has his interview at Oxford for a scholarship, he comes back home to await the results with great anxiety and says, "Since the day I was born, I've been a prisoner behind a stone wall, and now someone has given me a leg up to have a look at the other side. They cannot drag me back again. They cannot. Someone must give me a push and send me over." In true Hollywood fashion (this is an American film), he wins the scholarship and other complications are resolved.

In *Stand and Deliver* (1988), Jaime Escalante (Edward James Olmos) tries to prepare his students to overcome the double barriers of ethnicity and class. He tells them, "There are people in this world who will assume you know less than you do because of your name and your complexion. But, math is the great equalizer." Escalante is right about prejudice. When his students score well on the Advanced Placement (AP) Calculus test, their scores are invalidated because of what the test officials term mysterious similarities in their answers. A repeat test proctored by test officials yields similar scores. As this film confirms, most political projects in the movies are only marginally political. Escalante wants his students to succeed in the dominant culture rather than to challenge or dismantle that culture. The dedicated teacher helps students learn to take the AP calculus test; he does not question the validity of that test or the validity of the practice of administering standardized tests to students.

In *Sarafina!* (1992), the political involvement of teacher Mary Masembuko (Whoopi Goldberg) is central to this story about student resistance in the face of injustice in South Africa's Soweto. This is the only one of the films I have viewed in which the political project is both central to the film and radical. Sarafina is a student in Masembuko's history class and relishes the lessons about her heritage. Like the other students, Sarafina recognizes from Masembuko's lessons that history exists in a cultural context. It is these lessons that help ignite student resistance at the same time that they validate student self-worth.

At one point in the film, Sarafina visits Masembuko in her home. The student watches as her teacher embraces her husband behind the house and says goodbye to him; it is implied that he is active in the resistance and living underground. While the two adults talk, Sarafina inadvertently finds a gun hidden in the kitchen beside the stove. In a subsequent conversation, Sarafina tries to find out from her teacher how she can respond politically to the injustice around her.

Sarafina:	The boys, they can fight. What can I do?
Teacher:	There are other ways, Sarafina.
Sarafina:	Like what?
Teacher:	You know what they say, "If you want to find a way, you must first know where you're going."
Sarafina:	No way …
Teacher:	That's not true. What do you want?
Sarafina:	What do you want, mistress?
Teacher:	Me? I want very many things. I want the war to be over. I want the hate to be over. I want my Joe to be back in my arms. I want quiet days and loving nights. I want babies. I want to come home to kindness.

Sarafina walks over to the gun, brings it from its hiding place and lays it on the table between them.

Teacher:	Would you believe me if I told you this was not mine?
Sarafina:	Yes.
Teacher:	I've never even held it in my hands. It's Joe's.
Sarafina:	He uses it?
Teacher:	He has done.
Sarafina:	I won't tell anyone.
Teacher:	I meant what I said. I hate the killing. I hate the violence. But, I cannot stand aside and let others die for me. I will fight, too. I can't kill. Don't ask me to kill. It's the same old argument. What if they come for you … come to the door … kick it in? Do you reach for the gun? Do you shoot? Do I? I don't know. I don't know.

When the soldiers come to the door of Mary Masembuko's classroom and arrest her for teaching "additional material" to the "authorized syllabus," she goes proudly with her captors, probably aware that she is going to her death. She pauses once before she is pushed into the government vehicle to turn toward the student faces pressed against the classroom window and raise her clenched fist over her head.

Notably, *Sarafina!* is listed as a joint venture of U.S., British, and French producing entities. Yet, casting Hollywood star Whoopi Goldberg in the lead follows the standard industry practice of signing "names" to try to increase box office revenues. Various filmic elements work at once to identify this movie as a South African narrative and to separate it from standard Hollywood fare. It is not only the location work and inclusion of elaborately staged musical numbers that make this film exceptional; the film is separated from other movies about teachers by the directness with which it addresses politics. While mainstream American films often contain an element of cultural politics embedded as a subtext in the overall narrative, *Sarafina!* offers a story that foregrounds political struggle as the teacher and her students directly challenge the government itself and along with it the dominant ideology of racism and other violations of human rights that the South African government represents. Masembuko, Sarafina, and other students are clearly engaged in resistance against oppression rooted in inequalities perpetuated by governmental institutions.

In the other films discussed here, the audience is allowed a measure of comfort at the implications of the struggle between the force of resistance (the good teacher) and the forces of social conformity (the institution and those representing it). It is easy to read the teacher as a wild-eyed idealist who manages to keep the institution honest or, at least, more humane in its dealings with students than it would be without the actions of the teacher who challenges its dominance. But, it is also quite possible for audiences to read that same teacher as a radical and to feel relieved that while she may challenge the dominant educational institution, she will never demolish it. After all, many people find comfort in the sense of security they glean from the status quo, security in believing that institutions and ideologies are distant and benign. Hollywood's good teachers and the institutions in which they labor play out the "dialectics of culture" by offering a recognizable pattern of resistance and social conformity. Mary Masembuko and her students know that ideologies are not benign and institutions are only as distant as they choose to be.

Hollywood teachers reveal their political projects in various ways.[5] Anna in *The King and I* (1956), a frothy musical, tries to improve the role of women in Siam and makes strong anti-slavery statements. Mrs. Wilkinson (Julie Walters) tries to convince homophobic family members that a boy should be allowed to learn ballet and develop his talent for dance in *Billy Elliot* (2000). Ms. Rain (Paula Patton) works with students the rest of the world has given up on and thrown away, but she goes even beyond her commitment in the classroom to bring a student who is a new mother into her home when the girl has nowhere else to go in *Precious* (2009). Rick Dadier (Glen Ford) continues to teach in an inner-city school even after he is beaten, his wife is frightened into premature delivery of their son, and he is stabbed in class in *Blackboard Jungle* (1955). Denzel Washington plays Coach Herman Boone in *Remember The Titans* (2000), which is based on a true story. In this case, Coach Boone is a black coach charged with leading a high school football team during its first season as a racially integrated squad. Washington also plays the good teacher in another true story, *The Great Debaters* (2007), a film he also directed. As professor Melvin B. Tolson, Washington encourages his students to form a debate team, and the Wiley College debaters go on to compete against Harvard in 1935.[6] In *X-Men* (2000), Patrick Stewart plays Charles Zavier, a professor who has assembled and trained children born in the future with an X-factor in their genes that gives them special powers and also targets them for destruction by people who fear them. Elna Penleric (Jane Adams) and Harriett Tolliver (E. Katherine Kerr) start a school in Appalachia in *Songcatcher* (2000) with the idea that education there should involve asking the "mountain people what they want and what they need." *Songcatcher* is set in the past while *Starship Troopers* (1997) presents a celluloid future filled with intergalactic battle and a teacher, Jean Rasczak (Michael Ironside), who inspires students to earn citizenship through military service then leads some of them in battle as their lieutenant.

But, my favorite scene of the overtly political in the movies I have watched occurs in *Conrack*. Conroy has just lost his job for taking the children in his class trick-or-treating. He is driving a beat-up van with big speakers mounted on top in a middle-class, white neighborhood in Beaufort, South Carolina. It is the neighborhood where he grew up. From a microphone inside the van he calls out:

Conroy: Ladies and gentlemen, I don't mean to take you away from your daily routine. I know you've got stores to open, clothes to wash, marketing to do, and other chores. But, I just lost my job, and I want to talk. My name's Pat Conroy. I was paid $510.00 a month to teach kids on a little island off this coast to read and write. I also tried to teach them to embrace life openly-to reflect upon its mysteries and to reject its cruelties. The school board of this fair city thinks that if they root out troublemakers like me, the system will hold up and perpetuate itself. They think as long as blacks and whites are kept apart, with the whites getting scholarships and the blacks getting jobs picking cotton and tomatoes, with the whites going to college and the blacks eating moonpies and drinking Coca Cola that they can weather any storm and survive any threat.

Well, they're wrong. Their day is ending. They're the captains of a doomed army retreating in the snow. They're old men, and they can't accept a new sun rising out of strange waters. Ladies and gentlemen, the world is very different now. It's true this town still has its diehards and nigger-haters, but they grow older and crankier with each passing day. When Beaufort digs another 400 holes in her plentiful graveyards, deposits there the rouged and elderly corpses, and covers them with the sandy Low Country soil, then the old South will be silenced and not heard from again.

As for my kids, I don't think I changed the quality of their lives significantly or altered the fact that they have no share in the country that claimed them, the country that failed them. All I know is I found much beauty in my time with them.

My point is not that Conroy did nothing for the children in his class. Those children felt his love for them and returned it. Over the course of the film, Conroy shakes those children from a listless slumber, helps them connect with the world around them, and helps some of them dream of the world beyond the salt water that divides them from the mainland.

The point is well-taken, however, that one teacher projected as a light in a darkened schoolhouse is not enough. Without the power of a collective force, Conroy probably did all that he could do, and the character is right in realizing that his solitary effort is insufficient. It is unlikely that commercial Hollywood films will often offer audiences other, more radical narratives. As Kellner writes:

... mainstream Hollywood is severely limited in the extent to which it will advance socially critical and radical positions. Hollywood film is a commercial enterprise and it does not wish to offend mainstream audiences with radical perceptions and thus attempts to contain its representations of class, gender, race, and society within established boundaries. Radicals are thus usually excluded from Hollywood film or are forced to compromise their positions within accepted limits. (1994, 102)

Watching one Hollywood teacher making a grand gesture and offering eloquent speeches may make us feel good about the teachers in the movies who do care about students and feel good about ourselves as an audience, but it diverts our attention from the larger cultural issues these films could address but do not.

Conclusion

The Hollywood construction of teacher and the aesthetic-ethical-political language spoken by that model is not unrepresented in the professional discourse of curriculum, as Huebner and the others quoted in this chapter demonstrate, but it is virtually the only model of good teachers and good teaching present in popular culture. There must be reasons that this particular construction of teachers and teaching has been so pervasive and enduring. In *Media Culture: Cultural Studies, Identity, and Politics Between the Modern and the Postmodern*, Douglas Kellner cites Ernst Bloch's argument that "radical cultural criticism should seek out those utopian moments, those projections of a better world, that are found in a wide range of texts" (109).[7] Kellner writes, "Extending this argument, one could claim that since ideology contains rhetorical constructs that attempt to persuade and to convince, they must have a relatively resonant and attractive core and thus often contain emancipatory promises or moments" (109). In Hollywood films the "emancipatory promises or moments" are made manifest by the aesthetic-ethical-political language of "good" teachers presented on-screen. It matters less in these films that Mary Masembuko is murdered, that Conroy is fired, or that Anna leaves Siam to return to her native England than that these teachers stand in our stead to battle oppressive forces and fill us as well as their students with heartfelt, if ultimately fleeting, hope. When Jaime Escalante, Rick Dadier, and Alex Jurrell reach out and connect with the most difficult of their students, we are given the message that in that process liberation from various sorts of oppression is possible for the student through the connection forged with the teacher and often a metaphysical emancipation accrues for the teacher from that same relationship. This pocket of utopia arising in the connective space between (the good) teacher and student satisfies the audience's need to maintain hope for a better world. The dramatic arrival of these utopian relationships is invariably foregrounded in these films against an unchanging background of oppressive institutional hierarchy or more general cultural oppression. While the foregrounded relationship may appear to contradict the backgrounded ideology, the dominant ideology of social conformity is never threatened.

Notes

1. To read more about ideas related to the collective cultural subjective, see Casey on the "text in context" (1993); Gramsci on "collective subjective" (1980); and Fish on "interpretive community" (1980).
2. See footnote 8 for Chapter 1. In Anyon's research on what she termed "Working-class Schools," she found that all subjects were taught in a way that emphasized rote, mechanical work with very little explanation and placing in context.
3. Kliebard describes the metaphors of production, growth, and travel.
4. They identify five conceptions of curriculum: the cognitive processes approach, curriculum as technology, curriculum for self-actualization and consummatory experiences, curriculum for social reconstruction, and academic rationalism (3).
5. Ironically, American history professor Michael Faraday, played by Jeff Bridges in *Arlington Road*, sets out to expose right wing terrorist organizations operating in the United States and ends up being framed for bombing the FBI headquarters in Washington, DC.
6. To read more about *The Great Debaters*, see R. Jarrod Atchison's essay "*The Great Debaters*: The Inspiring Story of Melvin B. Tolson" in *Screen Lessons: What We Have Learned from Teachers on Television and in the Movies*.
7. Kellner adds that identifying utopian moments in apparently ideological texts was undertaken by Bloch in *The Principle of Hope*, which was translated into English in 1986.

· 4 ·

THE TECHNICAL-SCIENTIFIC VALUE FRAMEWORKS OF BAD TEACHERS IN THE MOVIES

Introduction

In Chapter 2, I introduced The Hollywood Model as the system that commercial films use to evoke images of the good teacher. At every level, Hollywood's bad teachers arise in contrast to that outline. I have described the good teacher as an outsider, one who is not well-liked by other teachers. The bad teacher is generally presented as neither liked nor disliked (by other teachers) but as part of the system embedded so deeply into the structure of the school as institution that he or she must be accepted or at least tolerated. While good teachers get involved with students on a personal level and seem genuinely to like them, bad teachers are typically bored by students, afraid of students, or eager to dominate students.[1] The good teacher often has an antagonistic relationship with administrators while the bad teacher fits into the administration's plans for controlling students. Finally, as good teachers personalize the curriculum to meet everyday needs in students' lives, bad teachers follow the standardized curriculum, which they adhere to in order to avoid personal contact with students.

When Huebner discusses his five value frameworks for curricular thought – technical, scientific, (a)esthetic, ethical, and political – he argues that none of the five values he proposes exists in a vacuum separate from the other four and that none is inherently good or bad. Instead, Huebner points out the positive and negative aspects of each value framework. In Chapter 3, I proposed that Hollywood constructs good teachers as those who use some combination of aesthetic-ethical-political values in the sense Huebner writes of those frameworks. Recall for a moment Pat Conroy in the film *Conrack* (1974). He obviously operates from each of those three frameworks. He brings aesthetic experiences to the classroom with his use of music and takes students beyond the classroom walls to experience the beauty of the world around them. He develops a personal relationship with students and visits in their homes. Coming to know his students and recognizing their oppression at the behest of his own white culture leads Conroy to try to make them aware of the world outside their island and foster the origins of a political consciousness.

Hollywood films also present images of bad teachers although, not surprisingly, they are seldom the central figures in commercial films. Instead, the bad teacher in the movies is generally presented as a counterpoint to the good teacher lionized on celluloid or as a potential foil for a band of spirited teenagers.[2] In either scenario the bad teacher is clearly a supporting player, and in most cases that teacher exemplifies Huebner's technical or scientific value system. The exception tends to be instructors of physical education; they generally demonstrate none of the value frameworks but are nevertheless presented as bad teachers. Most physical education teachers are not shown in the process of teaching. They are yelling at students, otherwise humiliating students, or engaging in sexual escapades or ridiculous hijinks. It is interesting to note that the latter characterization is often true also of college professors, which is undoubtedly linked to the anti-intellectual thread that runs through the most commercial of Hollywood films. Bad teachers in the movies are also signified by the absence of the aesthetic-ethical-political value frameworks in their teaching.

The Technical Value Framework

Of these two value frameworks, the technical and the scientific, almost all of the bad teachers in the movies represent the negative side of technical values. Huebner presents the technical value framework as one centered on measurable outcomes. Technical values include an effort toward efficiency and a focus on evaluation with probable moves toward quality control. He writes:

> Current curricular ideology reflects, almost completely, a technical value system. It
> has a means-ends rationality that approaches an economic model. End states, end

products, or objectives are specified as carefully and as accurately as possible, hope-fully in behavioral terms. Activities are then designed which become the means to these ends or objectives. The primary language systems of legitimation and control are psychological and sociological languages. (223)

Huebner maintains that this curricular discourse, which is undoubtedly the dominant discourse, is both valid and necessary, but it is reductive to take the whole of human knowledge and individual expression and contort the richness of that experience to fit within the confines of this very narrow edu-cational model. To do so "weakens the educator's power" (224). For admin-istrators in the movies, the technical framework is clearly dominant and is centered on improving test scores and achieving order as the desired ends. Whether implicitly or explicitly, these same goals are generally shared by bad teachers in the movies. One of the best-known characterizations of the con-trolling, stodgy teacher dates to the early days of sound cinema. In Josef von Sternberg's 1930 cinema classic *The Blue Angel*, Emil Jannings plays Immanuel Roth, whose students caricature him as the devil. His serious and unyielding persona in the classroom makes his subsequent downfall, inspired by a show-girl played by Marlene Dietrich, even more precipitous. Once established, the traditional portrayal of controlling teachers takes root and thrives.

In *Fast Times at Ridgemont High* (1982), *Ferris Bueller's Day Off* (1986), and *Dead Poets Society* (1989), bad teachers are presented as colorless men who drone unmercifully in abstraction about subjects students find boring. They expect order in their classrooms and use grades to enforce it. In *Fast Times at Ridgemont High*, Mr. Hand (Ray Walston) locks the door when the bell rings and opens the first class of the semester by telling students that there will be a twenty question quiz every Friday and that their grades in the class will result from the average of their quizzes, their midterm, and their final with each component worth a third. He is shown more often enforcing his rule against eating in class and needling a pothead surfer named Jeff Spicoli (Sean Penn) than talking about his subject, U.S. History. In *Ferris Bueller's Day Off*, the situation requires even less of a presence onscreen for bad teach-ers to be amply represented. Over the course of the film, there are several shots each of two teachers, one teaching economics and the other English. Both deliver meaningless monologues in a mind-numbing monotone as cutaway shots reveal students falling asleep or struggling to keep their eyes open. The scenes are brief, but the impression they leave with viewers is unmistakable.

In *Dead Poets Society*, the final scene shows Mr. Nolan (Norman Lloyd), who is the Headmaster at the school, taking over Keating's class in the wake of the younger teacher's firing, creating an effect that is equally dynamic. In an early scene, Mr. Keating (Robin Williams) had ceremoniously urged students to rip out the introduction to their poetry text because those pages dictated a means of assigning value to poems by graphing them mathematically instead of taking a more aesthetic approach. As the final scene opens, Mr. Nolan begins anew by following the outline in the text. Clearly, Mr. Nolan wants the boys to play by the rules and follow the assigned text uncritically instead of learning to think for themselves. That is his formula for having them arrive at the desired outcome – acceptance at a prestigious college. This scene reinforces themes from an earlier conversation cited in Chapter 3 in which Nolan calls Keating down for letting the boys think for themselves. Nolan maintains that the curriculum at Welton Academy is "set" because it is "proven." After all, the faculty, alumni, and students at this prestigious New England prep school have come to believe that the honor bestowed on the school – and their own personal accomplishments – rest atop the school's four pillars: Tradition, Honor, Discipline, and Excellence. Their means-ends rationality positions them all to believe that their privileged status comes as their due in the meritocracy; no one ever recognizes that they are beneficiaries of a system created to make them reach the desired outcome time after time, generation after generation.

In *Fame*, Alan Parker's 1980 film about life at New York City's High School for the Performing Arts, we see the bad teacher represented by Mrs. Sherwood, an English teacher played in the movie by Anne Meara. The other teachers featured in the film teach in the arts – dance, acting, and music. Sherwood is the only teacher in an academic area featured in *Fame*, and her character plays out the tension between the arts and academics through her relationship with Leroy Johnson (Gene Anthony Ray). The film unfolds in sections beginning with "The Auditions" and ending with "Senior Year." Early on, the audience meets Leroy Johnson when he accompanies a young woman from his neighborhood to serve as her dance partner during auditions.

He's in, she's out, but Leroy's ride through the program is not altogether a smooth one because of his difficulty in Sherwood's class. This exchange occurs during the section of the film titled "Freshman Year."

Sherwood:	Why are you here, Mr. Johnson?
Leroy:	'Cause I'se young and single and I loves to mingle.
Sherwood:	Speak English.
Leroy:	I speaks like I likes.
Sherwood:	This is my homeroom. You'll speak as I like. I teach English. Now, if that's a foreign language, you're gonna learn it. This is no Mickey

	Mouse school. You're not getting off easy because you're talented. You'll work twice as hard. Now, I don't care how well you dance ...
Leroy:	Bitch (and something unintelligible).
Sherwood:	... or how cute you are, or how many colored tutus you have. If you don't give your academic subjects equal time, you're out.
Leroy:	Bullshit.

From this point, their relationship spirals downward.

Leroy is habitually late turning in assignments, and Sherwood fails to work on the real problem: her student's poor reading and writing skills.

Leroy:	I forgot it [his homework].
Sherwood:	For two weeks?
Leroy:	I told you. I done it, and I forgot it.
Sherwood:	My hearing is fine. It's your homework that's missing. And, these couple of pages I have, they're unintelligible.
Leroy:	It's a secret language, all right. It ain't meant for whiteys to understand.
Sherwood:	This isn't a joke.
Leroy:	I got lots of jokes.
Sherwood:	This is garbage.
Leroy:	My pen broke.
Sherwood:	It's in pencil.
Leroy:	That broke, too.
Sherwood:	Hey, you can't learn to read; you can't learn to dance. You're flunking out.
Leroy:	I can read.
Sherwood:	Terrific, go ahead. Surprise us. Sarah, give 'im your book. Pay attention, class. Mr. Johnson is gonna read.
Leroy:	I said I can read.
Sherwood:	Then read.
Leroy:	No.
Sherwood:	Read!
Leroy:	No!
Sherwood:	Read!

Leroy answers her, "No, you fuckin' bitch," and continues with his tirade before stalking out of class and breaking a series of glass bookcases in the hallway outside the door. Inside the classroom, Mrs. Sherwood smiles and puts upright a chair Leroy overturned on his way out.

Later on, the audience sees Leroy on the street where he is presumably living. By dim firelight, he struggles to read a manual for a Maytag washing machine. His is a life Mrs. Sherwood either cannot envision or does not care to envision. The next year begins with Leroy stopping by Sherwood's office as she stands on a ladder replacing books on an upper shelf. He has evidently turned in a book report on "The Best of Playboy," and Sherwood suggests *1984*, *Huckleberry Finn*, *Great Expectations*, and *Treasure Island* as more suitable texts. When Leroy answers that reading is "not my style," Sherwood pulls down a book and tosses it to Leroy. "Then try *Othello*," she says. "He's black. A thousand words in two weeks." Perhaps Mrs. Sherwood really believes that Leroy will respond to the material and find meaning in its pages because the character Othello is black. Not Leroy. Not at this point in his life. But, all that matters for Sherwood is the outcome, the one thousand words.

There is one final altercation between Leroy and Mrs. Sherwood in a hospital hallway where her husband is a patient. He tells her that he must pass her class to graduate and join a professional dance troupe. She tells him that this is neither the time nor the place for that discussion. The scene ends without resolution. Both are angry. They are unable to find common ground. Evidently Leroy passes the English class because he dances in the graduation program in the film's final scene, but we do not have reason to believe that he ever learns to read and are not sure, given the caustic presence of Mrs. Sherwood, that he should want to.

Teachers (1984), a film that gives us an illustrative example of the good teacher in Mr. Jurrell, also provides a memorable bad teacher in the form of Ditto. Ditto, played by Royal Dano, earns his nickname because of the way he hogs the hand-crank mimeograph machine each morning in the school office. In his classroom, the student desks are placed in orderly rows facing away from his own desk. Students are in their seats and quiet before the bell rings. As the bell rings, the students at the end of each row walk to Ditto's desk and pick up worksheets to pass forward to the other students sitting in their rows. Each class begins that same way. When the papers are in the hands of the students, they begin to work silently, and Ditto begins to snooze behind his newspaper.

Ditto's students and colleagues all know what goes on in his classroom. In the following exchange in the teacher's lounge, a teacher has just asked the assistant principal to put a particular student in Ditto's class because the student has bitten that teacher and because the assistant principal insists that he can't expel the student, since to do so would violate the boy's civil rights. When Ditto begins to speak, Jurrell cannot pass up the opportunity to voice what everyone else probably believes. This scene brings the hero in *Teachers* face-to-face with the film's composite character representing bad teachers.

Ditto:	Well, that's fine with me. I'll handle him.
Jurrell:	You'd bore him to death.
Ditto:	What's that supposed to mean?

Jurrell:	Whatdya think it means, Ditto? Your class is boring. Your students don't learn a thing. If it weren't for tenure, you'd be selling vacuum cleaners. Have I left anything out?
Ditto:	I don't have to take that from you. I have received three consecutive teaching awards for the most orderly class.
Jurrell:	Oh.
Ditto:	Three consecutive awards for the most orderly class. And, what do you think about that, mister?
Jurrell:	Gee, Ditto. Your shit don't stink.

It is no accident that later on when the cadence of Ditto's snore during class is interrupted and his eyes fly open before his final gasp, no one notices. His class is orderly, and students keep their eyes forward as they complete their worksheets. The bell rings, and students file out without noticing anything amiss.

Another period begins and ends, and still another follows. Ditto, whom we finally learn is really named Mr. Styles, remains behind his desk when emergency medical technicians burst into the room. The school nurse sits quietly in one of the desks, which she has turned around to face the front of the room, and smokes a cigarette. One of the medical technicians exclaims, "This guy is dead!" The nurse deadpans, "Really? How can you tell?" For Ditto, his technical value framework revolved around maintaining order and continuing his supply of worksheets for students to complete during each class. In the end, his objectives were met, but no one stopped to notice because no one really cared.

Figure 4.1. Royal Dano as Ditto Styles in *Teachers*, 1984. Mr. Styles maintains absolute order in the classroom and structures lessons with such precision that there is very little contact with students. No wonder it is several periods after his death at his desk that anyone notices.

Possibly the cruelest of the "bad" teachers is Eve Tingle, played with chilling precision by Helen Mirren in *Teaching Mrs. Tingle* (1999). Her military bearing and manipulative nastiness is enough to make even the school principal cower. She criticizes her students in history class when they present their projects and finds ways to push personal buttons for each one to maximize the hurt she inflicts. Mrs. Tingle targets Leigh Ann Watson, played by Katie Holmes, a smart girl whose mom is a waitress struggling to support the two of them. Leigh Ann has worked hard to win a lucrative scholarship, and Mrs. Tingle gleefully dashes the student's hopes. When two of Leigh Ann's friends try to help her, Mrs. Tingle ends up their captive in her home. Mrs. Tingle never does learn the lessons of fairness and kindness the students hope to instill, but she does end up fired from her position after attacking her pet pupil in a case of mistaken identity. And, yes, Leigh Ann wins the scholarship in the end.

Perhaps the most compelling, and certainly the most extreme, examples of the technical value framework come from *Class of 1999* (1989) and its sequel *Class of 1999 II* (1994). The action of the first film takes place in Seattle's Kennedy High School and the free-fire zone surrounding the school. Free-fire zones are gang-controlled areas that police do not enter. The film opens with the school principal, Mr. Miles Langford, played by Malcolm McDowell (who also plays a blustery principal in the 2010 film *Easy A*), and other school officials meeting with Dr. Forrest (Stacy Keach). Forrest is head of a company known as Megatech, and he labels himself and his employees "automation and robotics specialists." He is trying to close a deal by which his company would provide Langford and the others from the "Department of Educational Defense" with three "super teachers." As Forrest puts it, these "artificially created tactical education units have been thoroughly programmed in history, chemistry, all mathematics, of course physical education, and also come equipped with the optional XT6 hardware to deal with discipline problems." Almost immediately, that optional hardware goes haywire, much to Forrest's delight.

Discipline is, after all, the name of the game in Kennedy High School in 1999. As the school day begins, the audience watches Cody Culp, played by Bradley Gregg, make his way through gang skirmishes to arrive at the school barricades. Culp has just been released from prison for gang activity and is trying to avoid being sent back. A loudspeaker message greets him at the school guard tower, "Welcome students to Kennedy High School. All weapons must be surrendered before entering the school grounds." Besides the students, the school is populated by SWAT-team goons wearing Darth Vader style hats.

We never see any teachers other than the three "super teachers" produced by Megatech. When these teachers enter the classroom, they begin to subdue students by beating them to a pulp or, if they persist in their resistance, killing them. Once order is established, these teachers move toward their secondary objective. As the history teacher puts it, "I operate from a model of absolute zero tolerance."

Meanwhile, Cody and the principal's daughter have become interested in one another and set out to confirm their suspicions about the new teachers. They confront Principal Langford who, unable to ignore the growing body count of student casualties, in turn confronts Dr. Forrest. Langford learns that the "super teachers" are, in fact, reprogrammed military surplus "battledroids."

Langford:	So, they've been waging war with my students?
Forrest:	Isn't that what all teachers do? But, my people aren't just fighting, Miles. They're winning.
Langford:	Whatever happened to education?
Forrest:	The students can learn if they want to. They simply have to make the right choice.
Langford:	Sure, learn or be killed. I want you to turn them off. I'm terminating this project.
Forrest:	I'm afraid that's the bad news, Milesy. You see, once this program has been implemented, I'm afraid it can't be turned off. The bottom line is "kill the enemy."

With that, Forrest has one of the "super teachers," the physical education teacher, kill the principal. The three have effectively become the efficient killing machines originally intended. They take out the Megatech technicians monitoring their activities from a control center inside the school, wage war against the gangs (which, ironically, have united against the killer teachers), and finally kill Forrest before a few enterprising students dismantle the droids.

In the sequel to this film, the killer teacher turns out to be Dr. Forrest's "mental" son, who thinks he is a battledroid. Posing as a substitute teacher in various schools, John Bolen, played by kickboxing champion Sasha Mitchell, runs around saying things to other teachers such as "Discipline is necessary to maintain order," "Order is necessary to prevent anarchy," and "If you allow a student to gain control of a situation, the result is anarchy." Before he kills unruly students, Bolen usually manages a silly one-liner. At one point in the film, for example, he says the following before incinerating a student: "You've been more than a bit of a discipline problem. Now we're going to have to do something about your attitude. In fact, you're on permanent detention …

School's out." *Class of 1999* and its especially inane sequel may seem to be vastly different from the other films cited in this section. Still, they share several elements in common. Schools are driven by adults who do not care about students on a personal level but instead care only about measurable outcomes. For administrators and teachers alike, those outcomes are discipline and, sometimes, test scores. In most of the films, bad teachers do not literally kill students who get in their way, but in the end is it such a different thing to kill their spirits?

The Scientific Value Framework

Huebner writes that "scientific activity may be broadly designated as that activity which produces new knowledge with an empirical basis" (225). In terms of curriculum values, Huebner acknowledges that a "packaged curriculum" may be useful to produce information and determine how students respond to a particular curriculum but warns against the narrow conception of "educational activity valued only for the change produced in students or for the support it brings to teachers" (226). While most bad teachers in the movies are presented as caring only about achieving perfect discipline or some vague notion of academic outcome, there are two compelling examples of bad teachers who manipulate the scientific value framework for their own benefit.

In *Real Genius* (1985), Dr. Jerry Hathaway is a brilliant, though greedy, professor of physics at Pacific Tech. Hathaway (William Atherton) has assembled a team of top science students, including a 15-year-old prodigy, to help him with "The Crossbow Project." The students, who include Chris Knight (Val Kilmer) and prodigy Mitch Taylor (Gabe Jarrett), do not realize that their research is feeding a lethal CIA military project and is being turned over by their professor to a military contractor for big bucks. Hathaway's utter disdain for other people is evident throughout the film. At the beginning of the movie, when he goes to a science fair to tell Mitch that he's been accepted into Pacific Tech and will be part of Hathaway's own research team, Hathaway confides in the boy, "Mitch, there's something you're going to have to understand. Compared to you, most people have the IQ of a carrot. We're different than most people, Mitch … better." Later, near the end of the film, Hathaway hands out the final exam in one of his classes.

Hathaway: All right. We have exactly three hours for this. And, remember, we believe in the honor system here, boys and girls, though it will be

readily apparent to me how many of you have absorbed this material
and how many of you haven't. Take one [paper] and pass them back
just like your IQ was normal.

For most of the students on the research team, creating new knowledge is
intrinsically worthwhile. Knight, in particular, turns his research into amuse-
ment by designing elaborate pranks and planning pleasant surprises for his
fellow students. For Hathaway, the bad teacher, the motivation is quite different. Dr. Hathaway seeks recognition as the best and a pile of money to go
along with it. He does not care that The Crossbow Project is designed to use
lasers to kill humans on battle stations locked in space. All Hathaway seems
interested in is remodeling his expansive Victorian home, accumulating a lot
of costly fixtures and trinkets, and being sure that at least one of the students
on his research team will act as his flunky. Clearly, he represents only the most
negative aspects of the scientific value framework.

Professor Gerry Lambeau (Stellan Skarsgård) in *Good Will Hunting* (1997)
may or may not have mass destruction on his mind, but clearly he does hope
to enhance his own academic reputation by exploiting the unschooled genius
of a local kid he discovers solving a complex problem on a hall blackboard.
Will Hunting (Matt Damon) works as a janitor at MIT by day and hangs out
with his buddies in South Boston by night. Somewhere in between, he manages to read and remember a virtual library full of books. When Hunting is
arrested for assault and facing active time because of his previous arrests, Lambeau steps in to keep the young man out of jail so long as Hunting works with
the professor and undergoes therapy with Lambeau's former college roommate
Sean McGuire (Robin Williams).

McGuire, who teaches at a community college, places students above
research and tries to protect Hunting's best interests. This proves a difficult
task in direct opposition to Lambeau's desire to realize his own goals through
Hunting's intellectual gifts.

Sean:	You wanted to talk about Will?
Lambeau:	Seems like it's going well.
Sean:	I think so.
Lambeau:	Well, have you talked to him at all about his future?
Sean:	We haven't really gotten into it.
Lambeau:	Maybe you should. It's pretty exciting actually. My phone's been ring-ing off the hook with job offers for this boy.
Sean:	How does anybody even know about him?
Lambeau:	Well it's tough to keep something like this a secret.

Sean:	Jobs doing what?
Lambeau:	Math-related fields.
Sean:	What? Defense contractors?
Lambeau:	A number of different fields, Sean. The point is he should be doing something with his talents.
Sean:	Well Gerry, this kid's not here for nothing. I need time to figure out what I'm dealing with and how to help him. And if that means he doesn't punch the clock right away, then that's what that means.
Lambeau:	Don't think he comes in and talks to you because he likes you. The boy comes in because he's ordered by the court to do so, Sean.
Sean:	I know that.
Lambeau:	If we don't show him that there's value in what he can do, when this is over he's going to go right back to where he was when I found him.
Sean:	And if we try to jam an agenda down his throat–
Lambeau:	–O, for God's sake, Sean.
Sean:	No, Gerry. Stop! Just stop it! It's not about what you want him to do. It's about the boy's best interest.

Later in the same scene:

Lambeau:	This boy could make contributions to the world, Sean. I can help him do that.
Sean:	I imagine you'd like that.
Lambeau:	Look, it's important to start early on these things. I was doing advanced physics when I was 18-years old and it still took me 23 years to win a Nobel Prize.
Sean:	Maybe he doesn't care about that, Gerry. Give him time to figure out what he wants.
Lambeau:	Sean, I came here today out of courtesy. I wanted to keep you in the loop. Believe it or not, some people do have their priorities straight. As we speak the boy is in a meeting I set up for him over at Raytheon.

Lambeau walks away, but the final chapter has not been written. Following The Hollywood Model, McGuire's concern and focus on Hunting's welfare prevail. Hunting spurns Lambeau's contacts, walks away from a job the professor arranges, and follows McGuire's advice to put personal relationships first in his life. Once again, the bad teacher is thwarted in the final reel.[3]

Lambeau's self-absorption and elitism are common characteristics among screen professors. In *Wit* (2001), Emma Thompson plays Vivian Bearing, an English professor specializing in 17th century poetry, whose scholarship is more defining to her character than her teaching and whose interactions with students are presented as generally adversarial. Similarly, John Nash (Russell Crowe) in *A Beautiful Mind* (2001) walks into a stuffy, MIT classroom in his tee shirt to face properly attired students because his mind is somewhere else. He's late to this class and wouldn't have thought to come at all if colleagues had not reminded him. Nash closes the window to block out construction sounds outside and proclaims, "Your comfort comes second to my ability to hear my own voice" then adds that the class will be a waste of their time and, what is infinitely worse, his time. He is a brilliant mathematician whose interest does not extend beyond his research projects into the classroom. Soon he is dating a student, which is a common behavior among teachers of advanced students in films such as *Animal House* (1978), *Top Gun* (1986), *The Nutty Professor* (both versions, 1963 and 1996), and even more serious films such as *Looking for Mr. Goodbar* (1977) and *Elegy* (2008). We'll return to this topic near the end of the chapter and again in Chapter 7.

In something of a role reversal, Indiana Jones (Harrison Ford) trades in his swashbuckling persona for glasses and a stuffy suit when he enters the classroom in *Raiders of the Lost Ark* (1981). The camera reveals that his class is filled with mostly females who appear on the verge of swooning, despite his dry lecture style. One attractive blonde in the front row has "love" and "you" inked on her eyelids so that even the largely oblivious professor cannot overlook the message when she closes her eyes. Whether or not they are lascivious, and lasciviousness does make their motives and actions suspect, college professors are generally presented as more distant from students than teachers of high school and younger students; their distance is often a product of their intellectualism and self interest, which presents them in marked contrast to Hollywood's good teachers.

The Special Case of Physical Education Teachers

Instructors of physical education merit a separate section in this discussion of cinema's bad teachers. There are many indelible moments in Woody Allen's 1977 Oscar-winning comedy *Annie Hall*, but one of them springs readily to mind here. Picture a 1940s-era, public school classroom in the Coney Island area of Brooklyn then imagine Allen's alter ego Alvy Singer saying, "Those who can't do teach, and those who can't teach teach gym." As Charles A. Duncan et al. discovered in a survey of films with physical education content, there are several themes that are common to multiple films. These themes are overwhelmingly negative and include the locker room as a place for humiliation and aggression, extreme images of female physical educators, and negative teacher attitudes toward students (38–45). Most gym teachers are relegated to this category without the benefit of any particular curricular value framework because most of them are not portrayed in the process of teaching. Carol A. Smith discusses the negative stereotypes of physical educators – the teacher as bully; the dumb jock, who is often depicted as oversexed; the dual role of the former athlete pigeonholed as a coach; and, women in physical education who are depicted as the masculine female (103–05).

Miss Mann (Jayne Trcka), for example, is presented as a perverse joke in *Scary Movie* (2000). Coach Calhoun (Sid Ceasar) from *Grease* (1978) and *Grease 2* (1982) is presented as generally clueless while the PE teacher in the movie *Clueless* (1995) is alternately snide and easily manipulated by the film's main character, a spoiled, Beverly Hills high schooler named Cher. Alicia Silverstone plays Cher, and early on her narration reduces the PE teacher to a standard cliché, "And, in the grand tradition of PE teachers, Miss Stogner (Julie Brown) seemed to be same-sex-oriented." In *Teachers*, we see Mr. Troy usher an attractive student into his office next to the gym then looks around to be sure there are no witnesses to their assignation. Later, he is presented in tears before school officials as we learn that he has impregnated not one but three students at the school. In *Mean Girls* (2004), Coach Carr (Dwayne Hill) teaches abstinence-only sex education classes while he, unbeknown to the students for most of the film, has romantic relationships with two girls in the "Cool Asians" clique at the school. In *Class of 1999*, it is no accident that one of the killer droids placed in the school as "super teachers" is a physical education teacher. In one scene, he nearly kills a student on the wrestling mat before actually killing another one on the high-gloss wood floor of the basketball court. Similarly, it is no accident that the abusive football coach in *The Faculty* (1998) (played by Robert Patrick) is the first of the teachers and administrators at an Ohio high school to be taken over by an alien being before he begins to forcibly take over other faculty and students. Two films, however, merit special attention.

In *Porky's* (1981), a raunchy "coming of age" flick set in Angel Beach, Florida, in the late 1950s, there is an assortment of physical education teachers to discuss. Boyd Gains plays Coach Bracket, a 23-year-old teacher who ogles students and two other teachers before ultimately admitting he is the "worst coach that ever lived" and joining up with a rowdy group of students involved in a dangerous prank. Miss Walker is a sexy teacher who wears shorts that reveal more than they should and appears in the film mainly to entice Bracket and the male students without ever uttering a line. Miss Lynn Honeywell (Kim Cattrall before her iconic turn as Samantha on *Sex and the City*

[1998–2004]) is the main object of Bracket's desire. At first he thinks she is a virgin. Later a colleague urges him to get Honeywell into the boy's locker room during class one day, and Coach Bracket quickly learns why Honeywell has been dubbed "Lassie." She becomes aroused by the smell of the boy's locker room, makes sexual advances toward Bracket, and begins to howl loudly while they are engaged in intercourse. Students and teachers alike hear them from the gym below. Most of the students laugh, but Beulah Balbricker (Nancy Parsons) is not amused. Of all of the physical education teachers in the film, Balbricker has the most screen time. She is the object of fat jokes and pranks and is known by everyone as "Kong." Like Honeywell, even her name evokes a particular image that is used to identify her character. Throughout the film, a group of boys have been spying on girls in the shower through secret holes in the wall. One day, after some of the girls discover them, one of the boys sticks his penis in the hole. Unbeknown to him, Miss Balbricker has entered the shower. She is appalled by their behavior and grabs the boy's penis as if she can use it to pull him through the wall and take him to the office. Later, after he has escaped her grasp, she tries to convince the school principal that she could identify the penis in a line-up. Finally, she is arrested for pouncing on the boy she suspects as the culprit and trying to pull down his pants to identify his penis. Throughout the film, Balbricker is presented as a joke, as a bad teacher out to "get" students.

Betty Buckley plays a more complex character in Brian De Palma's 1976 horror film Carrie, which is based on a best-selling novel by Stephen King. Buckley's Miss Collins tries at first to protect a high school student who has begun her first menstrual period in the showers after gym class. Carrie (Sissy Spacek) is the daughter of a deranged religious fanatic. She has not been given any information about menstruation and is obviously terrified. The other girls in the class begin to pelt Carrie with tampons and sanitary napkins while chanting, "Plug it up. Plug it up. Plug it up." Miss Collins breaks through the circle of girls, pushing some of them forcefully away. Carrie is hysterical, and Miss Collins slaps her across the face, a slap accompanied by a sound effect worthy of the most outlandish martial arts picture. After hitting the girl, Miss Collins croons, "Now relax … calm down …" and cradles the student like a child. The dualism in Collins' character is evident throughout the film. She punishes the class for ridiculing Carrie by forcing them to work out 50 minutes after school in a grueling regimen for a week or take suspension and miss the prom. When one student challenges the punishment, Collins slaps her hard across the face. Yet, she also admits to a school administrator that she shared the contempt and disgust that the girls felt for Carrie during the locker room scene. On the one hand, Collins tries to help Carrie, while, on the other hand, she cannot completely hide her own revulsion when confronted with the girl. Carrie trusts the teacher at first, but she later has second thoughts after a group of students play a cruel prank on the girl at the prom. It turns out that Carrie has amazing telekinetic powers. She slaughters many of her classmates, electrocutes an English teacher who made fun of her in class during an earlier scene, and crushes Miss Collins by releasing some stage scenery suspended above her. Is Miss Collins bad or merely ambivalent about her students? As Carrie walks out of the fiery high school gym alone, wearing a blood-soaked dress, the answer seems to present itself.

In "I Teach Jim and Jane; I Don't Teach Gym," Smith discusses the pedagogical implications of negative stereotypes of physical educators in popular culture on teacher candidates, who will more than likely be taking classes from professors of kinesiology or health and exercise science or anything but physical education, a name change that reflects the evolution of the field of study. She cites three important ways that teacher educators can "work with preservice teachers to counter negative stereotypes in order to adopt the professional dispositions of physical education teachers" related to professionalism, curriculum, and lifelong learning (106). Smith recommends that teachers dress professionally at all times and eschew coaching attire or clothing that accentuates the body in the classroom. She says the course of study should exceed "sports-oriented skill development" and emphasize "knowledge pertaining to health and wellness" with assessment of learning that is "authentic and credible" (106). Finally, she promotes the importance of continuing education through professional workshops, conferences, and seminars to stay current with the field of study. All of these strategies would be helpful, but there is a long tradition of negative stereotyping of "gym teachers" in popular culture to overcome.

A Note on Ambiguous Exceptions

While most Hollywood movies paint teachers, students, and schools in broad strokes with predictable patterns, there are always exceptions. This is particularly true in some recent films featuring predators and professors. What is particularly interesting in some of these cases is the deliberate ambiguity of these characters. First, let's take a quick look at the teachers. While the teacher in *Blue Car* (2002), David Strathairn as Mr. Auster, is clearly a predator who discovers a young girl's particular vulnerabilities through her writing then methodically exploits her for his own ego and sexual desire, not all of the cases are so clear-cut. *Notes on a Scandal* (2006) is an interesting example. Cate Blanchett plays Sheba Hart, an art teacher who is having an affair with a 15-year-old student, and Judi Dench plays Barbara Covett, an older teacher who befriends her. The curious thing about this film is how the story, as it is presented, inverts what we would know from reading tabloid headlines about the situation. One would assume that the art teacher is the predator when, in the reality created by the film, the student and the other teacher are the predatory ones. Furthermore, in an aside that could easily go unnoticed in the film, Sheba Hart's relationship with her husband began when he was her professor. In this film, Sheba Hart is about the only person who is not a predator. Other stories are similarly ambiguous. Also in 2006, *The History Boys* (Alan Bennett's screenplay based on his play), features Richard Griffiths as Hector, the favorite teacher in a boys' grammar school in Sheffield. Clearly, he's taught them something to get them to a place where a group of them prepare to take entrance exams hoping to get places in Oxford or Cambridge, but he also habitually gives them rides home in turn after school on his motorcycle and fondles them. The boys talk about this and laugh it off, and while there are repercussions for Hector in the film, there is a tone of ambiguity throughout. The 2008 film *Doubt* (written and directed by John Patrick Shanley from his play) is similarly nuanced. Both *The History Boys* and *Doubt* consider whether truth is static or dynamic – in the classroom and in life. In *Doubt*, Philip Seymour Hoffman plays a priest, Father Brendan Flynn, who oversees a school. Sister Aloysius Beauvier (Meryl Streep) doesn't like his liberal approach to education or theology, and she becomes convinced that he has molested a student at the school. Has he? The title of the film reflects its conclusion on two levels about the nature of doubt.

I have one final observation about ambiguous exceptions, and that is the role so often played by professors. Even when they fit The Hollywood Model in other ways, professors in the movies are often questionable in one regard or another. Think of all of the flirtations or affairs with students. Sometimes those are presented as harmless (*Teacher's Pet*, 1958), sometimes the professors are smarmy (*Animal House* and *Legally Blonde*, 2001), sometimes the professors are pitied (*Educating Rita*, 1983), sometimes the professors are seduced (*Kinsey*, 2004), sometimes the professors may be harassers (*Oleanna*, 1994), sometimes the professors become caretakers (*Elegy*, 2008), and sometimes the professors are disappointments who impregnate the University Chancellor

(*Wonder Boys*, 2000). In *A Single Man* (2009), George Falconer (Colin Firth) skinny dips with a student then takes the young man home with him, but the context provided by the film makes their romp take on an unexpected tone as the student tries to save his troubled mentor. These teachers are presented as a motley crew. The space these characters occupy is small in comparison to more popular representations, but it is rich and worth exploring, as we will more fully in Chapter 7.

Conclusion

There is little room for ambiguity in the Hollywood curriculum. Good teachers are set apart from the rest by their undivided commitment to students in the school setting.[4] For Miss Collins, failure to commit to Carrie completely and save the pitiful girl relegates her to the ranks of the bad teachers. For Miss Balbricker, to be unattractive and unsympathetic is to be bad. For Bracket and Honeywell, to have needs of their own and human failings is to be bad, or at least unworthy. And, for the other bad teachers, the label means even more. To be a bad teacher in the movies is to place measurable outcomes – be they test scores or orderly classrooms or big payoffs from secret military weapons – above unselfish interaction with students. In addition to the technical and scientific values presented in these films, there are at least four other modes in which bad teachers are represented, most appearing in tandem with Huebner's two relevant value frameworks. Throughout the films, there are many examples of the boredom of schooling, the bad teachers' limited tolerance for difference, the suppression of the erotic, and the use of technical surveillance in schools. In most of the films, bad teachers are also presented as boring. Recall Ditto for a moment. When he dies in *Teachers*, no one notices for hours. As a teacher, he was not only boring, he was also bored. He "tuned out" long before the current crop of students appeared in the rows of his classroom. We never see the faces of his students, and neither does Ditto. In other movies, such as *Ferris Bueller's Day Off*, for example, we see many shots of students dozing in class or mugging before the camera or trying to communicate with other students as the teacher drones on about remote ideas or disconnected facts that have no relevance to the lives of the students in the classroom. In the movies, good teachers care and try to make their classes interesting while bad teachers are the opposite. Those bad teachers don't even seem to care about their own subjects, so why should their students?

The majority of these films feature white teachers and white students. Intolerance for difference is seldom an issue because Hollywood classrooms are basically homogeneous. It is the good teachers who attend to issues of race if not gender. Conroy challenges his superintendent over segregationist policies; Escalante and Clarke deliver the message that being Latino or black means you have to be better than the white competition to succeed; even Anna in *The King and I* (1956) tries to convince her monarch employer that women are not property and that neither men nor women should be enslaved (the same theme is explored in two other film versions of the story released over 50 years apart, *Anna and the King* in 1999 and *Anna and the King of Siam* in 1946). That is the province of the good teacher. Bad teachers respond as Mrs. Sherwood does to Leroy. She ignores his heritage and personal background just as she glosses over his literacy problems. This white English teacher cavalierly tosses her student a copy of *Othello* and expects him to find resonances between the text and his own life because the main character and the student are black! Sherwood's myopia is overwhelming. Her lack of sensitivity transcends indifference and skirts overt intolerance. Just as Mrs. Sherwood ignores Leroy's difficulty reading and writing, she also manages to marginalize his greatest talent, dance. She denies the value of the body and supports a mind-body dualism that hierarchically elevates cognition above movement. In the case of Leroy, there is also an implicit suppression of the erotic in this enforced dualism. Dance is the means through which Leroy is able to form relationships, particularly relationships with female dancers. He is as spectacularly successful on the dance floor as he is miserably unsuccessful trying to perform in Sherwood's class. I would be interested in seeing someone, especially a dance educator, make a systematic study of films featuring dance and dance instructors in the context of depictions of teachers and teaching in popular culture, particularly since so many of these films focus on the erotic dimensions of dance.

Other times in these films, teachers represent an explicit suppression of the erotic. Balbricker stands before one of the peepholes male students have discovered on the other side of the wall of the girls' shower, and she obscures a particular student's view of the naked female students. Dr. Hathaway shows up at a party Chris Knight has arranged and stops the "nerds" from getting together with the women Knight has invited from a nearby beauty college. Mitch Taylor is practically pulled from the arms of a nerd co-ed by his professor, who tells the boy he has made a mistake by not spending his evening working on the assigned project. Coach Carr preaches abstinence and scare tactics in place of comprehensive and scientifically accurate sex education.

The suppression of the erotic and the denial of the importance of the body and of its pleasures is simply one more way these bad teachers try to control their students. These teachers are not concerned about sexually transmitted infections or even some vague notion of morality; they are trying to use their positions to exert control over students and reassert their own dominance. There are a few examples of teachers who create a sexually charged atmosphere in the classroom (*Waterland*, 1992, and *The Mirror Has Two Faces*, 1996, come to mind), but these examples, like those of teachers who have sex with students, are presented with a curious ambiguity. Many of these flawed characters – just like Ryan Gosling's Dan Dunne in *Half Nelson* (2006), a teacher whose drug addiction interferes with his pedagogy – are presented otherwise as teachers who fit the characteristics of the good teacher outlined in The Hollywood Model. The complexity of these representations, while not always easy to watch, represents a revisionist storytelling that signals a willingness on the part of filmmakers and audiences to deal with difficult issues and complex characters more openly than ever before.

The metaphor of school as prison is not a new one, and modern technical surveillance makes the task of spying on students efficient and unobtrusive. Armed guards, suspicious public address systems and massive chain link fences and gates are commonplace in these films and are linked with bad teachers, but the theme is best expressed in *Class of 1999*. The battledroids-turned-substitute teachers are the ultimate technical surveillance machines. Their eyes record images of their students and transmit those images to a secret command station hidden deep inside the school building. Next to these technical manifestations, the metal detectors at the front door, or even the watchtowers at the school gate, seem commonplace if not reasonable. It is the idea that a researcher would be able to put killing machines in the schools under the guise of technological advancement that should give us pause. At first this story line seems farfetched, but how far is it really from the traditional metaphors we use to relate school and prison to an advanced technology that links school and battlefield with disastrous results? In any case, the bad teachers and their counterparts, the bad administrators, use devices of technical surveillance to further separate themselves from students while simultaneously increasing the power and control they have over their charges.

Many of these films are targeted at teenagers and young adults. Why do these age groups appear to respond to these images and characters in such a way that causes filmmakers to repeat the patterns over and over again until a formula is established? It seems evident that the audience, all of whom are students or former students, find pleasure in seeing the bad teacher ridiculed, scapegoated, and even killed onscreen by students who take up the fight that audience members either left off or never entered. The recollection of bad teachers (or parents or bosses) from their own lives who have exerted power over them at will is enough to align an audience with the student or group of students onscreen who are battling oppressive forces represented in the films by the bad teachers. The crime committed by these bad teachers, whether they are killer androids, boring economics teachers, or out-of-control gym teachers, is that they are one-dimensional representations of the oppressive force of social control. They are the front line warriors in a celluloid war against student freedom and self-determination. In these films, student efforts at resistance propel them past the front line much to the delight of the audience, but the larger conflict remains unresolved. Students, like the good teachers who join them, seldom accomplish much in the battle against the institutional hierarchies backing up the bad teachers. The shows are entertaining, but when the applause fades away, dominant forces of social conformity are still intact and shoring up for the next skirmish with the forces of resistance.

It is most telling that as Vivian Bearing lies alone in a hospital bed with ovarian cancer killing her body, she thinks about her life as a teacher and the dehumanizing, competitive manner she adopted in interacting with her students. She has spent her professional life preferring research to humanity, but what she longs for as death approaches is what she was never able to give to her students: kindness. She exerted control in the classroom and produced positive, measurable outcomes among her students, but she never formed the personal connections in life that she comes to see are more valuable than scholarly output and fearful respect in the classroom. When I say that there is little room for ambiguity in the Hollywood curriculum, I am not suggesting that complex representations are totally absent. From *Rope* (1948) to *Whiplash* (2014), there have been teachers who defy neat categorization as good or bad. Alfred Hitchcock's thriller is best known as an experiment with long-take sequence shots, but it is also the story of a charismatic teacher, Rupert Cadell (James Stewart) who unwittingly motivates two students to commit "the perfect crime" based on ideas he promoted in class about the superiority of some human beings over others, an ideology he renounces when he is confronted with the effects of it. Is he good? Is he bad? It is hard to know. On the surface, Fletcher (J. K. Simmons in an Ocsar-winning performance) is clearly a bad teacher who berates students mercilessly and even bullies one into committing suicide at a fiercely competitive conservatory. The story focuses on a talented drummer who falls under the sway of Fletcher and suffers for it. The entire film leading up to the climax seems to suggest that Flether's techniques are inhumane (they are) and counterproductive (they seem to be) only to be contradicted in the final scene. The message delivered at the end of the film is that only by pushing students to the brink can some of them reach their highest potential. Is it worth it? The answer to that question will come from individual viewers, who are unlikely to reach a consensus. Is Fletcher unkind? Yes. Are his methods effective? Sometimes. Is he a bad teacher? I don't know, which is one reason among many this film is brilliant.

It is the intertextuality weaving these films together at the same time that weaves them into our larger cultural canvas and into our own lived experiences that makes us look beyond the basic patterns and metaphors linking these films to Huebner's clearly delineated value frameworks, so we can explore the less readily visible patterns embedded in these film texts. Since the last iteration of this book, there has been a turn of sorts toward depictions of the bad teacher as an anti-hero – a simplistic attempt at revisionism – and nowhere is that pattern more clearly expressed than in the 2011 comedy *Bad Teacher*, with Cameron Diaz in the eponymous role as Elizabeth Halsey. The logline speaks volumes: A lazy, incompetent middle school teacher who hates her job, her students, and her co-workers is forced

Figure 4.2. Cameron Diaz as Elizabeth Halsey in *Bad Teacher*, 2011. Rather than teach her classes at the beginning of a new academic year, Ms. Halsey shows them videos of good teacher movies and sleeps off her hangovers at her desk.

to return to teaching to make enough money for breast implants after her wealthy fiancé dumps her. To say that I find this movie silly and offensive does not in any way suggest that I do not take it seriously. In 2013, I wrote an essay that was published in the *Journal of Popular Film and Television* establishing a context for evaluating bad teacher characters and provided a close reading of *Bad Teacher* by focusing on the plot, the depiction of major characters, and aesthetic elements before assessing the implications of this film for viewers. That essay, "*Bad Teacher* is Bad for Teachers," is open access, so I will not engage in detailed analysis of the film here, but it is important to note that if reducing teachers into discrete categories of good and bad is dangerous, then presenting narratives in which all of the teachers are bad is even worse. In this type of media landscape, which is beginning to dominate film and television, trust in educators, in their training, and in their professionalism is eroding. The effects of this decimation of reputation and regard will be difficult to overcome, but in no small way, our future depends on our ability to change the narrative.

Notes

1. Sometimes all the teacher has to do to appear bad is to discourage a student's dreams. In *Rudy* (1993), a priest calls attention to the fact that the title character is failing civics then keeps him from a class visit to Notre Dame, his dream school, with classmates by telling him that "Not everyone is meant to go to college." This contrasts vividly with the reform school scenes in *Sleepers* (1996). By night four boyhood friends are repeatedly beaten and raped by vicious school guards, but there is one scene during this sequence in which a caring teacher notices one of the boy's interest in classwork and gives him a copy of *The Count of Monte Cristo* to keep as his own. In this case, a teacher is the only one to encourage an abused boy's dreams, perhaps the only one outside of his friends to see him as human. The scene is short and singular, but it is powerful.

2. Or, sometimes the bad teacher is a minor character without serving as a counterpoint for the storied good teacher. In *South Park: Bigger, Longer & Uncut* (1999), Mr. Garrison is such a character, proving that animated teachers can still make a lasting impression and, as bad teachers, are capable of breaking nearly every standard of professionalism.

3. In *Good Will Hunting*, there are two teachers with vastly different approaches and perspectives who both work with a gifted student. This is essentially the same construct that is found in *Searching for Bobby Fischer* (1993), except that the two teachers, played by Ben Kinglsey and Laurence Fishburne, in this film ultimately unite in support of a seven-year-old chess prodigy in this touching, well-done film.

4. An interesting counterpoint to this standard is the film *187* (1997). The movie stars Samuel L. Jackson as an involved teacher with a good sense of humor at a high school in New York City before he is knifed and nearly killed by a student whom he refuses to pass.

Fifteen months later, he has sufficiently recovered to relocate to the West Coast and begin teaching again. Soon, it becomes evident that his recovery has been physical and that the emotional scars from his attack have dramatic repercussions. Ostensibly a good teacher, Jackson's character, Dennis Broadway, is caring in the classroom so long as students play by his rules. When students refuse to play by those rules, he murders them. He was a victim once and refuses to play that role again.

· 5 ·

DIVIDED LIVES

The Public Work and Private Pathos of
Women Teachers in the Movies

Introduction

Carol Witherell and Nel Noddings write that good stories allow us to "both know and imagine our world" (1). Whether or not the stories are "good," stories are used by most of us to construct some meaning for our existence and to find ways to form connections with other people. Our very lives become stories when we move from the feeling of them to thinking and talking about them. And, as Fiske points out, these stories of our lives are inextricably linked to the stories we hear about the lives of others. This chapter discusses how feminist scholars have positively influenced the way we understand teachers' lives with regard to gender, an influence generated largely through the use of narrative research techniques. At the same time, the narratives of popular cinema continue to either ignore women teachers or to recast them in stereotypical roles. There is a remarkable intertextuality between the research conducted by feminist scholars on women teachers' lives and the lives of women teachers in the movies. Over the last couple of decades, there has been an active group of researchers in various disciplines working on narrative research projects. Some of these researchers have moved from traditional ethnographies into a more critical (and inclusive) stance, some have come out of oral history traditions, and still others come from various feminist perspectives. What is important is the shared commitment these researchers have to letting research "subjects" become "participants" by giving them a voice in the research project. When researcher and subject become less divided by hierarchy and enter into dialogue, participants in research projects are given what Casey terms the "response-ability" to establish their own "author-ity" (1993, 23). In another article Casey writes, "The social relations of research are transformed when teachers are presented as subjects in their own right, not as mere objects of research. Teachers can be seen as authors of their own lives, and, in their roles as educators, as co-authors of their students' lives as well" (1990, 301).

It is an undeniably feminist principle that people have the right to name their own experience. But, there are also benefits to the research itself for undertaking this type of inclusive project. Researchers report (see Casey 1993, and Nelson) that listening to other people describe their experiences in interview situations adds to the richness of the analysis and introduces ideas that would have otherwise never occurred to the writer. I do not mean to suggest that there is no role for the researcher in the process. Of course, someone must make decisions about meaning and context in addition to performing necessary groupings and editing. My point is simply that "objective" observers are, in fact, as "subjective" as the objects of their gaze. Including research subjects as participants in an intersubjective dialogue creates a richer discourse that openly acknowledges the complexities of our subjectivities. My purpose here is not to theorize the self; others have devoted extensive energy to that process (Casey; Denzin; Flax; Witherell and Noddings 1991, to name a few). I will, however, draw parallels and outline discrepancies between the recounted lived experience of women teachers and the cinematic depictions of women teachers' lives. To that end, I need to demonstrate that there is a reason to draw connections between the lives of women teachers constructed in their own narratives and the social construction of women teachers in popular culture, which, in this case, is represented by commercial films.

Witherell argues that the process of forming the self involves a dual process: the social formation, which comes out of the ways we "define and are defined by our social and cultural contexts"; and the relational formation, which gives us "our sense of self in connection with other selves and the meaning systems that evolve from our mutual predicaments and possibilities" (85). Writing on the subject of interpretive biography, Denzin makes an even more direct case for investigating connections between the lived experience of women teachers and the characterization of women teachers' experience in the celluloid world of the movies.

Lives and biographical methods that construct them are literary productions. Lives are arbitrary constructions, constrained by the cultural writing practices of the time. These cultural practices lead to the inventions and influences of the gendered, knowing others who can locate subjects within familied social spaces where lives have beginnings, turning points, and clearly defined endings. Such texts create "real" persons about whom truthful statements are presumably made. In fact, as argued above, these texts are narrative fictions, cut from the same kinds of cloth as the lives they tell about. (26)

Denzin goes on in a later section to say that "ethnographies, biographies, and autobiographies rest on *stories* which are fictional, narrative accounts of how something happened" (41). I think the key in working with stories, throughout the process of piecing together stories from multiple storytellers and even from different formats of storytelling, is never to lose sight of the context in which the story is told. In the introduction to *Studying Teachers' Lives*, Ivor Goodson points out that one possible consequence of engaging in "life story work" is to "de-politicize" inquiry by working at the individual level and being cut off from "wider social forces" (9). This is precisely why it is critical to ground the work at the individual level in analysis that examines the broader social context influencing that lived experience; it must be determined what social forces are tugging at the corners of the particular that make it *that* particular.

In the course of my research on teachers in the movies, I have viewed a number of Hollywood films that have teachers as central characters. In previous chapters, I have analyzed the films using Huebner's five value frameworks of curriculum and looked at the characteristics that are common to the good teachers, who are the heroes of these films, and the bad teachers, who are generally less significant. It is now my task to look more deeply into these films, particularly into those that star women as the central character, and see the difference that the gender of the teacher character appears to make in the development of these film narratives. In subsequent sections, I will discuss the following: the role of nurture in teachers' work lives; the historic and contemporary constraints placed on women teachers; the teachers' acts of resistance in the contexts of dealing with the administration and of political action; and, the divided lives that teachers have been forced to lead in our neighborhoods as well as on our local movie screens.

The films I use to frame my ideas in this chapter have been divided into three categories. The films in which the good teacher is the primary character or one of the primary characters are as follows: *Bright Road* (1953); *Boyhood* (2014); *The Children's Hour* (1961); *The Corn Is Green* (1945); *Dangerous*

Minds (1995); *The English Teacher* (2013); *Freedom Writers* (2007); *Good Morning, Miss Dove* (1955); *The King and I* (1956); *Little Man Tate* (1991); *Looking for Mr. Goodbar* (1977); *Mean Girls* (2004); *The Miracle Worker* (1962); *Mona Lisa Smile* (2003); *Music of the Heart* (1999); *Rachel, Rachel* (1968); *Still Alice* (2014); *Then She Found Me* (2007); *These Three* (1936); *Unexpected* (2015); and *Up the Down Staircase* (1967). The film in which the teacher is not, perhaps, good, but is the central character, is *The Prime of Miss Jean Brodie* (1969). The films I have chosen to discuss here in which the woman teacher is a supporting character to the male teacher emphasized in the film are as follows: *Blackboard Jungle* (1955); *Hoosiers* (1986); *Lean on Me* (1989); *Only the Strong* (1993); *Stand and Deliver* (1988); *The Substitute* (1996); *Summer School* (1987); and *To Sir, with Love* (1967). While these films may fit loosely into the model established in Chapter 2, they are important to consider separately in terms of their presentation of the gendered teacher. Tying everything together are stories. Witherell writes of "… the narrative structure of the self that is woven within an intricate tapestry. The tapestry is composed of interlocking patterns of cultural-historical, individual-biographical, and interpersonal-relational threads" (84). Each thread is a story or, perhaps, many stories.

Nurture

The Ethic of Care

From Carol Gilligan's groundbreaking work, *In a Different Voice*, to the work of Witherell and Noddings cited here, including stops between and since, there have been many words written about the ethic of care. Witherell and Noddings write that it is "our belief that to take seriously the quest for life's meaning and the meaning of individual lives is to understand the primacy of the caring relation and of dialogue in educational practice. Our use of the term *caring relation* assumes a relational, or connective, notion of the self, one that holds that the self is formed and given meaning in the context of its relations with others" (5). The maternal seems to be embedded in the ethic of care, but conceptually they are not the same thing. While scholarly discourse and the films considered here are ambivalent about the concept of "teacher as mother," teachers themselves and teachers in the movies are generally committed to caring for children. Casey finds that commitment to care is a recurrent theme in her analysis of the life narratives of women teachers: "Even though the life histories which I will discuss contain conflicting evaluations of the maternal in education, in these narratives women teachers consistently talk about students in I-thou terms. This seems to me to be a distinctive and essential element of any feminist definition of nurture in education (1990, 318)."[1] The ethic of care Casey finds among the teachers she has interviewed, a notion that has been largely written out of public discourse on education (1990, 301), is also common to most of the women teachers presented in commercial films.

Of those teachers who are the central characters in films and portrayed as good, most teach students who are prepubescent. In the cases of *Looking for Mr. Goodbar* and *Rachel, Rachel,* having the central characters work with small children clearly removes sexual tension from the classroom. Those particular teachers, Theresa Dunn (Diane Keaton) and Rachel (Joanne Woodward), are presented in psychosexual crisis throughout large portions of the films, and their onscreen personas are shown nurturing innocent, young children as a counterbalance to the other scenes. The first day Theresa enters a classroom of hearing-impaired children, she sits down on their level to talk with them. Her demeanor is kind and reassuring, and she touches the children. Touch is also part of Rachel's interaction with her students. Most of this film centers on Rachel's mental instability and sexual insecurity, but the classroom scenes reveal a kind, typically competent teacher. Rachel is both playful and tender with the small children she teaches. She believes the best of the little ones, and she sings to them during naptime. She realizes that her role as a nurturer is different from their mothers' but not unrelated. At one point Rachel muses, "It may be that my children will be temporary, never to be held. But, so are everyone's." Rachel and Theresa Dunn spend most of their screen time out of the classroom. Rachel spends her summer vacation losing her virginity in a relationship that is destined to end and avoiding the tentative advances of a female colleague. Theresa Dunn, in a script based on a "true" story,[2] spends her evenings cruising singles bars and winds up dead long before she learns to elude her Catholic guilt, to live with the trauma of a childhood illness and resulting deformity, or to get beyond an affair with her married college professor that ends badly.

For the teachers who spend the bulk of their screen time in the classroom, the story there is pretty much the same. Certainly, Miss Moffat's nurture in *The Corn Is Green* is rooted in political action, and Annie Sullivan's in *The Miracle Worker* springs from a desperate attempt to save a child from isolation, but the net result is not much different in terms of tangible pedagogical exchanges between these teachers in the movies and their students. In the classroom projected onto the silver screen, it is the relationship between the teacher and student, the "caring relation" exhibited by the teacher, that is paramount. And so it is for women teachers working in real classrooms. In her analysis of teachers' narratives, Casey found recurring themes over and over: "Many women define being a teacher as a fundamental existential identity ... These women work for children, not for those who pay their wages" (1992, 206). Clearly, for these women, teaching is much more than paid employment.

Teacher as Mother ... Teacher as Other than Mother

The research of feminist scholars has opened discussion on many areas related to the social and psychological meanings of motherhood, to the social construction of gender, and to the many values associated with women's paid and unpaid work. Rather than attempt to pull bits and pieces from vast sets of literature to demonstrate connections between motherhood, the feminization of teaching, and the social construction of woman as teacher, I will instead limit myself to what I think are direct connections between our apparent ambivalent regard for the "teacher as mother" metaphor and the manifestation of that ambivalence in cinematic portrayals of women teachers. It did not surprise me to find that women teachers represented as central characters in the movies tend to work with younger children while men teachers tend to work with high school (as well as college) students. It would present a more accurate representation of actual statistics to find women teachers the majority in both settings. Hollywood decision makers respond to the market forces that label male stars more "bankable" than female stars, however, and they put men in the lead roles with greater frequency than they do women.

Recall here The Hollywood Model of good teachers outlined in Chapter 2. The good teacher is usually an outsider, someone not well-liked by colleagues. He or she gets personally involved with students, learns from those students, and has an antagonistic relationship with administrators. Often these teachers personalize the curriculum to meet the everyday needs in their students' lives, and sometimes they have a ready sense of humor. Women presented as good teachers fit the model in all of the critical ways. The only gender-based difference at this level is that the women teachers in the movies do not tend to be equipped with a ready sense of humor. To find the influence of gender on the construction of teachers in popular film, it is necessary to look at deeper levels than this model provides. What is it that makes Bette Davis's Miss Moffat different from Robin Williams's Mr. Keating (in *Dead Poets Society* [1989]) and Anne Bancroft's Annie Sullivan different from Nick Nolte's Alex Jurrell (in *Teachers* [1984])? I assure you it is more than the dollar value of their paychecks unadjusted for inflation.[3]

There are the unavoidable connections for Miss Moffat and Annie Sullivan between their roles as teacher and the maternal manifestations of their characters. Neither Moffat nor Sullivan has children of her own, and both characters are forced to address issues of parenting within their respective films while the men cited do not. This is not a coincidence. Women teachers in the movies regularly deal with this issue in one way or another, either explicitly or by implication, while it is not an issue for the male characters. In *The Corn Is Green*, Miss Moffat takes a particularly talented boy from the coal mines and pushes him academically. This boy, Morgan, is like a son to her, a fact she reveals after he complains about all of the extra work she gives him. Morgan asks, "How can you be interested in a machine that you put a penny in and if nothing comes out you give it a good shake?" Miss Moffat tells him that she has spent two years on him because she has "great interest" in him. She confides that she stays awake in the middle of the night making plans for him. It is an emotional scene. Later, after Morgan receives a scholarship to Oxford, the school Miss Moffat attended, she hides the fact that a local girl is pregnant with his baby. To keep Morgan in school, Miss Moffat first pays off the girl, Bessie, then finally adopts the baby to rear as her own child. Is it Miss Moffat's own displaced ambition that propels her to urge Morgan forward in place of herself and Bessie? Not insignificantly, the baby she adopts is a boy.

Nancy Chodorow's widely read book, *The Reproduction of Mothering: Psychoanalysis and the Sociology of Gender*, uses object-relations theory and feminist analysis to explain why it is almost exclusively women who mother. The cultural norm is for women and men to take for granted "women's unique capacity for sacrifice, caring, and mothering, and to associate women with their own fears of regressions and powerlessness." At the same time, men are seen as having the ability to aid separation and integration into the wider society and are associated with "idealized virtue and growth" (83). Applying Chodorow's premise to an examination of the interplay between gender and teaching, it becomes clear that the nurturing behavior of women teachers is accompanied by unstated negatives that lie beneath the surface and add tension and complexity to the relationship between students and women teachers, while men teachers are able to integrate nurturing behaviors into their relationships with students without inspiring a similar fear of "regressions and powerlessness." In *Feminine Fictions: Revisiting the Postmodern*, Patricia Waugh writes:

Most men and women in this society will have been "mothered" in early infancy in terms of a fairly exclusive emotional attachment (though the actual *forms* of this will differ according to variations determined by historical factors including class, education, region, state intervention, etc.). "Father" tends to appear as breadwinner/ support though not as a primary pre-oedipal figure; so, while mother *appears* (as in Freud and Lacan) to be part of the "natural" order, father is conceived in the terms of the "culture." "Mother" will thus carry our ambivalence not only about dependency but about the "natural," and she will continue to be experienced in part as tied to regression to a pre-social, primitive state whose emotional uncertainties undermine our "sophisticated" secondary socialization. (63)

Obviously, children bring their prior relationships with gendered adults into the classroom with them.

For children, the first years of school provide a transition between the private world of the home and the public spaces beyond. Grumet writes poignantly about the difficulty women teachers experience when they try to shut off their inclination to nurture in order to comply with the stated curriculum supplied by their institutional hierarchy. In the following passage from *Bitter Milk: Women and Teaching*, Madeleine Grumet writes about the role teachers play in helping children fashion an escape from their dependency on their mothers:

It is the female elementary schoolteacher who is charged with the responsibility to lead the great escape [of children from their dependency on their mothers]. At the sound of the bell, she brings the child from the concrete to the abstract, from the fluid time of the domestic day to the segmented schedule of the school day, from the physical work, comfort, and sensuality of home to the mentalistic, passive, sedentary, pretended asexuality of the school-in short, from the woman's world to the man's. She is a traitor, and the low status of the teaching profession may be derived from the contempt her betrayal draws from both sexes. Mothers relinquish their children to her, and she hands them over to men who respect the gift but not the giver. (25)

All of this brings us back to Annie Sullivan.

In *The Miracle Worker*, Annie Sullivan spends most of the movie in a battle with Mrs. Keller over young Helen. The girl was left blind and deaf after an illness in her infancy. She has passed the age when other children are learning in school, and her whims control the household. Helen does not have a common language with anyone in her family; her father hires Annie Sullivan to live with the family and teach his daughter. Over Mrs. Keller's frequent objections, Annie uses firmness to arrive at the point of nurturance. The teacher introduces the student to language and, thus, gives Helen the tool she needs to extricate herself from her mother. It is near the end of the film that Annie helps Helen make the connection between the letters she is signing in the girl's palm and the water they are pumping from the outdoor well. In her joy at the discovery, Helen leaves Annie for a moment to stand with her parents on the front porch. She hugs her parents but only stays briefly. The connection has been broken. The scene ends with Helen leaving her mother and father to go back to her teacher. Later that night, Helen comes into Annie's room and kisses her. The film ends with Annie cradling the girl in a rocking chair and signing into her hand, "I love Helen." The connection between Helen and her mother no longer has the primacy it once did; and, the connection between Helen and Annie has been made and secured, establishing teacher as maternal but not mother.

Constraints

Historic and Contemporary

It is evident that women teachers in the movies emerge as images constructed for our viewing pleasure. Most of the characters on the list of women teachers who are central characters in films are "pretty, young things" or, at least, attractive women. Even the rare older woman, such as Jennifer Jones's Miss Dove, is shown in classroom flashbacks as a younger woman, a worthy object of the gaze. Laura Mulvey and Teresa de Lauretis are only two of the many scholars who have written about the politics of representation in the cinema and about the effect of the presentation of women as objects of the masculine gaze. Indeed, women teachers are included in supporting or minor roles only as the love interest or potential love interest for the male teacher, who is the film's central character, in movies like the following: *Hoosiers*; *To Sir, with Love*; *Summer School*; *Blackboard Jungle*; and *Only the Strong*.[4] In the terminology of screen narrative, they provide "complication." John Berger writes about the politics of representation in the larger sense in *Ways of Seeing*:

> Men *act* and *women appear*. Men look at women. Women watch themselves being looked at. This determines not only most relations between men and women but also the relation of women to themselves. The surveyor of woman in herself is male: the surveyed is female. Thus she turns herself into an object – and most particularly an object of vision: a sight. (47)

Is it any wonder that the traditional image of the stereotypical schoolteacher wears a blouse buttoned up to her neck, a skirt that falls far below her knees, and a severe hairstyle? If she must be looked at as she stands in front of the class, she certainly does not want to be actually seen. To invite the gaze of students or visiting administrators is to challenge the constraints placed on women teachers to keep them from behaving like other women.

While she was researching her book (1992) on the life histories of women teachers teaching in Vermont between 1900 and 1950, Nelson writes that she posted a copy of regulations for rural schoolteachers on her bulletin board. The rules, which she calls typical, were as follows:

> Teachers will not dress in bright colors. Dresses must not be more than two inches above the ankles. At least two petticoats must be worn. Their petticoats will be dried in pillowcases. [Teachers] will not get into a carriage or automobile with any man, except her brother or father. Teachers will not loiter at ice cream stores. Teachers are expected to be at home between the hours of 8 P.M. and 6 A.M., unless in attendance at a school function. The teacher will not smoke cigarettes or play at cards. She will not dye her hair under any circumstances. (178–79)

Perhaps most telling of the preceding rules is the edict that teachers must dry their petticoats in pillowcases. These women were not to be considered human beings like the rest of us; their "unmentionables" must literally be neither mentionable nor visible. It was common practice during the time period Nelson studied for women teachers to be dismissed when they married, or, if they were allowed to marry, they were not generally allowed to remain in their teaching position when they became pregnant. Through her analysis of interviews with fifty women teachers and her examination of pertinent written documents, Nelson has uncovered evidence that the constraints placed on teachers were not uniform and that their daily lives in the classroom were not always as imagined by those of us who look back through the filter of history. The teachers themselves provided anecdotal evidence that marriage, and even pregnancy, were not always grounds for dismissal. Often the terms of their employment depended more on the availability of qualified teachers than on proximity of their own due dates (173–76). Several of the women interviewed mentioned that they brought their children with them to school on a regular basis because other childcare was not available (175).

Nelson was even more surprised to find evidence in the interviews that these young female schoolteachers had to deal with what appears to be an old problem that has been given a relatively new name – sexual harassment (171–76). Just like the teachers in the movies, who present unfailingly virtuous images publicly while privately living life as human beings, real-life teachers in Vermont chafed at the restrictions placed on them. Nelson writes:

"One teacher said she 'outwardly' conformed to the requirement that she act 'like a lady'; she added 'inwardly I rebelled.' Another teacher summed up the effects of these policies in a poignant way: 'Teachers were a thing apart,' she sighed, 'you couldn't do anything that other people did'" (179). Nelson cites Tyack and Strober[5] for their assertion that the feminization of teaching had an effect on the constraints placed on teachers. They feel that adult men would not have been treated the same way as these women teachers (179). Still, the question arises, why did these women teachers who benefitted from a labor shortage by being able, in some cases, to teach after they married and while pregnant comply with other restrictions placed on them? Nelson reports that although the teachers interviewed for her project may have minded the restrictions, they still recalled them with a certain pride, and "they link them with both protection and status" (180). Negotiating between their public and private selves amid the constraints imposed upon them from their supervisors and from their communities has historically been a perilous balancing act for women teachers.

As some of the historical constraints on women teachers have relaxed, new restrictions have emerged. Sandra Acker points out the inequities in career opportunities for women teachers according to the age level and subject they teach as well as the size and type of school in which they are employed. Teachers in secondary schools, for example, have greater opportunity to increase their salaries by taking on management responsibilities (10). Notably, the one teacher in the movies who takes advantage of that opportunity, Raquel Ortega, the math department chair in the film biography *Stand and Deliver*, is portrayed as a bitter, negative woman who tries to hamper the creativity and downplay the accomplishments of the film's central character, Jaime Escalante.

There are also larger societal issues to consider. Casey and Apple point out that teachers have become scapegoats as economic crises place millions of people in positions of unemployment or underemployment. Rather than consider changing the economy, vocal constituencies cry out for changing the school curriculum (172). Later in the same article in a section called "The Teacher as Female Worker," Casey and Apple write about changes in the job market related to changes in the sexual division of labor. Jobs filled by women are structured so that there are greater attempts to control the content of the job and how that job is performed (179–80). It is little wonder that, as Casey writes, women teachers often identify with their students on the basis of their mutual powerlessness (1990, 306). But, as we shall see in the next section, women teachers have not let the constraints of their workplaces and communities shackle them into immobility; both in Hollywood movies and in American classrooms, women teachers have found and formed pockets of resistance.

Resistance

Administration and Political Action

The literature on teachers' acts of resistance seems rather slim when placed next to writings about the oppression and victimization of teachers. Still, there are scholars writing about the troubled relations between women teachers and administrative hierarchies and about the political action of women teachers, and this same discourse is occasionally found in motion pictures. Nelson finds that the teachers interviewed for her project often converted the rules that constrained them into something they could use to their own advantage: "Rather than a simple mark of their oppression, these restrictions became a resource, the basis for the accumulation of influence within the community, the school and their personal lives. The fact that they could even abandon them, on occasion, suggests that we should see teachers as a relatively powerful and inventive group" (184–85). Still, it would be wrong to infer from Nelson's work that women teachers' dissatisfaction with their position in the workplace, their very real feelings of oppression at the hands of administrators, are mitigated by being able to manipulate on occasion the rules that signify that oppression. Casey finds that one of the reasons women who are progressive activists leave teaching is their persistent problems with school administrators, problems that have not been studied in great detail. Casey (1992) writes:

> Perhaps the most serious omission in the literature on teacher retention is its neglect of the antagonism between teachers and administrators, a major explanation in these narratives. This exclusion is partly due to the widespread and unquestioning adoption of an administrative perspective by writers on the subject; it is also caused by the not-unconnected selective filtering of women's experiences through male, and in some cases, masculinist perspectives. (206)

That antagonism is a major theme in the motion pictures that star men; not coincidentally, many of the films with male central characters are also more recent films.

In a recent film, however, there is a very telling scene that shows a woman teacher vent her frustration with the amazingly authoritarian tactics of principal Joe Clark in the biopic *Lean on Me*. This is the only scene in the film to feature the music teacher, Mrs. Elliott, but it is a powerful example. Clark has taken over a failing inner-city school. Twenty years earlier, he was a teacher in the same high school when the hallways were clean, and the students were middle class and white. In this scene, Clark has called Mrs. Elliott into the hall after bursting into her class and interrupting a rehearsal to demand that she teach the entire student body the school song.

Clark:	Mrs. Elliott, I don't like being ignored like that.
Elliott:	I'm sorry, Mr. Clark, if you weren't getting enough attention, but I'm trying to train a chorus.
Clark:	And you don't think the school song is important enough to warrant a little interruption. Is that right?
Elliott:	The school song is fine, but we were doing Mozart. I was right in the middle of a difficult part. If you would like us to respect your work, you could try to appreciate ours.
Clark:	Who do you think you're talking to?
Elliott:	A man who seems to be threatened when any other adult in this school does something that the children like.

The two continue to bicker in the hallway.

On a whim, Clark cancels the students' annual concert at Lincoln Center and charges Mrs. Elliott with "rank insubordination" for not clearing the trip with him personally, despite the fact that she filed the appropriate paperwork with his office staff.

Clark:	You've questioned my judgement, my competence, my intelligence …
Elliott:	Look, I don't want to get into this. You are the one who comes around here to bother me. You are a bully, a despicable man. I have nothing to say to you.
Clark:	All right, let's just accommodate that, Mrs. Elliott. You're fired.
Elliott:	You need a psychiatrist.
Clark:	Get out. Right now …
Elliott:	Fine. Fine. Fired … fired. You will hear from my lawyer.

Mrs. Elliott is left in the hallway beside the open door to her classroom to slap her hand futilely against the cinderblock wall. Joe Clark strides purposefully down the hallway with his bullhorn pointed back at Mrs. Elliott, calling to mind the proverbial "eyes in the back of the head" that such authoritarian figures often claim to have.

As the character Joe Clark so ably demonstrates, there are clear limits on a teacher's autonomy, not to mention limits on her resistance. Nelson writes:

Schoolteachers could violate rules, but they could not change them. To the extent that they embraced restrictions as a source of personal empowerment, they eliminated the possibility of achieving a collective basis for effective resistance. Outward conformity to the norms of lady-like behaviour – though paired with inward rebellion – limited the terms in which the battle for occupational improvement could be waged. (185)

Of course, there are examples of individual acts of resistance. In her book *I Answer with My Life: Life Histories of Women Teachers Working for Social Change*, Casey found numerous examples of women committed to political action, even though many of those same teachers might not have labeled themselves activists. She identified an existential discourse of Catholic women religious teachers, a pragmatic discourse of secular Jewish women teachers, and a signifying discourse of black women teachers. The metaphors are different for the different groups of women, but the commitment to children is tangible. Yes, these teachers nurture children, but that nurture is expressed as "political responsibility, not domestic duty" (1990, 306).

What is the political project of teachers in the movies? It varies from film to film, but the project is typically one of the factors that motivates the teacher to teach. Hollywood teachers reveal their political projects in various ways.[6] Although some of these films were produced before the Second Wave of the American women's movement, they can be read as feminist texts. Several generations of young girls sat in darkened movie houses watching women schoolteachers in roles that must have appeared remarkably autonomous and important. That these characters appeared more self-determining in that context than they do through our contemporary, feminist lenses was, of course, not a concern to the original audience. Anna in *The King and I* may try to improve the role of women in Siam and speak out against slavery, but her political positioning is integrated into the narrative largely to provide conflict between the teacher and the king to intensify their relationship. *The Corn Is Green*, which has also been cited before, offers a better example. Miss Moffat uses her Oxford education and her inherited wealth to bring young boys up out of the coal mines and keep them in school until they reach the age of sixteen. There is also, implicit in many of these films, the notion that the ethic of care that women (and good male teachers) bring to the classroom offers important progressive dimensions that transcend classroom teaching to become counter-hegemonic. In this sense, the act of caring for children is double-edged and reinscribes women teachers at the same time it offers a serious critique to the dominant ideology of educational institutions, an ideology that views schools as a giant sorting machine used to direct children to their respective slots in the world of work. If only flesh and blood teachers could command the resources and take advantage of the fortuitous good fortune that accrues to Hollywood's anointed ones. While there are parallels between the representation of women teachers in films and the lived experience of women teachers working in American classrooms, there are few, if any, actual teachers whose work for and nurture of children is repaid with the immediacy and intensity accorded to teachers in the movies.

Divided Lives

Public Work and Private Pathos

Undercutting all of the other categories are the divided lives that are imposed on female teachers in the movies and in local classrooms. Historically, women have been asked to choose between caring for the children of other women and having children of their own (Nelson 173), a decision not forced upon male teachers. Still, I think the divisions between public and private are much deeper than the categories we assign to our lives at work and our lives outside of work; there is more to this issue than labeling women as "married" or "not married" and "mothers" or "not mothers." We must consider the ways in which female teachers are asked to deny their experience as women in their teaching. Grumet writes: "Convinced we are too emotional, too sensitive, and that our work as mothers or housewives is valued only by our immediate families, we hide it, and like Eve, forbidden to know and teach what she has directly experienced, we keep that knowledge to ourselves as we dispense the curriculum to the children of other women" (28). It seems to be this larger bifurcation just addressed by Grumet that is played out in films with "unmarriedness," "childlessness," and a litany of other maladies acting as metaphors for the ways in which women teachers are forced to alternately draw upon and deny their femaleness, as in being asked to nurture but not to mother the children they teach.

In films, most women teachers are single and childless, or their marital and maternal status is not revealed to the audience. While many of the male teachers portrayed in films are also single, some are not, and the issues are different. In the movies, male teachers are allowed to have happy, full lives outside of the classroom *and* to be heroes at school. They are also allowed a range of moral ambiguity or ambivalence that is not open to female teachers.

Figure 5.1. Robert Stephens as Teddy Lloyd, Maggie Smith as Jean Brodie, and Jane Carr as Mary McGregor in *The Prime of Miss Jean Brodie*, 1969. Mary McGregor is shocked to see her idolized teacher kissing another (married) teacher in the empty classroom.

Consider the on-screen persona of Jean Brodie and her ultimate downfall. Keroes advances an interesting analysis of this character in writing about the film and novel versions of *The Prime of Miss Jean Brodie*: "As a character, Miss Brodie embodies powerful desires that threaten to disturb the social order and that make of her a transgressive figure, attractive and frightening at the same time. As she resists the constraints her world imposes on her, it must in turn resist her efforts" (33). Keroes argues that Jean Brodie's downfall results in part because "she makes explicit and, more importantly because she exploits what for a woman teacher especially must remain tacit – the seductive power of teaching" (37). For the male teachers with empty private lives, or with serious personal problems, the implication by the end of the film is usually that the emptiness will be filled or the problem resolved. Often, the heroism demonstrated in the classroom by the man teacher, which translates into power in ways deemed acceptable, is parlayed into a solution for his personal deficits.

For women teachers, the opposite is true. Hollywood plays out the stereotype that women cannot balance a successful career and private life and must, instead, choose one over the other. The choice to privilege her career, a choice seemingly made without regret until she faces death, is the path chosen by Dr. Vivian Bearing in *Wit* (2001). Or, as is often the case for women teachers, they must pay for professional success with personal misery. In *Dangerous*

Minds, Michelle Pfeiffer plays LouAnne Johnson in a heroic story based on Johnson's autobiographical book on teaching. From the beginning of the film we learn that Johnson is in dire financial straits following her divorce. During a later scene in a dim stairwell outside a rundown apartment, Johnson makes a home visit and tries to keep a bright student from leaving her class to attend a special school for pregnant girls. The teacher confides in the student about beatings she received from her former husband and tells the girl she had an abortion and implies that her own personal life is wretched. "Sometimes you start out wrong and just keep going," Johnson says.[7] It is worth noting here that Johnson's "heroism" is problematic in ways other than her gender. In his book *Hollywood Films About Schools: Where Race, Politics, and Education Intersect*, Ronald E. Chennault looks primarily at films that focus on teachers and principals that were released between 1980 and 2000 and were widely seen by audiences either in theatrical release or on cable and home video. Like others writing about race and representation in teacher movies, Chennault is particularly interested in *Dangerous Minds*, which he cites for its "regressive and demeaning" racial representations (118) and its attempts to "reestablish white supremacy" as part of the natural order of things (121). Robert Lowe also identifies *Dangerous Minds* as a "blatantly racist film" (212), and Giroux writes that the film "attempts to represent 'whiteness' as the archetype of rationality, authority, and cultural standards" (46) in a review of the film published in *Cineaste*.

There has been less criticism of another biopic. Roberta Guaspari enters teaching after her husband leaves her for another woman in *Music of the Heart*. In fact, the film opens with a montage that conveys her hurt and anger over her husband's infidelity. Guaspari's subsequent attempt at a relationship ends when an old friend turned lover is unwilling to commit to her. Other possibilities for relationships over the years are precluded because of her hesitance. Her older son, Nick, misses having a dependable, male presence in his life and blames his mother, "The problem with you is that you're mean to everybody and then they don't want to be with you." He throws down his violin, tells his mother he hates the instrument, and tells her it's her fault that his father left and that the boyfriend she has briefly after she starts teaching is going to leave. "You're gonna be all alone, and I'll have to take care of you!" His mother tells him that their father met someone else and that she can take care of herself and him and his brother, but even in this sympathetic portrait of a gifted and devoted teacher, it is clear that juggling a romantic life and developing a music program for under-privileged children are competing interests that cannot be balanced. As the years pass, however, her sons do not give up. They place a personal ad for their mother without her knowledge. They tell her what they have done at the dinner table only after the responses to the ad begin arriving.

Roberta:	Listen, don't you think it's a little weird that you're trying to get your mother a date?
Nick:	Don't you think it's a little weird that you're not even interested in dating?
Roberta:	Look, even if I were interested in dating, which ... which I'm not, I don't have time to do that and, besides, you know, I have my teaching ... which I love ... I have you (touches his younger brother's face) ... and you (touches Nick's face). That's all I need.

She follows through on a date with a perfectly nice journalism professor and has a great time but tells him that she's not ready for a relationship; this is several years after the end of her one post-marital relationship. The film concludes, in this regard, just as it begins: Roberta Guaspari does not have a life partner. It is not entirely clear in the film how she feels about this state of affairs.

Consider the film *Little Man Tate* as another example. Dianne Wiest plays Dr. Jane Grierson, a former child prodigy who heads the Grierson Institute and devotes her life to studying academically and artistically gifted children. She meets Fred Tate (Adam Hann Byrd) and is so impressed with his abilities that she wants him to live with her for the summer and attend college classes while she makes a documentary about him. Jodie Foster directed the film and plays Fred's mother, a waitress named Dede Tate. The two women spend most of the film vying to gain physical and emotional control over Fred. Jane's attempts to "mother" Fred while he spends the summer with her are alternately ridiculous and frightening. She feeds him a macrobiotic diet, ostensibly for his stomach ulcer, and the food causes him to vomit. On another occasion, she is furious when the boy eats dinner without her. Most tellingly, Jane does not know what to do when Fred has a bad dream. His real mother, Dede, is shown in an earlier scene crawling into bed with him to comfort the boy. Jane is portrayed as an egghead without common sense. The sterility of her elegant home and her failure to sustain emotional ties with others is played off against her successful academic career. Of course, it is not surprising that the film manages to reconcile Fred's real mom and his surrogate in the final frames, but discerning viewers will, I think, find the resolution a little too pat and will also find that the stereotypes preceding the final scene linger after the film ends. This is only one example of the private pathos of female teachers in the movies; there are many others, some of which can be difficult to watch because of our helplessness as viewers to reach out and help teachers in need of support.

One needs only to consider Theresa Dunn's multiple one-night stands and excessive use of drugs and alcohol, Rachel's mental instability, and Martha Dobie's tragic death in *The Children's Hour*. Shirley MacLaine stars as Martha and Audrey Hepburn as Karen Wright in this 1961 version of Lillian Hellman's play about two teachers who become the victims of a lie one of their students tells. When they punish one of the girls enrolled in their boarding school, the girl tells her grandmother that the two women are lesbians. The old lady gossips, which causes most students to withdraw from school. The teachers are in financial ruin, and even Karen's fiancé begins to question the relationship between the two women. Martha is forced to acknowledge that her feelings for her friend do exceed the bounds of friendship and hangs herself. Even though the little girl's lie has been publicly exposed, there will be no place for an openly lesbian teacher in the movies for decades to come, a condition that will be explored more fully in Chapter 6. The film ends as Karen walks silently past her fiancé, the old woman who perpetuated the lie, and other townspeople at Martha's funeral. Significantly, Karen is alone.

Even in more recent films, little has changed. In *Mona Lisa Smile*, Julia Roberts plays Katherine Ann Watson, a free-thinking art history professor at

Figure 5.2. Shirley MacLaine as Martha Dobie and Audrey Hepburn as Karen Wright in *The Children's Hour*, 1961. A student's malicious lie has tragic consequences for these two teachers.

Wellesley who tries to teach her students to look beyond the proscribed roles of wife and mother. As Fisher et al. put it in *Education in Popular Culture: Telling Tales on Teachers and Learners*, "Katherine has a mission at Wellesley, but it is not really about art history; rather, it is about questioning accepted values, including gender roles, in society" (41). She begins a relationship with an Italian professor but ends it after she discovers he has lied about his past. At the end of the year, she is not only out of the relationship but out of the job, deciding that this particular classroom is not for her. Helen Hunt (who also directs) plays first grade teacher April Epner in *Then She Found Me*. Her husband, who teaches a class across the hall, leaves her almost as soon as the film begins. As soon as she starts dating after his departure, we almost never see her in the classroom again. In *Mean Girls*, the unflappable math teacher Ms. Norbery (Tina Fey) begins the new year revealing to the principal that she is now divorced. When she tells promising student Cady Heron (Lindsay Lohan) that she doesn't have to hide her aptitude for math to get boys to like her, the student just looks at the primly dressed teacher wearing glasses. What Norbery says confirms all of our preconceptions: "I know, how would I know, right? I'm divorced. I'm broke from getting divorced. The only guy that ever calls my house is Randy from Chase Visa, and you know why? Because I'm a pusher. I push people. I pushed my husband into law school. That was a bust. I pushed myself into working three jobs. And now, I'm going to push you because I know you're smarter than this." True, she dances with the goofy principal at the end of the movie, but it is hard to pull for that union. In *Boyhood*, things are not much better for Patricia Arquette, who plays "mom." In this unprecedented film, a longitudinal narrative feature shot over a period of years, we see a single mother go back to school, get out of an abusive second marriage (to her former professor), have some "not quite right" boyfriends, and end up alone by the time her kids leave the nest and after she has become a professor herself. This bifurcation between the public and the private is standard in the movies for women teachers.

Words and Pictures (2013) is a movie worth watching for many reasons, but the best of them is to see Juliette Binoche's performance as Dina Delsanto, an artist with disabling rheumatoid arthritis who has been hired to teach an advanced art class at Croyden, an upscale, co-ed prep school in Maine. Her rival-turned-romantic-interest is a writing teacher, Jack Marcus (Clive Owen), whose students engage in a competition with hers to prove which is more important – words or pictures. It is remarkable to see a teacher depicted who is at once physically infirm and sexually attractive. What is her punishment for being sensual and expressing sexual agency? Her partner is an annoying alcoholic who plagiarizes his son's work. There is the hint of a thaw between them at the end of the film after his misdeeds have come to light, but I hope Delsanto finds a partner who matches her strength instead and does not return to the dubious charms of Marcus. Julianne Moore has recently played two notable teacher characters that challenge but do not reject the pattern when it is applied broadly. She won an Oscar in 2015 for playing a linguistics professor diagnosed with early-onset Alzheimer's disease in *Still Alice*. Moore's depiction of the character Alice Howland is remarkably good and saves the film from falling into too much predictability in terms of story, but nonetheless her successful career and strong marriage slip away as she loses her ability to use the thing that has defined her life more than any other: words. There is a more familiar pattern with a twist in *The English Teacher*. Linda Sinclair is introduced with a montage narrated by someone (never introduced in the film as a character) with an English accent. The point seems to be that her life is like an Austen or Brontë novel – at least until it isn't. She is a dedicated teacher who grades all of the men she meets for dates (really, marks from a red pen magically appear onscreen) and finds them lacking. When a talented former student comes to town planning to give up his writing dreams for law school, she jumps in to help by getting the school to stage his unproduced play. Encouragement and nurturance lead to a frenzied tryst on her desk, which turns out to be a bad idea as much because he is a heel as because it leads to a series of events that cause the temporary loss of her job. As the narration foreshadows, it all ends well with the restoration of her job and a date with a man (the former student's father!) who seems a fit, but there is a false note to it all. And, surely she is unduly punished for the lapse in judgment that comes with expressing her sexuality with a less than worthy partner. I can't quite place *Unexpected* (2015) in the same category as the other films and count it as an exception to the rule. Samantha Abbott (Cobie Smulders) does have a stable relationship with her partner, which breaks with the standard narrative, but the inner-city high school teacher wants to leave the classroom for a museum job even before she discovers that she is pregnant.

Consider *Freedom Writers* as another recent, and widely seen, example. Liberal idealist Erin Gruwell (Hilary Swank) shows up for a job interview in a nice suit and expensive pearls. She has chosen a school participating in a voluntary integration program and counters the skepticism of her interviewer (who also reveals her racism during the interview) by telling her, "I know I have a lot to learn as a teacher, but I am a very good student." Her husband is lukewarm in his encouragement from the beginning, but he becomes increasingly jealous of the time and attention she spends with her students. Clearly, the message is that this teacher cannot manage both the students and the marriage. For the good teacher, there is no balance if she is a woman. Her husband feels crowded out, which is no wonder because she can't seem to talk about anything but her students and classes. As the movie progresses, more and more of her time after class is spent on projects for the students. The first time I watched *Freedom Writers*, I kept hoping that the pattern would be broken and that a woman teacher could finally manage to have it all. I hoped that her husband, Scott Casey (Patrick Dempsey), would meet her halfway and that she would learn to carve out time for their marriage. When Gruwell takes a part-time job at a department store to buy books for the kids (which rattles administrators because the books she buys are not part of the standard curriculum), she is oblivious to his displeasure. Later, she goes on to take a weekend job at the Marriott. He is reasonably frustrated that she didn't even consult with him before taking the two extra jobs. As she becomes the super teacher, his ambition dwindles. We can see that the marriage is in trouble even if Gruwell doesn't have time to notice. Until he begins to challenge her, that is. Until he tells her that he feels he is living a life he never agreed to and leaves

Figure 5.3. Hilary Swank as Erin Gruwell in *Freedom Writers*, 2007. When Erin Gruwell comes in late from work one evening bubbling over with news about her students to find her husband's bags packed, we aren't terribly surprised. After all, this is the pattern for women teachers in the movies.

the marriage. The break-up scene is painful to watch. Is Erin Gruwell a good teacher? Undeniably, yes. Does she have the balance to sustain the intensity of her work? I don't think so. When watching a biopic like this one, it's impossible to know just how much art imitates life. The film does indicate at the end that Gruwell left the classroom after several years to take a college teaching job. Are there any happy endings for women in the movies? There are very few of them. I think *Precious* (2009) offers a welcome bit of progress for women teachers, and that will be noted more specifically in the next chapter.

Conclusion

If the forced split between the public and private is the defining feature of women teachers in the movies and a very real factor in the lives of actual women teachers, it seems appropriate to consider in conclusion the elements with which we began: the self and public culture. Waugh writes that the development of selfhood balances the necessity of separation against the process of individuation, a process that occurs in the relationship with the primary parenting figure, who is generally the mother:

> The ability to conceive of oneself as separate from and mutually independent with the mother develops with the ability to accept one's dependency and to feel secure enough to be able to relax the boundary between self and other, to allow for the ambiguity which resides at the *interface* between subject and object ... If selfhood is conceived in terms of disidentification with the mother and identification with a father who symbolizes the larger culture, it is the father who is seen to carry the reality principle. (72)

According to Waugh, this configuration constructs "truth" in the "real" world of knowledge in such a way that necessarily devalues the "personal" and provisional "truths" of the familial world. Flax points out that related arguments by feminist theorists about our early primary relations and the repression of "relational aspects of our subjectivity" fall into a pattern that is necessary for replicating male-dominant cultures (232). While Waugh and other feminists have embraced postmodern discourse as a relaxation of (artificial) boundaries around categories and an opportunity for redefining the patriarchy, Jane Flax cautions that postmodern theories may not be the panacea others hope:

> A feminist theorist might well ask whether certain postmodernist deconstructors of the self are not merely the latest in a long line of philosophic strategies motivated by a need to evade, deny, or repress the importance of early childhood experiences,

especially mother-child relationships, in the constitution of the self and the culture more generally. Perhaps it is less threatening to have no self than one pervaded by memories of, longing for, suppressed identification with, or terror of the powerful mother of infancy. (232)

Instead of proclaiming the self to be fictive, Flax suggests that the self is social and, in important ways, gendered. She adds that a feminist deconstruction would locate the self and its experiences in "social relations, not only in fictive or purely textual conventions." There is a political purpose to her work; Flax sees the self, or concept of it, as a "lever" to be used against essentialist or ahistoric notions of the self. The problem with postmodernist discourse, finally, is its difficulty in discussing terms like "freedom" and "emancipation," terms connected to broader issues of justice and power that are so very important to all women (232–33).

Casey (1993), too, struggles against the narrow notion of the postmodern self. Her analysis of the life histories of women teachers draws on Bakhtin's theory that only in relationship to the other can the self be defined. When faced with the stories of living, breathing participants, Casey arrives at her own way of thinking about the self: "Unlike the alienated persona of post-modern discourse, the self is not a jumble of fragments; she can articulate her own coherence. Acting within the limitations constructed by others, she nevertheless has some choice, and she has some power" (23–24). I like this description of the self. Casey writes about a self with purpose, not a rigid set of values and tasks, and certainly not a self exhibiting an absence of values. Casey's female teachers tread the ground between those poles. They have choice and power, but they also face limitations. The work of feminist scholars has opened our eyes to the lived experience of women teachers. Their research provides a valuable contribution toward helping us understand the roles gender construction and power relationships play in their lives and in their teaching. At the junctures of private and public, of self and culture, it becomes critical to look at the other forces that influence the way we think about women teachers. Certainly, one of these forces is popular culture. Commercial films not only tell women teachers how other people construct them and re-articulate them as characters on the movie screen, but also shape the way students and parents respond to teachers and the way women teachers respond to public opinion in the construction of their own lives. It is my hope that revealing the implications of gender in these films will help to free women teachers from the tyranny of the images these films project. One glimmer of that hope arrives in form of Dr. Louise Banks (Amy Adams) as a linguist who plays multiple roles as an accomplished academic and loving mother who saves the world from its tribal competitions when extraterrestrials come to Earth in *Arrival*. Yes, she also reclaims romantic love in the process, but this wonderful film remains an outlier among stories of women teachers. Ironically, television has been a more progressive medium in recent years in terms of allowing women teachers to express themselves sexually in loving relationships without limiting their effectiveness in the classroom (in the quirky *Boston Public* [2000–04]) or the front office (in the exquisite *Friday Night Lights* [2006–11]).[8] It is counter-intuitive to think of television as a more progressive medium than motion pictures, but in this case the small screen leads the way in offering a wider range of representations of women teachers. It is past time for film to catch up.

Notes

1. Another theme Casey finds in the narratives, interestingly, is that "nurture is necessary, but it is not sufficient" (1990, 318).
2. The book, which has the same title, was written by Judith Rossner.
3. Bette Davis's film was released in 1945, Anne Bancroft's in 1962, Nick Nolte's in 1984, and Robin Williams's in 1989. I do not know what each actor was paid for starring in these films, but suspect that my point is nonetheless well taken.
4. In two other films, the Adam Sandler vehicle *Billy Madison* (1995) and the soft-core, serial killer movie *The Teacher* (1974), the young, attractive woman teacher serves as the love interest of her male student. *The Teacher* is notable as what I would consider the very worst of the films discussed in this book. I would be remiss not to mention the surprising casting choice of Jay North, better known as Dennis The Menace on television, as the student turned lover. In *Varsity Blues* (1999), sex education teacher Miss Davis, played by Tonie Perensky, strips at a club called the "Landing Strip" where a group of her students, who also happen to be on the high school football team, come in to enjoy the view and enjoy drinks with their teacher after finding out about her moonlighting. In *Meet The Parents* (2000), a pretty, sweet elementary school teacher is the love interest of the main character who is neither a teacher nor her student. In *Rushmore* (1998), everyone seems to be in love with elementary school teacher Rosemary Cross, played by Olivia Williams. And, *Back to School* (1986) stars comedian Rodney Dangerfield as a rich man who falls in love with his professor when he returns to college to encourage his son.
5. Nelson's footnote cites Tyack and Strober (1981).
6. Sometimes the classroom project is oblique, as during one of the last scenes of *Malcolm X* (1992) in which child after child stands up after hearing their teacher talk about the slain leader and proclaims, "I am Malcolm X." An oblique political presence is preferable to the out of touch or revelevant (Look at this) presence of teachers in other classrooms populated by students of color as seen fleetingly in *Boyz n the Hood* (1991) and *Menace II Society* (1993).

7. Interestingly, the film as originally shot included scenes with actor Andy Garcia playing a romantic interest for Pfeiffer's character. Including such a character might have helped expand on the typical portrayal of the "gendered" teacher. Those scenes, however, were cut before the film was released and ensured that the character of the woman teacher would conform to the stereotype prevalent in other films.

8. See *Teacher TV: Sixty Years of Teachers on Television* and the essay "I Believe in Love and *Friday Night Lights*," which I have contributed to *Screen Lessons: What We Have Learned from Teachers on Television and in the Movies*.

· 6 ·

HERE BUT NOT QUEER

The Mainstreaming of Gay Teachers in the Movies

Introduction

When the first edition of this book was published, there was little need to include a separate chapter on gay teachers. Several films released since the late 1990s, however, suggest that the time had come by the publication of the second edition to take a look at how Hollywood constructs gay teacher characters and to contrast the portrayal of these male characters with that of a lesbian couple who open their own school in *Songcatcher* (2000). Not surprisingly, given the arguments advanced in Chapter 5, women teachers do not fare so well as their male counterparts, though one related factor is certainly that theirs is a period narrative. The other major film texts considered in this chapter are *In & Out* (1997), *The Object of My Affection* (1998), and *The Opposite of Sex* (1998).

Queer theory has gained a sophistication, and perhaps even a cachet, in the last couple of decades that far exceeds the depth of the film texts considered here. The richness of the analysis of complex texts and the interplay between various theoretical constructs, autoethnographic essays, and various media forms are expansive in the literature. Thirty-five years ago, Richard Dyer and others were writing about the importance of critiquing media stereotypes and were, at the time, particularly concerned with the damaging cultural influence of repeated "negative" portrayals. Larry Gross and James D. Woods drive home the point in a discussion of *The Boys in the Band*, released in 1970, and its context:

> When the central character surveys the wreckage of his apartment at the end of the party and says, "You show me a happy homosexual and I'll show you a gay corpse," he was summarizing an entire genre of movies: out of thirty-two films with major lesbian or gay characters between 1961 and 1976, thirteen feature gays who commit suicide and eighteen have the homosexual character murdered. (293)

While the range of portrayals of LGBTQ characters has evolved to the point that critics and theorists have the occasional complex, ambiguous, and sometimes in-your-face character to consider,[1] Hollywood has been slow to place gay characters in the classroom. It is little wonder, actually, that an industry reluctant to present the straight, (mostly) white, teacher heroes of the silver screen as particularly political – not to mention radical – would be especially cautious when writing these characters as gay.[2]

My choice of the terms gay and lesbian when writing about the teachers in this chapter is carefully considered. I am comfortable in a post-binary world where gender and sexuality are fluid constructs while mainstream Hollywood is still tied to the industry imperative to make profits and tends to "play it safe" even as we begin to see a more expansive range of representation. Though there is no consensus about a definition for the term "queer" – and I am not suggesting there should be – I will borrow from Alexander Doty in making the case that gay teachers have arrived in Hollywood, but they are careful constructions, nonetheless, and clearly not queer. As Doty suggests, "queerness has been set up to challenge and break apart conventional categories," and this is not the political project of Hollywood's gay teachers (xv). The three male teachers, though two of them are paired with women through parts of the first two films considered, are all wearing firmly established sexual identity labels by the final reel, which belies the most compelling uses of "queer" as distinguished by Doty:

> … I like those uses of "queer" that make it more than just an umbrella term in the ways that "homosexual" and "gay" have been used to mean lesbian *or* gay *or* bisexual, because queerness can also be about the intersecting or combining of more than one specific form of nonstraight sexuality. (xvi)

If, as some argue, there has been a backlash against the early preoccupation with "positive images" of gays in cinema (Hanson 9) and wider appreciation for the critical readings and connections made by queer theorists, these films will not prove challenging subjects for textual analysis. Taken in the larger context of teacher movies, however, they do provide another set of interesting insights about how Hollywood industry executives perceive the larger culture. Technology is facilitating some inroads into expanding the range of representations. There were over 400 scripted television shows on broadcast networks, basic and pay cable networks, and internet platforms in 2015, motivating some to call this the era of "Peak TV" (Stanhope). Although retired as a professor when the series begins, it is not surprising that one of the upstarts, Amazon Studios, brings us the first transgender teacher character in the groundbreaking and celebrated series *Transparent* (2014–), a series that includes other LGBTQ professor characters, some still active in the classroom.[3] It is not unprecedented that television leads the way occasionally on some social issues, but that is a topic discussed more fully in *Teacher TV: Sixty Years of Teachers on Television*.[4]

Although we have made big advances socially, politically, and legally in terms of securing some rights (not all that are needed) for people who identify as LGBTQ, there is still work to do, and films such as those explicated in this chapter have played a role in preparing the mainstream audience to take a more progressive stance on sexuality or, at least, to connect with the humanity of gay characters. I believe that, at least in the cases of the most mainstream films *In & Out* and *Object of My Affection*, writing gay teacher characters is a way of putting a new spin on a dusty, stock character, but the way these particular characters are written still makes them safe and acceptable to a mass audience.[5] They are all good teachers as defined by The Hollywood Model advanced in Chapter 2 and, as far as we can tell, they practice the aesthetic-ethical-political value frameworks discussed in Chapter 3. For all practical purposes, these are conventional teachers who just happen to be gay. Just as with progressive representations of women teachers who act on their sexuality without being punished in one way or another, television has paved the way for depictions of gay teachers in these films with the introduction of the first gay teacher and the first gender non-conforming teen depicted in the classroom during primetime on the series *My So-Called Life* in 1994–95, a representation preceding the earliest of these films by a couple of years.

In & Out

As this film opens, Mr. Howard Brackett (Kevin Kline) is introduced as the quintessential good teacher in the bucolic town of Greenleaf, Indiana. He teaches English literature and Romantic poetry. He coaches the track team, who must be winners since team members are shown dousing him with champagne. He has been engaged for three years to a younger colleague, Emily Montgomery, played with great humor and pathos by Joan Cusack, and they are mere days away from the planned nuptials. Howard's parents are played by the appropriate icons: Debbie Reynolds still evokes wholesome perkiness after all these years, and Wilford Brimley looks like a codger while we all know he is the "salt of the earth" with a "heart of gold." Greenleaf, marked by a sign that reads "A great BIG small town," looks like the kind of town Hollywood presented in the glossy, studio pictures of the 1940s and 1950s to represent small-town perfection. Greenleaf is quaint and clean and safe, and the town itself is flanked on all sides by pristine farms and rural spaces that hark back to an undefined earlier time that we have been trained to think of as simpler.

As the film opens, townsfolk are in a tizzy. Local boy made good Cameron Drake (Matt Dillon) is up for a Best Actor award at the Oscars, and the whole town is set to watch the event. Earlier in the evening, Howard quips at his engagement party that he had always said he wouldn't get married until Cameron was nominated for an Oscar. It's an interesting comment that says more about his reluctance to get married to Emily than about his interest in his students. By the time the big show starts, Howard and Emily sit on his sofa with his arm draped casually around her shoulders. Cameron Drake is nominated for his role as a "brave, gay soldier" in the "breakthrough" film *To Serve And Protect*.

Predictably, he wins, and there are various shots showing the townsfolk going wild at their various gatherings. Then comes Cameron's acceptance speech, and the same townsfolk are stunned into silence because after he thanks a lot of industry folks and nameless gay soldiers, he thanks a special teacher:

> Cameron: I'm just an actor playing someone. This really belongs to all the gay soldiers and sailors, and other guys and women who defend this country to keep us free but can't date. (He's interrupted by applause.) So, maybe I should thank someone else, someone who's really been there, someone who taught me a lot about poetry and Shakespeare and just like, you know, staying awake, man, someone who's an overall great guy and great teacher, Howard Brackett from Greenleaf, Indiana. And, he's gay.

Howard's wrist drops on cue in an insert shot to a limp position then the shot returns to Cameron's speech.

Cameron: I've decided to dedicate this night to a great, gay teacher. Mr. Brackett, we won!

Immediately, Emily turns a questioning look at her intended, and Howard's parents ring the doorbell before he can respond to her. When he opens the door, he immediately declares, "I'm not gay."

Howard is outraged. He threatens to sue Cameron then accuses him of being under the influence or a member of a cult. His mother's response is interesting, "We'll love you gay, straight, or if you kill someone as long as you get married." In another telling moment, Howard tells Emily he loves her, offers her a chaste kiss, and sends her off with his parents. Howard may think everything is settled, but dramatic complication is needed to fill out the rest of the narrative. In fact, Mr. Brackett has been outed before he has even admitted to himself that he is gay, which leaves the issue open for viewers.

The next morning Howard leaves his picturesque, white, two-story house for school on his bicycle.[6] The teacher is greeted by a feeding frenzy of media representatives at the school, and Peter Malloy (Tom Selleck) is established as a reporter for an entertainment news show. Howard's students are uncomfortable, and one throws him a note that reads, "Best Actress Mr. Brackett." When he tells them that he's not gay, the students are relieved because they have never dealt openly and honestly with homosexuality or, probably, with many controversial issues. Judging from the responses of the students, the school principal, and others, the biggest thing about this "great BIG small town" may be the closets.

Once order has been temporarily restored in the classroom with Howard's assurance that he is not the dreaded "other," the students tell him they believed Cameron because the teacher is, after all, prissy, smart, clean, head of the Drama Club, a bike rider, well-dressed, and engaged for a long time. One student then sums it up, "Smart, clean, totally decent human being – gay." Clearly, this is a line penned by a Hollywood screenwriter reflecting a particular political agenda rather than an attempt to reflect an authentic response of a student in a school that has already been established as more of an idealized 1950s institution than any school, idealized or not, representing the 1990s. Just as Howard Brackett is squeaky clean in all of the personal and professional habits we are privy to and he is presented as a dedicated teacher in the mold of all "good" teachers presented onscreen before him, the most threatening element of the student population in this Indiana High School is a brawny jock whose comments – on any topic – are obtuse and sometimes insensitive.

Students are uncomfortable with the idea that a favorite teacher may be gay because this turn of events challenges the values they have grown up with and tacitly accepted, but the school principal poses a direct threat of his own when order is questioned. Tom Hallowell, played by Bob Newhart as something of a nebbish himself, initially accepts Howard's statement that he is not gay but later calls him in for a meeting because of complaints from some parents. Hallowell cannot say the word "homosexual" but conveys that he is once again interrogating the teacher about his sexual orientation. The scene is played for laughs during the early minutes, but the final threat is completely serious.

Howard:	Tom, do I look like a homosexual?
Tom:	Would you walk for me?
Howard:	Excuse me?

Howard starts to walk out of the room.

Tom:	Howard, do you enjoy teaching?
Howard:	No, I don't enjoy it. I love it. It's my life.
Tom:	Then you'd miss it?
Howard:	Are you threatening me?
Tom:	No, now, I'm your friend. Friends don't threaten.
Howard:	No, they don't.
Tom:	Friends warn. And you are getting married, aren't you?
Howard:	Are you saying that if I weren't getting married, I'd be fired?
Tom:	But, that's not an issue, is it?
Howard:	No.

The men shake hands, but both are uncomfortable.

Some years ago I had a student in an undergraduate film class make a comment that struck a chord with the other students. She was talking about *Birdcage* (1996) and how she thought the film was commercially successful because it presented such stereotypical images of gay men that the film perpetuated an us-them dichotomy and the resulting chasm created a distance founded on difference that made straight audiences, even some homophobes, feel comfortable enough to plunk down their money and see the movie. Her comment, perhaps particularly since it came from a student, was revelatory for some other students, who undoubtedly saw themselves in her description. There is a section of *In & Out* during the second act that references these stereotypes and even mentions the earlier film. Responding to the media barrage, Howard answers his phone, "I have no thoughts on gay marriage, I did not see *Birdcage*, and I'm just trying to have my dinner."

At his bachelor party, Howard acts really macho; he fondles a blow-up doll and smokes a cigar. This is a façade, and everyone there knows it because the guys have brought *Funny Girl* (1968) to watch together at the party and share fond remembrances of the Barbra Streisand movie festival Howard organized the previous year. Howard goes to a priest for advice, a curious choice because he is not Catholic, and reveals that he has not had sex with Emily. He goes to Emily's place and tries to ravish her but is distracted by an image of Richard Simmons on her television and leaves abruptly. He has a near collision with Peter Malloy that includes Peter's revelation that he's gay, advice that "Sometimes the worst thing you think can happen turns out to be the best thing," and a kiss at the conclusion of the scene. Howard listens to a tape on being more masculine and learns that "manly men do not dance" but cannot hold himself back when the disco music pounds, and – for the first time in the entire film – we see Howard Brackett break loose and boogie to the disco beat. What role did the kiss have in effecting this liberation? Like everything else in life, Howard's recognition is a process, and its trajectory is uneven.

It is not until Howard stands that the front of the church facing Emily at the wedding that he seems to realize that saving embarrassment in the short-term is a recipe for amplifying hurt in the long-term. The exchange of vows begins. Howard takes on a shell-shocked expression, and instead of replying, "I do" at the first prompt, Howard says, "I'm gay." Emily keeps muttering that she lost 75 pounds for Howard and for this ceremony. Before she punches him in front of the guests, Emily shows enormous self-awareness and offers interesting cultural critique that, in its obviousness, again reveals the influence of the politically engaged screenwriting. She tells her would-be husband that she has waited for him not just three years but has waited her entire life and based her entire system of self-esteem on the fact that he was willing to marry her. She rages while he listens. She punctuates her tirade with a punch then runs out of the church. It is Peter who congratulates Howard for doing the right thing, and we finally see Howard start to marvel at what he has done, "I just came out at my wedding ... in front of everyone."

Is there a "happily ever after" Hollywood ending? Not without some further complication and a suitably dramatic resolution. Howard is fired and stripped of the "Teacher of the Year" award he habitually wins. Cameron comes to town and ditches his vacuous, painfully thin, supermodel girlfriend for Emily, whom he had met years before and was attracted to when she was a student teacher and he was her student. Howard's mother gets the wedding she always wanted as she renews her vows with his father, an event Howard attends with Peter. The resolution to Howard's professional situation occurs just before the wedding in a climactic scene in which Howard surprises Mr. Hallowell by turning up at the school graduation ceremony and sitting down in an empty chair on the stage. When the "Teacher of the Year" award is presented to someone else, Cameron Drake interrupts the ceremony, and an uproar ensues. Mr. Hallowell admits that Mr. Brackett has been fired because the community believes there is a "question of influence" and is thus ineligible for the award. The principal says he's taken this action to protect the students and concedes that he was afraid others would "become gay."

The scene continues in a manner reminiscent of *Spartacus* (1960) with the townspeople aligning themselves publicly with Howard Brackett. One student, whose character has been written with enough ambiguity that he may or may not actually be gay, stands and comes out to the crowd, "It must have rubbed off – I'm gay." Other students follow one after another standing and saying, "I'm gay." Mr. Hallowell blunders and thunders that the community has spoken, but Howard's brother and father both stand and declare themselves gay. His mother, played by the irrepressible icon of American wholesomeness that is Debbie Reynolds, stands and says, "I'm Howard's mother, and I'm now very proud of him, and I'm a lesbian." As broad and calculated a comedic moment as this is, it is difficult not to laugh out loud and to feel proud of Howard's mother for standing up and coming out in principle. Others, including the town hair stylist and the mail carrier, follow suit, and Cameron gives Howard his Oscar.

After this Hollywood moment and the renewal of vows that follows, what happens to Howard Brackett? That is not for us to know because Hollywood stories like this one, and the next film we will consider, end with the loose ends apparently tied up in a bow denoting promise for a rosy future. Just as in the films discussed in previous chapters, the status quo is evidently intact, since Mr. Hallowell's job has never been in question and another teacher is presented as eager to capitalize on Howard's fall from grace to claim the teaching award for himself. Questions linger, however, about Howard's life, which, as he has told us himself, is teaching. Does he get his job back? That is unclear. Does the larger community accept him so that he can continue to call Greenleaf home? There were, evidently, some parents who called for his ouster, and we cannot safely assume they disappeared forever into the crowd at the graduation ceremony. It is not the purpose of this film to answer these questions;

Figure 6.1. Kevin Kline as Howard Brackett and Bob Newhart as Tom Halliwell in *In & Out*, 1997. The film seems quaint by today's standards.

it is the intent of *In & Out* to tell us that these questions are irrelevant. The film has a broadly liberal political focus geared toward convincing viewers that Howard's sexuality is not the issue because he is "one of us" and thinking of him as "other" is misguided. In other words, he is here but not "queer," and that is supposed to allay our fears. Once again, Hollywood has given viewers feel-good moments in place of an exploration of serious concerns and meaningful political action.

The Object of My Affection

This film opens with a musical adaptation of *The Little Mermaid* performed by first graders at an upscale private school in Manhattan. George Hanson, played by Paul Rudd, is directing the show but is distracted and disappointed because his partner does not show up, as promised, to share the event. It is unclear just how out George is, but he is invited to a posh dinner party by the parents of one of his students and brings along his boyfriend. At the party, he meets Nina Borowski, a social worker played by Jennifer Aniston, who tells him how sorry she is about his breakup, which is how George learns he is about to be dumped. It is interesting that George's boyfriend is a professor, another of those lascivious professors, who has begun seeing one of his students.[7] With no other place to go, George ends up moving in with Nina, who has an extra room to rent. They become close friends almost immediately.

Very little of the film deals with George as a teacher, though we do see occasional scenes in the classroom and observe that he is gentle, creative, and very engaging with the small children. When Nina turns up pregnant by her abrasive boyfriend, who is a legal aid attorney, she decides she wants the baby but not the father and asks George to help her raise the baby. At first George is reluctant. After watching a boy and his dad play catch in a recreation area, he agrees. George says this is because he's not content to teach other people's children then always have to say goodbye; he wants to be the one who gets to tuck a child in bed and say goodnight. George and Nina cuddle together in bed snacking and watching television, and he assures her that he does not miss men when he's with her. There is even a moment when we believe that because George loves Nina, and her attraction to him is palpable, they will make love.

Soon enough, the moment is gone, and George meets and falls *in* love with a handsome, young actor. Because of his commitment to Nina and the baby, George hides his love affair for a while, but Nina cannot overlook his distraction and frequent absences forever. Finally, at a wedding, Nina breaks down and tells George that what she really wants is for him to love her and marry her, and he admits that what he really wants is the man he loves. At this point, Nina tells George to move out. Her hope that they could live together as friends and raise her daughter as a family has always been predicated on her desire that George might someday return her romantic feelings; this illusion is destroyed by George's realization and revelation that he did not miss men when he was with Nina only until he met the right man, Paul, the man he wants as his life partner.

As expected, this romantic comedy with a twist offers us the proverbial happy ending – with a twist. At least six years have passed since the previous scene in which she asks George to move out, and Nina's daughter, Molly, has the lead in a musical produced by the Prospect Park Cooperative School where George Hanson is now the principal. Nina's father, who walked out in a snit before she was born because Nina wouldn't marry him, sits front and center looking happy and proud of his daughter. Nina sits with her boyfriend, a black police officer. Paul is there to support George at an event that is very important to him. And, in a final nod to inclusivity, Molly remarks to "Uncle George" that she has more people there than anyone. The contrasts between this musical program and the one that opens the movie are worth noting:

George is working at a public school instead of an elite private school; George is now a principal instead of a teacher; George is in a committed relationship with a man who supports his work; and, George has restored his friendship with Nina and developed a close, familial relationship with Molly. How all of this comes about is a mystery, but the Hollywood ending assures us that all is well that ends well. It is also notable that this resolution, one that suggests an unfocused but loosely liberal political agenda promoting "diversity," is achieved solely in the personal realm with virtually no implication that there may be professional consequences for gay teachers. Those consequences are explored in the next film considered, however.

The Opposite of Sex

With its provocative title, unconventional narrative, and edgy style, *The Opposite of Sex* stands with *Election* (1999), *Half Nelson* (2006), and *Detachment* (2011) as a rare film that revises and expands our understanding of the good teacher in the movies. This film presents a gay teacher, in a supporting role, who is strong, unapologetic, and unwilling to compromise his principles, despite the consequences. This is the story of Dedee Truitt, played by Chrisina Ricci, an incorrigible 16-year-old on the run from Louisiana who decides to escape a bad situation by seeking refuge in Indiana with her 35-year-old half-brother, Bill Truitt, played by Martin Donovan. There are a number of instances in the movie in which Dedee advances the narrative with voiceover narration, and this is how viewers are first introduced to Bill:

Dedee: Bill's like dozens of years older than me and an actual, real-life homo,
           and a teacher, which is kind of gross, I mean, the combo. But he had a
           lot of money from his last boyfriend who died of AIDS, and I needed
           a place to get my shit together.

Colleagues and other characters infer throughout the film that Bill is a good teacher, but there is little direct evidence of this fact onscreen. Representations of him at school are very limited – after all, this is Dedee's story – but there is an interesting scene early in the film that suggests Bill's sense of humor and comfort with his identity.

The scene takes place in the boys' bathroom at school, and a bell rings, causing students to scatter. One boy is writing graffiti on the wall about Mr. Truitt when Bill walks in and catches him in the act. He lets the student go and reveals that there is a sexually suggestive drawing of a woman – either this student is unaware that Mr. Truitt is gay or he is intentionally feminizing him. Alone in the bathroom, Bill tries to wipe off the graffiti. When the ink will not erase or smudge, the teacher modifies the drawing, deftly converting the woman's body into the face of a man. Another student enters the empty bathroom and seems perplexed to find a teacher writing on the wall.

When Dedee arrives at Bill's upscale home, the order and elegance of his life are immediately and irrevocably displaced. In a quirky turn of events, Dedee seduces Bill's current boyfriend, Matt, announces she is pregnant, runs away with Matt and $10,000 of Bill's money, and colludes with Matt's other boyfriend, Jason (whom Bill did not know about), on a blackmail scheme to get even more money from Bill. Only one part of this storyline relates to Bill as a teacher: the blackmail scheme. Jason confronts Bill and announces that he will tell the school that the teacher is gay if he does not come up with a substantial sum of money to support Matt and Dedee. When Bill says that his colleagues at school know he is gay, Jason ups the ante and says he'll tell people that Bill came on to him when Jason was a high school student.

When Jason carries through on his threat and goes to the local police, the resulting media frenzy is predictable. Even though a number of colleagues are supportive – Jason is not a very credible accuser – Bill is suspended from his job with pay. Dedee's narration minimizes the situation, "Bill just hired a lawyer, stayed at home, and worked on his garden." In fact, the story told visually is far more serious. Someone hurls a rock through the window of Bill's home one night, shattering a vase of flowers, and through the broken glass someone yells "Faggot." In the next scene, Bill gathers up a lot of rocks, which suggests there have been a number of vandals hurling epithets and stones, and puts them in one of his flowerbeds.

The resolution to this scenario is, not surprisingly, more complex than those in the previous two films. The charges against Bill are dropped when Jason fails to appear in court. Bill quits his job anyway, becomes something of a recluse, and plans to sell his magnificent home. It takes another visit from Jason, who brings a renewed blackmail threat several months later, to generate the righteous anger that will shake Bill from his lethargy. He starts by reaching out and twisting Jason's nipple ring, so that the resulting pain renders the punk helpless.

Bill: Listen to me, you little grunge faggot. I survived my family, my schoolyard, every Republican, every other Democrat, Anita Bryant, the Pope, the fucking Christian coalition, not to mention a real son of a bitch of a virus in case you haven't noticed. In all that time, since Laul Lynne and Truman Capote were the only fairies in America, I've been busting my ass so you'd be able to do what you want with yours. So, I don't just want your obedience right now, which I do want and plenty of it, but I want your fucking gratitude right fucking now, or you're going to be looking down a long road at your nipple in the dirt.

Bill orders Jason to take him to Dedee and Matt, which he does, but the story doesn't end there.

Jason not only recants but goes further and tells authorities that the Christian right put him up to making the charges. Bill is reinstated in his job, enjoys playing a major role in raising Dedee's baby, and begins seeing her parole officer. In this film, the gay teacher suffers serious consequences personally, as well as discrimination publicly and professionally because of his sexuality. Bill endures that suffering for prolonged periods of the film, and the outcomes in the public and private spheres of his life are in question until the final moments of the film. This teacher possesses a self-awareness and political consciousness that are not available to Howard Brackett or George Hanson as those characters have been written. Bill Truitt has lost his life partner to AIDS before the film begins, he loses his boyfriend to a scheming teenage girl, and he loses his job because of a false accusation that he molested a student four years earlier, but he never loses his ability to persevere.

The Double Standard Persists: Songcatcher

Perseverance is never in question for the Penleric sisters. Though they face numerous obstacles to their personal happiness, their effectiveness as teachers is never questioned in this film set in 1907 in the Appalachian Mountains. This lovely, evocative, independent film follows musicologist Lily Penleric (Janet McTeer) from an urban university where she is denied promotion to full professor (and fails to even get the vote of her married lover, who is a senior faculty member) despite a strong record of scholarship. Lily decides to spend her summer with her younger sister, Elna (Jane Adams), who has set up a rural school with a colleague, and Lily discovers the indigenous people of those mountains still sing English folk songs that have been handed down for generations, unknown to the outside world for 200 years. She begins to collect the songs with passionate enthusiasm. Along the way she finds love with a mountain musician and decides there is no place in the academy for her to pursue the work she really wants and to nourish her new relationship.[8]

It is the story of Elna and her partner in personal and professional life, Harriett Tolliver (E. Katherine Kerr) that is most relevant here. These two women have founded the Clover Settlement School and hope to make a difference in the community while Harriett is also working on a child labor project. Lily is so obsessed with her own work that she takes little notice of the other two women until she walks in on them making love in her sister's room one night. After a few moments, Elna comes to her sister's room and tries to talk with her.

Elna:	Lily, I'd like to talk with you.
Lily:	I'm very tired. I don't want to talk.
Elna:	I think we should talk.
Lily:	(sighs) How could you, Eleanor?
Elna:	You sound so like Father. I'm not a child.
Lily:	You're teachers! What kind of an example are you setting? You're disgusting.
Elna:	She's the finest person I have ever known.
Lily:	And I suppose Harriett is a lot older and more experienced than you, so … I suppose it's her fault.
Elna:	It's nobody's fault. We're in love.

Elna leaves, and for the moment her secret life with Harriett is safe. Lily returns to her work. The two women defend their school against the disapproval of the missionary board and the paternalistic support of a robber baron ready to mine the hills, but when a malicious boy sees the two women kissing in the forest and shares this information with a man Elna has kindly refused, their hatred fuels the flames they set to the wood frame building that serves as school and home.

The women sleep outside by the charred remains of the building, the three teachers and one teenage girl who boards at the school because she has no family. The school is gone, as are the songs Lily has collected over the summer. As dawn begins to break, Harriett strokes Elna's hair and murmurs to her sleeping love, "Goodbye, my darling girl." Harriett creeps away before the others wake. Later, the women remaining in the mountains wash out clothes in a creek.

Lily:	Elna?
Elna:	How am I going to live without her?
Lily:	Perhaps you could find her?
Elna:	She swore that if anyone ever found out, she'd leave … my Harriett.
Lily:	I'm sorry. I'm so sorry.

And, Lily is sorry for her sister's loss because she has grown over the course of the summer and learned that love takes root and blooms in unexpected places. Even under the best of circumstances, relationships must be worked at and nurtured, but for Elna and Harriett, there is no open place for their love to grow.

Conclusion

The first rule in the politics of representation is to look at who is included within the film frame and who is left out. The occasional gay teacher depicted in the act of teaching in the movies before the late 1990s has been an oblique presence, such as the PE character in *Clueless* (1995), or a character considered abnormal, such as Rachel's colleague in *Rachel, Rachel* (1968) or Martha Dobie in *The Children's Hour* (1961). To be dismissed as peripheral or treated as an anomaly constitutes an unsatisfactory set of portrayals, but these characterizations do constitute a presence on the movie screen for women teachers. It follows that once a presence is established, the next step is to critique those representations.

As bland as the two most commercial of the films examined in this chapter may be, *In & Out* and *The Object of My Affection* still signal a notable turn of events: gay men, long invisible in the celluloid classroom, are shown in the classroom and held up as role models of good teaching in mainstream, Hollywood films. In the first case, Howard Brackett realizes that he is gay, he comes out, and he begins to come to terms with his identity as a gay man. There really is no practice of his sexuality in this film; the kiss planted on Howard by a handsome, masculine television reporter is more a wake-up call than a romantic act. It is an interesting casting choice to have Tom Selleck play reporter Peter Malloy in the film. Selleck, sexy star of the long-running television drama *Magnum P.I.* (1980–88) is a cultural icon of heterosexual masculinity – the type of man, as the conventional wisdom goes, that all the women want and all the men want to be. Casting Selleck as Malloy calls all of that iconography into question, just as Howard's outing calls into question the values that have been tacitly accepted by the townsfolk of Greenleaf, Indiana. Deeper readings of *In & Out* offer interesting insights into the film, a film that might otherwise be seen as simplistic, and present the opportunity to make complex connections among various types of cultural texts. For example, Howard has been so steeped in the traditional values of his Midwest upbringing that it may have never occurred to him before, in any way he could address, that he is gay. Being gay is not an option that occurs to him because there is no model for it in his small community.

Perhaps Emily is drawn to Howard, and Howard to Emily, because she is also facing cultural pressure to be something she is not: thin. She laments the 75 pounds she lost for Howard, for the wedding, for everyone, it seems, except herself. Just as Howard finally acknowledges that he has been in denial about his sexuality, he admits to himself and his community that he is gay, and he begins to change the consciousness of that community about what it means to be gay, Emily finds a man who loved and desired her before she lost the 75 pounds. That this man is younger, a famous movie star, and that he has recently been dating a waiflike supermodel is a bit of a stretch, but the point is clearly made that there are all types of oppression imposed on individuals because of cultural expectations and that the results are painful and damaging whether the constraints and pressure to conform involve sexual identity or body image or some other oppressive expectation about what it means to be normal and acceptable to the dominant culture and even to our intimate friends and family.

In the second film, George Hanson is dumped by a self-centered boyfriend, finds refuge in his friendship with his female roommate until he heals, and, finally, he falls in love with a giving, loving man who fully returns his affection. The instant attraction between George and Paul and the romance of their developing relationship is not glossed over in the film. Their desire for one another is evident and strong while their kisses and touching also display tenderness and caring that indicates the depth and range of their feelings for one another. The fact that George is a teacher, and later a principal, and that he withstands the charms of Jennifer Aniston, whose success in the long-running and perennially popular sitcom *Friends* (1994–2004) has led to a string of commercially successful films and more magazine covers than one can count, presents the scenario as rather remarkable. How can he refuse her? Perhaps it is necessary to cast Aniston, who is sexy but still possesses a sweet, "girl next door" quality that makes her beauty approachable, to make the point to a mainstream audience that the man who can resist her must *really* be gay. Aniston's character, Nina, has a hard time believing that she can have a strong desire for George and that they can share such a close, loving friendship without him feeling the same degree of sustained, sexual desire for her. They do share a moment, of course, but loving is not the same as being in love, and Nina must come to terms with the fact that she is not, and never can be, the right life partner for George.

Howard and George are visible representations of "good gay teachers," but they are safe characters for us as viewers. These two teachers do little to challenge our preconceptions, except for the fact that they are gay, and in the nearly 20 years that have elapsed since these movies were released, those preconceptions have eroded.[9] These men are conservative forces, as presented, who are happy to scratch out a place for themselves professionally in the existing institutions of education and make a name for themselves by caring about their students and encouraging an aesthetic value framework in the classroom. Nonetheless, their presence is important for this very reason: Howard and George (even their names are rather bland) are "normal" teachers in the established mold of The Hollywood Model of the "good" teacher.

Bill Truitt offers a complementary character. His sex life is less circumspect than that of his cinematic colleagues, however, and he deals with serious consequences professionally for being out, gay, and unapologetic in *The Opposite of Sex*. As the film opens, Bill has lost his life partner Tom (who had been a very successful investment banker) to AIDS, and his live-in boyfriend is a much younger man (who works the night shift at a photocopying shop). The mechanics of the plot have been addressed earlier, but the emotional dynamics of the relationship between Matt and Bill are worth noting here. Matt is much younger than Bill, and he is very handsome. After Matt runs off with Dedee, thinking he has gotten her pregnant, and his affair with Jason (which overlaps with his relationship with Bill) has been revealed, Bill sees Matt and tries to convince him that what Matt has with Jason is "just sex" while the two of them have something more together. Matt, in a rare flash of insight, tells Bill that he has tried to make it more than sex because Bill really wants Tom back. The complexity, richness, and range of sexual connection among human beings and the emotional elements that sometimes accompany sexual expression (and sometimes do not) are central to this film for Bill, Dedee, and most of the other characters in the narrative.

It is true that Bill is first suspended then reinstated in his job as a teacher because of a false accusation by a former student of sexual misconduct, but the film narrative seems to suggest that this is a realistic consequence in the world we live in rather than some sort of appropriate retribution for Bill's comfort with his sexual identity.[10] While we do not have a clear sense of Bill Truitt's persona in the classroom, he is more politically aware than Howard or George, and he is angry enough and secure enough to stand up to the system, to refuse to return to teaching when first cleared of charges, and to come back to the classroom on his own terms. Still, there is no indication that Bill is interested in engaging in collective action to force political change on any front. As the film ends, he seems to have found peace in a domestic setting that includes a baby he is helping raise (Dedee's son) and a new relationship with a professional man (Dedee's parole officer) who seems a more suitable partner than Matt.

While these representations of gay male teachers introduce a presence that has been absent in preceding decades and offer us a vision of men who can find success in the classroom and fulfillment (or the promise of it) with their male partners, the portrayal of lesbian teachers continues to rearticulate the timeless message to all women teachers: their personal life cannot flourish if they express their sexuality. The double standard outside of the classroom persists, and it is rather surprising that this continues to be the case generally, regardless of the sexual orientation of the women teachers. Notice that Lilly Penleric, who is straight, must leave academia to find personal happiness while her sister, Elna, can only rebuild her school after her lover, Harriett, has left the mountains when their affair is discovered. That lack of progress noted, it seems appropriate to end this chapter on a positive note.

The late 1990s presented images of gay male teachers who, while not politically active in a radical sense, are finally here. They have achieved a presence onscreen. These are central characters whose ability as teachers, as good teachers, is never seriously questioned and who, in the latter two cases, are unapologetic about their sexual orientation. One advantage to these mainstream portrayals of gay male teachers is the gradual, less threatening progression we have already seen: Howard's sexuality and how it relates to his role as a teacher is *the* issue of the film; George's sexuality is *unrelated* to his performance in the classroom; and Bill's sexuality is relevant *only* because of a false accusation leveled by a blackmailer. As these issues have been more fully explored and the presence of gay teachers in movies more commonly accepted, a space has opened up for one lesbian teacher to enjoy the same balance between professional success and personal happiness that gay male teachers achieved earlier. In *Precious* (2009), Ms. Rain is shown in two scenes with her partner. They take Precious in when the teenager has nowhere else to go, and Precious is astonished to learn that her wonderful teacher has a woman partner. Quickly, though, the kindness the two women show her puts the student at ease. Now that more depictions of gay and lesbian teachers are emerging onscreen, the next step is an acceptance of teacher characters identified as LGBTQ, who are out, and who are engaged in radical political projects in ways that denote acceptance in cinema and connote acceptance in the larger culture.

Figure 6.2. Paula Patton as Ms. Rain in *Precious*, 2009. Ms. Rain is one of the few women teachers in the movies who has a stable and fulfilling personal life with a partner.

Notes

1. Ellis Hanson's commentary on *Bound* (1996) in the introduction to *Out Takes: Essays on Queer Theory and Film* is a useful example.
2. It is often the case, however, that women gym teachers are presented as lesbians. Invariably, these are small, throwaway roles, but the pattern is so persistent that it is parodied in *High School High* (1996).
3. Maria San Filippo, author of *The B Word: Bisexuality in Contemporary Film and Television*, has written a provocative essay on *Transparent*, "*Transparent* Family Values: Unmasking Sitcom Myths of Gender, Sex(uality), and Money," published in *The Sitcom Reader: American Re-viewed, Still Skewed*.
4. Stephen Tropiano, author of *The Prime Time Closet: A History of Gays and Lesbians on TV*, has written a moving, personal essay, "Out (and Proud) in America's Classrooms: Gay and Lesbian Teachers on 1970s Television," which explores the teachers who inspired him as a boy and gave him hope that he might realize his dream of teaching and also be true to himself as a gay man.
5. There is an interesting argument advanced in another popular culture text that portrayals of gay teachers designed to appeal to a mainstream, straight audience do not resonate with gay men. In *All Over the Guy* (2001), Tom, who is a special education teacher (though we almost never see him in the classroom), is on a blind date with Eli. Conversation is at a standstill until they begin to argue about movies and, not incidentally, provide the viewer with some insightful cultural criticism.

   Eli: Do you like movies?
   Tom: Yeah, I like movies.

Eli: Yeah, me too. I think it was gay night on cable last night. 'Cause I ...
           In & Out was on again.
Tom: Uh-huh.
Eli: I just thought it was great to see a movie like that with two guys. Not *with*
           two guys ... two guys who ... you know in the movie.
Tom: I hated it.
Eli: Oh, yeah, me too. I just thought it was light fun.
Tom: Fun?
Eli: Yeah.
Tom: Fun to see Kevin Kline get on his sorry-ass, middle-aged knees and give us
           a big old Hollywood blowjob by catering to every clichéd, homophobic,
           stereotypical idea of what it means to be gay? Without having the decency
           or the courtesy or even just the balls to drop a little trou and show us his ...
Eli: Wait a minute, come on! I thought it was nice to see a guy coming out to
           his family, his friends, not to mention his fiancé.
Tom: His fiancé? This loser bitch has been waiting her whole life to marry this
           Nellie barber loving, self-hating, geriatric English teacher who can't get it
           up for her, and we're supposed to feel sorry for her? Aw. No fucking way!
           I mean, you do the math. Where's the waiter with my drink? You want
           anything?

Tom gets up and walks off to find the waiter.

Eli: I'm not even gonna mention *Birdcage*.

6. Kevin Kline also plays Mr. Hundert in *The Emperor's Club* (2002), another dedicated,
   uptight teacher. Though Hundert has an implied longing for a married woman who later
   becomes his wife, it is hard to imagine the character having a passionate connection with
   anything or anyone except his dusty tomes.

7. See Chapter 7 for a brief discussion of professors who have sexual relationships with their
   students.

8. Lauded at Sundance and other festivals and given a limited theatrical release, this film has
   been criticized by some reviewers for perpetuating stereotypes of mountain people and,
   ironically, for presenting women teacher characters who exploit mountain culture at the
   same time their stated purpose is to preserve that culture. Those criticisms are noted here,
   but that is not my personal reading of the film.

9. Of course, there are still tragic stories of gay teachers, too, including the 2014 biopic of
   mathematician Alan Turing (Benedict Cumberbatch), *The Imitation Game*, which earned
   eight Oscar nominations and an award for Best Writing, Adapted Screenplay.

10. Sometimes a false accusation or questionable circumstance related to a sexual encounter
    is enough to end a teacher's career; this is what happens in *The Man Without a Face* (1993)
    when a male student fixates on Mel Gibson's character and causes a car accident in which
    the student is killed and the teacher disfigured.

POWER, PASSION, AND TEACHERS

Blurring the Line, Crossing the Line, Is There a Difference?

The story is not a new one – philosophers have debated such behavior at least since ancient Greece – but our penchant for "ripped from the headlines" cultural narratives in contemporary life puts a new twist on stories about teachers who engage in sexual relationships with their students. This essay explores links among those making arguments about the ethics of adults having sexual relationships with adolescents, the real-life stories of teachers who either face charges or marry their former students when the relationship is discovered, and movies that tell compelling stories about how such relationships may originate and unfold. Although other films will be referenced in the essay, the primary focus will be on two recent films: *Palo Alto* (2013) in which the "class virgin" is torn between her interest in a classmate and a flirtation with her soccer coach; and, *The Skeleton Twins* (2014) in which a man who has recently attempted suicide returns to his hometown and resumes an affair he had with one of his high school teachers. The surprising thing, perhaps, about the films, at least when compared with most of the news coverage of actual relationships between students and teachers, is how nuanced and emotionally complex the films tend to be. These teachers in the movies are not cut from a single cloth, and neither are the students who become involved with them. The films represent a range of predators, pederasts, and pedophiles along with the occasional teacher who is lured into an illicit relationship by a forward student or by falling in love. The laws and school conduct rules are clear, and there is almost universal agreement that romantic and/or sexual relationships between teachers and students are wrong. Yet, most communities deal with such inappropriate relationships on a regular basis. And, those are just the relationships that are discovered and reported. How many more of them are undetected? What can the movies, one of our major engines for cultural transmission, tell us about this type of relationship and how such relationships reflect our values and sense of humanity?

This chapter has been the most difficult for me to conceptualize and to write (it is new to this third revised edition of the book) because it fills me with ambivalence. Initially, the working title I settled on was "Predators, Pederasts, and Pedophiles: Movie Teachers Who Cross the Line," which is a fine fit for *Blue Car* (2002) but not for the bulk of Hollywood fare where students pursue teachers (from *The Prime of Miss Jean Brodie* [1969] to *The Boy Next Door* [2015]) or the relationships that are (at least nominally) consensual, which is the case for the bulk of films in which professors have sexual relationships with students as well as the two films that will be discussed in greatest detail in this chapter. If the law and school policies are clear in forbidding sexual relationships between teachers and minor-age students and most colleges and universities have adopted policies that forbid sexual relationships between professors and adult-aged students, that does not mean the problem has gone away, and it also doesn't mean that "blurring the line" and "crossing the line" have uniform meanings in each case. Think about how often you have heard an evening news report about a local teacher being arrested after the discovery of a sexual relationship with a student, have opened a newsmagazine to read about a long-term sex scandal at an elite, private school, or even have had the suspicion that something was "not quite right" about a situation you heard about or observed.

Many of these cases are clear-cut and not defensible on any grounds. Terry Abbott writes that there were 781 reported cases of teachers and other school employees accused or convicted of having sexual relationships with students in 2014. He says these illicit relationships are on the rise, that mobile phones and social media are contributing factors, and that "Classroom sexual predators have been exploiting these new, unsupervised modes of communication to develop improper relationships with students out of sight of parents and principals" (Abbott). Perhaps the movie that fits most closely with popular perceptions of predatory teachers is *Blue Car*. Christian Z. Goering and Shelbie Witte have written an important essay linking the depiction of systematic

grooming and abuse of a high school student by her English teacher to preparation that teacher educators can provide to help recognize troubling and
potentially transgressive behavior among their peers.

> Watching films such as *Blue Car* is unsettling for people who have spent their lives
> working in schools. Good teaching is blurred into sexual misconduct by a character
> who, through much of the film, appears to have his student's best interest in mind.
> The cold, hard reality of our situation as teacher educators is that there might not be
> anything we can do to prevent the future teachers we prepare from perpetrating such
> behaviors. Teachers who commit these acts are not easily defined into a subpopula-
> tion. Learning the signs of grooming behavior is a place to start. (121)

Examples in other films are well-known – a gym teacher who impregnates a
high schooler in *Teachers* (1984), a history teacher who fondles male students
during rides home on his motorcycle in *The History Boys* (2006), and dalli-
ances many of the professors depicted in movies have with their students – but
most are not presented with such evident trauma to the student as viewers see
in *Blue Car*.[1]

I remember the horror I felt reading about Mary Kay LeTourneau engaging
in an affair with her 12-year-old student when she was a 34-year-old mother of
four. I was sickened by the stories that popped up endlessly in the media. Two
jail terms and two children later, Mary Kay LeTourneau became Mary Kay
Fualaau after marrying her former student, Vili Fualaau, in 2005. As I finish
writing this chapter, Houston teacher Alexandria M. Vera faces charges for an
ongoing affair she had with one of her eighth grade students, and published
reports maintain that his parents approved of the relationship, which began
after an Instagram flirtation instigated by the student. Thousands of such
headlines have appeared between the two stories, and those are just the relationships that have been reported on by the media. It is hard to know how to
write about these relationships as a group. While the rules governing sexuality
are clear and broadly uniform, sexuality itself is variable, a condition cinema
taps into indelibly. James Stillwaggon and David Jelinek offer a long overdue,
systematic, psychoanalytic approach to teachers and teaching in the movies.
They write about the problematic model of teachers as heroes, the public
interest in teachers who have been involved in scandals, and the fact that
both impulses come from transference, the idea that is rooted in childhood
and sustained for most through adulthood that the teacher is the repository
of everything the child needs to know to create a happy and successful life.
The desire to know what the teacher knows can transfer into a desire for the
teacher, which is the psychoanalytic concept of transference. In their book,

Filmed School: Desire, Transgression and the Filmic Fantasy of Pedagogy, there are particularly insightful chapters analyzing *Notes on a Scandal* (2006) and *The History Boys*.[2]

Of course, when I say that the laws are uniform, that is more a present condition and a broad, cultural construct than it is historical truth As Gayle Rubin points out in her seminal essay "Thinking Sex: Notes for a Radical Theory of the Politics of Sexuality" and in three retrospective notes on the essay that can be found in *Deviations: A Gayle Rubin Reader*, we have largely operated under a sexual essentialism accepting sex as a natural force that is "eternally unchanging, asocial, and transhistorical" (146). Our culture "always treats sex with suspicion," "judges almost any sexual practice in terms of its worst possible expression," and considers "virtually all erotic behavior bad unless a specific reason [usually marriage, reproduction, and love] to exempt it has been established" (148). For most of our history, we have embraced a single sexual standard that valorizes procreative marriage for religious purposes and mature heterosexuality for psychological purposes (154), and teachers have often paid the price professionally for "unconventional" lifestyles that become known, sometimes even when the conduct is not illegal (161–62). When considering the sexuality of minors in an operational sense – without my making a personal judgment – the lines are sometimes blurry even if the rules are not. As Rubin writes:

> The law is especially ferocious in maintaining the boundary between childhood "innocence" and "adult" sexuality. Rather than recognizing the sexuality of the young and attempting to provide for it in a caring and responsible manner, our culture denies and punishes erotic interest and activity by anyone under the local age of consent. The amount of law devoted to protecting young people from premature exposure to sexuality is breathtaking.... The primary mechanism for insuring the separation of sexual generations is age-of-consent laws. These laws make no distinction between the most brutal rape and the most gentle romance. (161)

In one of her subsequent essays reflecting on "Thinking Sex," Rubin discusses ways in which our focus on the negative consequences of sex for young people and on "stranger danger" has been unexamined. "Hysteria, fear, and political opportunism have inhibited careful analysis and empirical research. Instead, many issues pertaining to sexuality and the young are riddled with unexamined assumptions, unverified claims, definitional incoherence, and muddled categories. Too often, scandal journalism has been a poor substitute for sober scholarship" (218). And, so it has. Some academics have grappled in provocative, if not wholly satisfactory, ways with arguments about sex and consent (MacKinnon, Primoratz, Ehman, Benatar), but the closest the culture at large seems to come to asking hard questions and providing nuanced answers may be in Hollywood movies.

I recently watched *Tea and Sympathy* (1956) again and was reminded just how unambiguous this film is (during the era of the Production Code, no less) in making the case that sex with the wife of a prep school housemaster and coach (a surrogate teacher) saves a young man's life. The film begins as Tom Robinson Lee (John Kerr) returns to school for homecoming 10 years after graduation and begins to reflect on the harassment he suffered – from his father and the housemaster as well as his classmates – for not conforming to standards of traditional masculinity. After a failed attempt to score with the town trollop leads him to attempt suicide, Laura Reynolds (Deborah Kerr) finds Tom and offers him much more than the recommended tea and sympathy. He goes on to become a successful writer, and she disappears but (in a nod to the Production Code) leaves a letter for him in the event he should return to the school saying that she should have been more patient with her boorish husband and could not stay married to him after seducing Tom. Okay, she didn't say boorish; I added that. The implication of the film is clear nonetheless: the affirming encounter with Mrs. Reynolds saves Tom's life and gives him the confidence to survive the damaging culture of the school and become a confident and successful adult.

In *The Prime of Miss Jean Brodie*, students are damaged, but by Miss Brodie (Maggie Smith) and her manipulation – which is its own type of seduction – rather than by the art teacher, Teddy Lloyd (Robert Stephens), who sleeps with one of them. Yes, Brodie schemes to get one of her students into Lloyd's bed in her place, but it is another student, Sandy (Pamela Franklin), who out-schemes the teacher to become Lloyd's lover then later to get the teacher she once admired fired for teaching "treason and sedition" to her students. Sandy's encounters with Lloyd – posing for him in the nude and having sex with him – are less about him than about her complicated relationship with Brodie. There is no indication that being sexually involved with Lloyd has any particular effect on the girl, but at graduation, Sandy sings a hymn and listens to a speech about the moral decisions the girls will have to make then walks alone after the ceremony with Brodie's voice from years before inside her head, "Little girls, I am in the business of putting old heads on young shoulders, and all my pupils are the crème de la crème. Give me a girl at an impressionable age, and she is mine for life." There are tears streaming down Sandy's face, and for all her machinations, she appears vulnerable. Vulnerability and strength seem to be opposing forces guiding Sandy, and the same might be said for characters in each of the two films to be discussed next, *Palo Alto* and *The Skeleton Twins*.

Palo Alto

There are two main characters in Gia Coppola's 2013 film *Palo Alto*, which is based on a collection of short stories by James Franco published in 2010. Teddy (Jack Kilmer) is a stoner teenager with an inclination for art and a best friend, Fred (Nat Wolff), who is unstable and always in trouble. Teddy has a crush on April (Emma Roberts), who is the class virgin, and she likes him back, though both of them are a little bit too shy to act on their feelings at first. The film is essentially the story of what separates them – misunderstandings about other encounters, friends who demand their attention, Teddy's scrape with the law, and April's affair with her soccer coach – before they cut through the clutter and make a connection. The mood of the film is reminiscent of Gus Van Sant's film *Elephant* (2003) with the same West Coast cool and ennui where parents are peripheral and what happens outside of the formal structures of school looms so much larger in the lives of students than the curriculum. These films give viewers a teenagers' perspective of the world where everything is relative and all the lines are blurred, which creates the perfect environment for a predatory teacher to identify and groom his targets with what appears to be minimal interference.

James Franco plays Mr. B, a young, handsome soccer coach, who often has members of his team babysit for his son when the divorced coach goes out on dates. The first scene of the film featuring April takes place at soccer practice where she is distinct within the group because of the bright, yellow sweatshirt she wears. As the girls stretch before practice, April's friends are talking about how much they want to have sex with their coach, whom they describe as a "hottie" and speculate about what kind of face he makes when he comes. Her friends laugh about their coach having a crush on April, and he later asks her to babysit then offers her the position of striker on the team. Mr. B reaches out and squeezes her upper arm before walking off, and her pleasure at the touch and being singled out is palpable. April's gaze follows Mr. B like a smitten schoolgirl. The night before she is scheduled to babysit, April and Teddy flirt at a party, but circumstances keep them from connecting with one another. The party sequence is followed by a scene in Mr. B's house. The teacher comes home from what he describes as "a shitty date"

Figure 7.1. James Franco as Mr. B and Emma Roberts as April in *Palo Alto*, 2013. The film is based on a collection of short stories written by James Franco.

and sits on the sofa beside April where she has been doing homework and watching a reality TV show.

April:	What happened?
Mr. B:	Nothing. Just like always. Teachers, they're so boring. Can't believe you guys have to sit there and listen to them all day. At least I can go home.
April:	Yeah, well, I don't really listen to them.
	She isn't looking at him much and seems nervous.
Mr. B:	Oh, really? You don't listen to me?
	He has turned the tables on her.
April:	I didn't mean you. Of course, I listen to you.
Mr. B:	You'd better.

There is an awkward silence following the exchange followed by pleasantries and April's departure.

The film unfolds in a very loose, episodic structure, alternating vignettes from Teddy's storyline with others from April's storyline. Back at school, April is sitting in her locker eating lunch when Mr. B comes up and says she has not been at practice for the last couple of days. April says that she fell behind on some schoolwork and asks if she can still play soccer. Mr. B reassures her that she can; he just wanted to make sure everything is all right. "You know you can talk to me, right? That's part of what a coach does." She laughs, and he continues, "If you need help with homework, I'm pretty good at that, too." He suggests that she bring schoolwork to his house the next time she babysits, and she says that she will. Later, when she goes over to his house for help with a history paper, things take a turn.

Mr. B:	Now, it's simple. The way to write a good history paper is to choose your event and just explain what happened. History is just explaining why things happened.
April:	But, what if I don't think there's a reason for something happening.
Mr. B:	Well, then you need to think harder.
April:	Yeah, but I do things all the time for no reason.
Mr. B:	Um-hmmm. It's because you're young, and you don't know why you do things. But, there's always a reason.
	She nods no …
Mr. B:	No?
April:	Umm-ummm.
Mr. B:	Okay.
April:	I mean, if you wanted to, couldn't you just say that the reason everything's happened is because of one thing that happened at the very, very, very beginning of time?
Mr. B:	Um-hummm. If you wanted to be a smart ass.

She hits at him. He leans in for a kiss, pulling her to him with his right hand on the back of her neck. Mr. B says, "Sorry." April says, "That's okay," and Mr. B replies, "I really like you." She gazes up at him and smiles, "I really like you." He looks at the girl intently, "Yeah, but, I'm older and I know that there aren't a lot of good things around, and I know that you are really good." After a pause, she leans in and gives him a very quick kiss on the lips. He grins at her. Later, riding in the back seat of a car, she holds her hand out the window and dreams, a feeling intensified by the use of slow motion.

At school, April and Teddy are aware of one another and attentive – it is clear that they like each other in a sweet way – but both of them are quite shy, especially without the social lubricant of alcohol or pot. This time at practice, Mr. B ignores April, who now wears a black hoodie with a skeleton on it, which is fitting since the coach acts as if he sees right through her. Later, she goes to Mr. B's house again where he offers her a beer as she is doing homework at his table and tells a juvenile joke about male endowment. When April, who seems more mature than her coach, asks why he doesn't talk to her at school anymore, he tells her he loves her. There is a back and forth in which she says this doesn't make sense, and he says they can figure it out, that they'll just say she's babysitting all the time. "I should be hanging out with boys my

own age," she says. "Why? Why do you want to hang out with a bunch of little boys? You're better than that. Just be with me." She nods no. "April, look,
please. All right, let's just start over. Let's just watch a movie. Find something
silly, like always, okay?" She leaves as he tries again to get her to stay. April
has two other interactions with school officials during the film, her history
teacher and her guidance counselor. The latter, who has a coffee mug that
reads "I like being friends with you!" is clueless. The plant in her office is
dying, reinforcing the point that if she doesn't water the plant, she can't nurture students. When the counselor asks April what she wants to do and be and
the student replies that she doesn't know, the counselor's only advice is that
the student should stay on the soccer team "because that could be so helpful."
From the counselor's office, April's next stop is the girls' bathroom where she
breaks down into tears, her most vulnerable point in the film. At home, her
mother says she loves her daughter, but as a parent, she is often distracted
and somewhat self-absorbed. Her stepfather is too interested in managing her
schoolwork and gives off a generally creepy vibe. And, her friends are mostly
interested in shopping and sex and exhibit flippant attitudes toward both. In
contrast, April tends toward the pensive but is not melancholy.

At April's next soccer game, it's no wonder that she messes up and misses
lots of chances to score. This is the first time viewers see the girls during a
game and learn that their uniforms are all black, like the clothing favored
by their coach, and their team mascot is the panther, a predator, again like
Mr. B. As the coach comforts another player, Raquelle, after the game, April
asks her friends if they think she's pretty. They do. She is. And, April must
wonder if the same thing is going to happen now that happened before at
the party when another girl maneuvered between her and Teddy. Mr. B turns
from Raquelle and asks if April and her two friends if they are upset then says,
"It's just a game" before offering to drive April home. But, that's not where
he takes her. Instead, they go back to his empty house where he offers her
some water, tells her it is nice to have her back there, and reassures her about
the game before they start kissing and stretch out on the sofa. Mr. B removes
April's shoes and sweatpants, revealing "Thursday" panties with a kittenish
animal in a snowsuit above the day of the week. A close-up of her panties
emphasizes April's youth. "I know it's not Thursday," she says. "I get the days
wrong." The two sit on the couch and begin kissing as Mr. B undresses April.
There is a gasp that suggests he enters her, and lots of close-ups of her face
separate from his, which makes her seem a little detached. One shot features
the gold necklace around her neck with a star nestled at the base of her throat,

as if she is earning a gold star from the teacher. At this point, the music turns a little ominous, and Mr. B's shadow covers April's face. The shadow moves away, and she appears sad before the shadow obscures her face once again. What is she thinking? She has felt rejected by Mr. B at the game, just as she has felt rejected by Teddy previously. If only she and Teddy had connected … she seems more wistful than traumatized.

The next morning, April's mom is on the phone with her friend (again) but hangs up to make breakfast. She seems to care for her daughter and says, "I just love you. You're such a good girl," but doesn't see her clearly and doesn't detect that anything might be amiss. Later, when April is babysitting, she smokes in the house, and Mr. B's son says she's not allowed to do that. "Are you going to tell on me?" She puts out the cigarette and starts playing a video game with him. When he wins, he asks for two cookies because he won. April asks, "Says who?" "Raquelle," the boy replies. To make sure she asks, "Raquelle?" He answers, "Raquelle's my other babysitter. She lets me have two cookies when I win." April will have to process this. She replies, "Well, okay," and lets the boy have all the cookies he wants. Later, when Mr. B. calls her, he says that what happened between him and Raquelle is nothing; it happened when April "broke up with him" and they "weren't talking to each other." The coach asks to see the student, who seems the more grown up of the two, and she says she doesn't want to come over to his house anymore. When he says that he loves her, April hangs up the phone. Now she understands that she has been played by the predatory coach, and this knowledge gives April the insight to untangle the complicated feelings associated with her teacher – attraction, curiosity, excitement, hesitancy, jealousy, doubt, distrust – and to walk away a stronger person than she was before.

Does Mr. B. cross the line? Of course he does. He is a predator who picks his victims, grooms them, and takes advantage. So far as viewers know, he may have been doing this for years, may continue for years to come, and may never get caught. His behavior is indefensible and – even separate from laws and school regulations – it is unclear whether or not April consents to their sexual encounter. But, there is also some ambiguity about their relationship. During a study session, she does kiss Mr. B. After she "breaks up" with her coach, April seems to have more confidence about connecting with Teddy. The film can be read in a way that suggests the relationship with her coach is an experience that helps her grow and become more independent without causing lasting damage. Just as there is a party near the beginning of the film, when Teddy and April express interest in one another but don't connect, there is another party near the end of the movie. At this party, April goes outside to sit with Teddy by a fire, which lights their faces with a nice, warm glow. He says she's crazy because she doesn't care about anything, and she replies that she wishes she didn't care about anything but that actually she cares about things too much. She says he's the one who doesn't care. When he answers that he cares about and loves her, April is confused because they haven't talked much to this point. Then they share a tender moment, and April looks softer, more open, and happier than she ever did with Mr. B. In a sense, the film suggests that the sexual playing field is now level between them. At the first party, Teddy is maneuvered into a sexual encounter with another girl when he really wants to connect with April, an incident that puts a temporary wedge between them. Her experience with Mr. B is presented in a similar context, almost as a distraction from what is really scary terrain: forming an emotional connection with someone else. At the second party, the teenagers make plans to get together, and the film ends later that evening as Teddy avoids a risky situation with his unstable friend Fred – something he fails to do earlier in the film with dire consequences – a parallel that implies both he and April have grown up. When Teddy receives a text from April as he walks home alone, it demonstrates that she is taking the initiative, and their growing connection makes him smile.

The Skeleton Twins

The stakes are higher than making a romantic overture for Milo Dean (Bill Hader) fifteen or so years after his affair with his high school English teacher. As the film opens, Milo's twin sister, Maggie Dean (Kristen Wiig), holds a handful of pills and is contemplating taking them when she gets a call that her estranged brother has tried to commit suicide. A montage of images that look like home movies from childhood show the twins dressing up for Halloween when their father appears in a gruesome skeleton mask. He has two rubber skeletons hidden in his closed fists. Young Milo, dressed in a female costume, chooses orange. The one Maggie chooses turns out to be blue. Maggie's voiceover sets the tone for the rest of the film. "I don't know. Maybe we were doomed from the beginning. I mean, it's not like dad was Mr. Sunshine. Sometimes I think all of our problems came directly from him. But, a lot of the good stuff did, too. Remember what he used to call us? The gruesome twosome. He told us to stick together no matter what." This sentence is punctuated by the orange skeleton floating to the bottom of a pool. Maggie continues, "But, what the hell happened to us?" The film starts with that question, and there are plenty of potential answers. Their father jumped off a bridge when they were 14 years old, their mother is distant with a feel-good, New Age persona that doesn't quite mask her self-absorption, and the twins share their father's battle with depression. Maggie's story focuses on the secrets she keeps from everyone but Milo. Beneath the beautiful façade of her life with the loving husband and graceful, old home, she is miserable and acts out with a series of affairs with other men. She also takes birth control pills on the sly while letting her husband think she shares his goal of becoming parents. After Maggie flies to California and convinces Milo to return to upstate New York with her, she eventually tells him her secrets, but he keeps one of his own.

While Maggie is at her scuba lessons – where the cool blue of the water is icy rather than reassuring and tranquil, reinforcing the emotional depths the twins share – Milo walks into a bookstore and surreptitiously watches a man working there. He walks over to the man, Rich (Ty Burrell), who is surprised and not pleased to see him. They go outside to talk, and Milo tries to connect with the older man, who tells him to go away. Milo tries again, "No, I … no, I … let's go hiking. Let's go to Case Lizzie Meadow and go to a harvest festival, and …" to which Rich replies, "Milo, you're out of your mind" before telling him not to come back to the bookstore.

Figure 7.2. Ty Burrell as Rich in *The Skeleton Twins*, 2014. Rich is shocked and afraid when a former student turns up after many years.

Later, he does return to the store and presents a copy of *Moby-Dick* over the counter. Rich smiles at the book cover, but his smile fades as he looks up and sees Milo, who says, "Someone told me to read this once." Their second encounter goes more smoothly than the first, and they continue talking in a car where they exchange information. Rich talks about his girlfriend, an optometrist named Melinda, and Milo has forgotten that Rich has a son, Eric. Rich asks why Milo is there besides "scaring the shit out of me." Milo, who has been waiting tables at "a shitty, tourist restaurant in Hollywood" instead of landing acting jobs, exaggerates his success by talking about having an agent and being there for a writer's retreat because he's working on a one-man show. Rich remarks that this doesn't surprise him at all because Milo was always a great writer. Milo returns the compliment, "Well … I had a … I had a good teacher," then things become awkward between the two men. Every time Maggie and Milo begin to reconnect, Rich will come between them, a rather elegant set-up that foreshadows the revelation about why the two of them have grown apart. Milo goes to pick up Maggie from her work as a licensed dental hygienist one day, and she cleans his teeth. They indulge in laughing gas and get silly together, and she reveals her self-destructive secrets. Milo answers his sister's confidence with a lie; he pretends to have an appointment with an old high school friend when he is really meeting Rich.

In the next scene, as Milo and Rich have drinks, they discuss *Moby-Dick*. Rich says, "I feel like I gave you a copper figurine for your birthday …" When Milo pulls the small whale out of his pocket, Rich is touched, "Wow! You carry that with you?" Milo says it is a good luck charm to which Rich replies, "It's working, Mr. Fancy LA Agent." Milo demurs but is pleased, and Rich says, "I should have kept that whale for myself. I think it's incredible. I always knew you'd do something amazing with your life. I'm proud of you, Milo." Now Milo feels a little conflicted and wishes he could be the person he has invented. When the younger man asks, "Do you want to get out of here?" Rich looks at him with discomfort, shame, and desire. In the next scene, they are smoking pot in a parked car talking about Rich's 16-year-old son.

Rich:	I'm old enough to have a kid that can drive. My god.
Milo:	Does he know about … about … me and you?
Rich:	No, no. God no. He knows I used to teach … and, uh … sometimes he asks why I stopped, you know, but …
Milo:	What do you tell him?
Rich:	That it wasn't my thing.
Milo:	I'm sorry, Rich.
Rich:	No, Milo. You don't ever have to apologize. You didn't do anything wrong. Understand me.
Milo:	(softly) Okay. Look, I know, I know what happened was weird … and illegal … and shit, but it really meant something to me. And, we're

adults. Well, I'm, I'm an adult. God, I feel like the freshman asking the senior to a dance.

Rich: It's part of the problem ... there's this freshman and senior dynamic between us.

Milo: Doesn't have to be ...

The next morning, they are together and both late for work. Rich hands Milo a script for a romantic comedy titled *Sunrise in Manhattan* and asks the younger man to read it and pass it on to his agent. After Milo agrees, Rich says, "I need you to leave," demonstrating a startling capacity to compartmentalize. Milo talks about their time together being a fun "blast from the past," and Rich says uncomfortably, "Yeah, uh, make sure the door locks when you close it." It is not coincidental that we never see the two men really together. Milo is in bed, naked beneath the covers when the scene begins, and Rich is dressed, even wearing layers – a red sweater with a shirt underneath – and wearing his glasses, both forming a barrier between them that makes true intimacy impossible.

That evening, Maggie is irritated with Milo for not coming home the night before and being late to the job he has taken working with her husband. After lying about whom he was with, Milo puts on the Starship song "Nothing's Gonna Stop Us Now" and starts dancing and lip-syncing. Maggie resists but eventually gives up and joins in the performance with Milo. It is in moments like this and the dental office scene that viewers see the afterlife of their childhood and glimpse how the twins coped with difficult situations. When they begin lip-syncing the lyrics "And if this world runs out of lovers, We'll still have each other, Nothing's gonna stop us now, nothing's gonna stop us now," she is motioning between the two of them, and it is clear that the twins have bonded again. Milo is listening to the song later on when he goes to Rich's house and pulls off headphones, abruptly ending the upbeat moment, when Rich's son Eric answers the door. The boy goes to get his dad, who drops his smile when he sees that the "some guy's at the door" his son refers to is Milo. Rich walks out closing the door behind him, "What are you doing? That's my kid in there! I have a life, Milo, I have a life." Clearly, Milo will not be part of it, and he is relegated to the shadows as the door closes in his face.

From Rich's house, Milo first goes to a bar and drinks then to a rooftop ledge and looks down at traffic. He takes the whale Rich gave him years before, holds it up and moves it as if the creature is swimming along the waves, then drops it into the darkness below. One police officer finds him on the roof, and another brings him home. Maggie is upset, and Milo tries to explain the episode by saying, "I get depressed about my life, and I do stupid things." When she tells her twin that she can't take it anymore, he apologizes. Maggie tells Milo, "Either we find a way to deal, or … I need to know you're not going to check out on me," and her brother tells his twin that he'll do his best. Later, when Milo reads Rich's script, he indicates to viewers non-verbally that it's not very good.

The film builds to a final resolution for Milo and Maggie with a Halloween set piece and a final confrontation between Milo and Rich. First, the twins go to their hometown's elaborate Halloween festival in costumes, reminisce about important events from their childhood over drinks, show one another their matching skeleton tattoos, and dance happily. Maggie looks at a cute photo of the two of them on Milo's phone while he is away from the table, and Rich calls at that moment. When Milo returns, his sister is upset.

Maggie:	Are you sleeping with him?
Milo:	Some of us have our secrets, and some of us have our reasons, Maggie.
Maggie:	Wow. So you're still attracted to child molesters. Is that it?"
Milo:	He's not a child molester.
Maggie:	You were fifteen, and he was your English teacher.
Milo:	You didn't see the way he treated me.
Maggie:	He wanted to fuck you.
Milo:	Who are you to judge, okay? You've had boyfriends since you were in the fifth grade. Okay? I was fifteen, and I hadn't even been kissed before. So what if he was my teacher.
Maggie:	So what?
Milo:	He made me feel, he made me feel better about myself.
Maggie:	I don't want to hear about how he made you feel. You know what, you want to go hang out with Rich Levitt, go ahead. I'm not going to stop you, but when all that shit went down, I know looking back I was right. And, I can't feel guilty about it anymore, and it could have been a lot worse. He could have gone to fucking jail, Milo. You realize that? He is lucky that we dealt with this quietly. And, I know that you blame me, and I know you think I ruined this blossoming relationship between you and him. I know you think that I ruined his life, that I ruined your life, but I did what I had to do.
Milo:	Look, it had nothing to do with you.
Maggie:	That's bullshit. You're my brother … and we're supposed to be there for each other … and if you don't get that by now … then … I don't know. I guess I'll talk to you in another ten years. This …
Milo:	Wait …
Maggie:	This sucks. I was having such a good night with you.

Now viewers know what came between the brother and sister years before, what remains unresolved. Maggie, in her cowboy costume, walks away from her twin. She leaves him standing alone in a drag queen costume, wardrobe that recalls the montage at the beginning of the film.

Angry, Milo reveals enough information for Maggie's husband to discover that she's been taking birth control pills. She is furious, and he throws her own words back at her by telling her that he is only trying to help her. During their argument, Maggie goes a step too far when she says, "Well, maybe next time you should cut deeper." As hurtful as her words are, something seems to have shifted for Milo. Coming home and confronting his past may be necessary for him to face the future, and the next step is for him to have another conversation with Rich. When Milo goes to Rich's house, he confronts his former teacher, "I know I'm not supposed to come over here, but I need to talk to you and I think you owe me that. You owe me. That's what I think." Milo asks how Rich makes juggling a girlfriend and a son with "guys like me" work, and Rich replies, "Well, there aren't a lot of guys like you." Milo answers, "Thanks, Teach." Rich says it's not a pattern for him, and Milo asks if he is gay. "I can make it work with Melinda, and I really want to," Rich says. Milo responds, "Well, good luck with that." When Rich leans over to kiss Milo, the younger man pushes him away.

Milo:	Don't … what am I? Some kind of forbidden fruit? Some kind of blowup doll? What am I to you?
Rich:	I treated you terribly. I know that, but it's not because I don't care or because I don't respect you or because I don't love you. It's because I'm a big pussy. That's it. I'm just a huge, pathetic pussy. I could never be you. You can crash on the couch if you want. (Rich walks away then turns back) Oh, um, did you by chance read my script?

Finally, Milo has the appearance of an adult; viewers see his face filled with resolve, sadness, and something else that turns out to be kindness. "Yeah," Milo says. Rich asks expectantly, "And?" Milo responds, "It's great. I'll definitely give it to my agent." For the first time, Rich smiles softly.

Milo sleeps on the sofa, wakes up, and pulls out a yearbook to look at a picture of Mr. Levitt then flips pages to photos of him and Maggie standing together. Turning the page on Mr. Levitt carries symbolism beyond the compassion and closure Milo now feels for his former teacher. He is ready to forgive his sister, too, and to save her. After receiving her message, "I finally did it. See you later," he knows where she has gone and what she has done. It turns out that she has changed her mind after submerging herself in the pool but that she cannot extricate herself from the weights that she counted on for drowning without help. Suddenly, Milo is in the water helping her, freeing her from the ropes. He soothes her. "You're here," she says. "I'm here," Milo answers, and viewers see young Maggie under water clinching the toy skeleton before she tosses it to Milo. There is one more scene in the film. The twins drive away together beneath the brilliant fall foliage; maybe this time the lyrics of the song they shared before will come to pass, "And if this world runs out of lovers, We'll still have each other, Nothing's gonna stop us now, nothing's gonna stop us now." They have shared their vulnerabilities, and viewers can hope that the twins will inspire one another to develop new strength. Was Milo being honest with himself and his sister when he told Maggie that Mr. Levitt is the one who gave him hope, made him feel good about himself, and made high school bearable? There is nothing in the film to suggest that the romance with his teacher (which a careful line reading of the dialogue suggests may not have been consummated at the time) was as damaging to Milo as his father's suicide, his mother's neglect, or his sister's betrayal. Despite his disappointment in discovering as an adult how feckless a man his teacher turns out to be, Milo might well argue that the relationship was a lifeline to him as a teenage boy who didn't fit in at school or at home.

As with *Palo Alto*, I am deeply ambivalent about *The Skeleton Twins*. Both of these films have been featured because of the emotional complexity they contain, but – unlike *Blue Car* – there is no evidence in either of the narratives that April or Milo have been damaged by their relationships with their teachers and some suggestion that the relationships positively affect (or, in the case of Milo, affected) the maturation process for both characters. It is important to note that both stories are told from the perspective of the student. If the teacher character had been the focal point of one of the movies, then there would be the possibility of reading the film from Mr. B or from Phil's perspective. In that case, viewers could persuasively argue that the teachers would have a vested interest in determining that their students benefitted in some way from the sexual relationship whether or not this account was supported by the students, effectively positioning the teachers as untrustworthy narrators. But, that is not how the stories are presented. On the one hand, it could be dangerous for these films to offer up a space where predators interpret their attention to students as having a positive outcome and, similarly, where students get the idea that such relationships are beneficial. On the other hand, there should be space for cinema – like all art forms – to go into difficult terrain and explore stories that contest commonly held assumptions.

My ambivalence reveals the crux of the problem because I simply can't foresee all of the implications, though if I have to err on the side of following a circumscribed narrative to avoid conflict or to risk failure and pain in the pursuit of authenticity, I will choose the latter.

A Word About Professors and Turning the Tables

In working on this chapter, I came across a file marked "notes on professors for essay." I found the line, "They inspire, they harass, and occasionally they actually teach. Professors on television, though not as well represented and iconic as high school teacher characters, have been represented on the small screen since the early days of TV ..." followed by pages of notations on professor characters for the book I co-authored with Laura R. Linder, *Teacher TV: Sixty Years of Teachers on Television*. Not surprisingly, many of these professor characters on television, especially those in guest starring roles, are seducers and cads, but I don't think the stereotype is nearly so entrenched on television as it is for professors in the movies.[3] Others have covered this ground much more thoroughly than I will here, but it is worth mentioning that the one thing many professors in movies have in common is that they sleep with their students, as William Deresiewicz notes when discussing films such as *Terms of Endearment* (1983), *Surviving Desire* (1993), *Oleanna* (1994), *One True Thing* (1998), *Wonder Boys* (2000), *The Life of David Gale* (2003), *We Don't Live Here Anymore* (2004), *The Squid and the Whale* (2005), and *Little Miss Sunshine* (2006). The pattern seems to be especially entrenched for professors of English and the humanities. Deresiewicz writes:

> In fact, lust is almost the only emotion that movie professors ever express toward their students. In the rare scenes in which these teachers actually teach, the point is to exhibit the classroom or office hour as a locus of sexual tension. The popular mind can't seem to imagine what other kind of relationship, let alone what other kind of intimacy, a professor and student could share. And it certainly can't imagine what other sort of gratification a person could derive from teaching in a university. (42)

While issues of consent are not the same in films featuring professors as they are in the major examples presented earlier in the chapter, the lines are certainly blurred when authority figures engage in relationships with partners who have less power and professional stature, and rules are usually broken, rules at the college and university forbidding such relationships and, quite often, marriage vows. Making the intertextual leap here from movies and television shows to real life, think of the professors you have known and make a mental checklist of how many of them have partnered with or married former students. Surely, some of those lines seem blurry.

While there are exceptions – in *Looking for Mr. Goodbar* (1977), a failed relationship with a professor and self-doubt lead Teresa Dunn (Diane Keaton) to pick up a succession of men in a bar, one of whom murders her, and in *An Irrational Man* (2015), Jill (Emma Stone) rather unconvincingly pursues her professor, Abe (Joaquin Phoenix), then he tries to murder her after she uncovers a crime he has committed – the effects on students of these affairs are downplayed in most of the films. The emphasis in Dale M. Bauer's work and, separately, in Jo Keroes's work is situated on the teacher. In "Indecent Proposals: Teachers in the Movies," Bauer argues that teaching, depicted once in the movies as a "profound calling," has become a "sexual proposition" (302). There are some intriguing critiques given to various films in her essay, which culminates in a call for a rhetorical intimacy related to teaching allegiance to the classroom community rather than the teacher. This redirection of desire functions as "a model of intellectual, even disciplinary commitment," a new calling that "does not offer the gratification of primary narcissism, where we measure success by our students' love for us" (315). Keroes provides a more expansive perspective. With an overarching argument that "teacher texts are fundamentally about love" (66), she argues that as a microcosm of the larger culture the classroom – with the teacher as an authority figure – presents gender and power relations and expresses "a connection between teaching and sexual politics" (9). Later, Keroes's argument, based on typical narrative patterns in teacher films, is developed further:

> When the teacher is male, he brings the force of public masculine power and all that it entails into the relatively confined psychic and social space of the classroom, where it may be subject to potential challenges but is almost always reconfirmed. When the teacher is a woman, she generates conflict between unleashed maternal (female) power and the alluring solace of domestic space. (15)

Keroes notes that men regularly "succumb to the erotic temptations teaching affords" (15) while the "erotic impulses of women teachers are usually suppressed, disguised, or demonized" (16). But, that pattern appears to be changing somewhat. From *Notes on a Scandal* to the torrid thriller *The Boy Next Door*, women teachers in movies can become the prey of predatory students who, in the case of the latter film, may turn the tables a second time and become psychotic killers when the teacher tries to break off the affair. While I am not making an argument that these relationships are justified let alone legal, the framework recalls the broader pattern of representation for women teachers that requires they be punished for acting on their sexuality and, in the case of transgressive relationships, that they are punished much more harshly than their male counterparts.

Conclusion

Where do we end up? I am as ambivalent about these films at the end of the chapter as I was at the beginning, but I think exploring them and thinking about the implications is an important exercise. It is tempting to be cautious, especially with education under siege from forces that want to privatize public education and vocationalize education at all levels. Under these conditions, how can we infuse the classroom with passion when lines can become blurry and risks seem outsized? Heather Weaver examines a gentler time in the movies if not in life in "Beyond Apples and Ice Cream: The Teacher-Student Relationship as Cinematic Romance 1909–39." Having never considered any of these films as primary texts in my own research, I am captivated to read her analysis:

> School is an emotional experience in these early films, not an intellectual one. It is a place where hearts are won, not minds. Here the teacher's role frequently corresponds to the hero of a romantic melodrama: the teacher meets the student; the student is unsure what to think of the teacher; the student falls into peril or otherwise demonstrates a need; and the teacher saves the student, thereby winning the latter's approval and affection. (10)

Later in the period she studies, the films in her survey move from melodrama toward comedy, but the teacher character continues to be depicted as a savior. "By saving a student, the teacher won, justified, and/or ensured that student's love. This, and not teaching, remained the teacher's primary role" (11). This remains a recognizable narrative pattern.

We come to teaching with a lot of baggage, both personal and cinematic. Perhaps we can begin by being honest with ourselves, which is a difficult but essential task. Before teaching became my career, I was a broadcast journalist, and I remember coming to the realization that objectivity is an impossible standard but identifying then bracketing our subjectivities is not. Erasing eros from the classroom is similarly impossible, but recognizing when the lines are blurred and choosing ethical behavior is an achievable standard. I was 21-years old when I taught my first class as a graduate student, younger than some of the undergraduates in the class, and 23 when I taught my first course as an adjunct instructor. Learning to acknowledge desire when it would arise then to put it away was an important step, another context for bracketing subjectivity and limiting involvement. Not being able to acknowledge and redirect that energy can wound students in unexpected ways, as bell hooks recounts in *Teaching to Transgress: Education as the Practice of Freedom*:

> During my first semester of college teaching, there was a male student in my class whom I always seemed to see and not see at the same time. At one point in the middle of the semester, I received a call from a school therapist who wanted to speak with me about the way I treated this student in class. The therapist told me that the students had said I was unusually gruff, rude, and downright mean when I related to him. I did not know exactly who the student was, could not put a face or body with his name, but later when he identified himself in class, I realized that I was erotically drawn to this student. And that my naïve way of coping with feelings in the classroom that I had been taught never to have was to deflect (hence my harsh treatment of him), repress, and deny. Overly conscious then about ways such repression and denial could lead to the "wounding" of students, I was determined to face whatever passions were aroused in the classroom setting and deal with them. (192–93)

To confront feelings and learn to channel them in productive ways is something most of us in higher education have learned to do with our research, scholarly work, and creative projects. Too few of us have managed to keep the fire kindled when it comes to our teaching. There are undoubtedly a myriad of reasons for that – our greatest public and monetary rewards come from publishing and producing, we are often drawn to the academy by love for our disciplines rather than teaching, and we become tired of mollycoddled students and their lack of engagement with the discipline we love – but one of the reasons our teaching suffers may be fear. We cannot let fear of blurring lines or fear that others think we are blurring lines stamp out love because the cost of that is too great.

To become or remain an involved teacher means staying connected to students and forging relationships with them. And, for those of us who embrace a critical pedagogy, it means taking risks because risk is a condition of changing consciousness. Eros may be the biggest risk, but, as hooks argues, the risk is worth it. "Understanding that eros is a force that enhances our overall effort to be self-actualizing, that it can provide an epistemological grounding informing how we know what we know, enables both professors and students to use such energy in a classroom setting in ways that invigorate discussion and excite the critical imagination" (195). My field is critical media studies, and my classrooms are filled with risk and possibility as I guide students who are willing to take the journey to a new way of thinking about their identity, the world, and their place in it through studying media texts. To do this work, I must remain open, authentic, and willing to let love into the classroom. I mean this in a broad sense because I'm thinking of my love of learning, my love of film and television, my love of my work, and my love of teaching and of my students. There's the potential for a lot of love in that space. I believe love is the energy that fuels the best of my classes, and nothing seems to come together quite so well when it dwindles.

Notes

1. There are several other essays in *Screen Lessons: What We've Learned from Teachers on TV and in the Movies* that address lines blurred and crossed between teachers and students. Suzanne Regan writes about the sexual impropriety of teachers in several recent cable series – *Girls* (2012–), *Shameless* (2011–), and *Ray Donovan* (2013–) – in "Bad Teacher: Bad Judgment, Bad Intentions, or Abuse?" Christine Mallozzi takes an autobiographical approach to her examination of a provocative music video in her chapter "When Worlds Collide: Van Halen's 'Hot for Teacher' and Gender in the Classroom." And, Jennifer S. Dean writes about "Teacher as Object of Desire in Wes Anderson's *Rushmore*."

2. If time and space permitted, it would be useful to examine the 1970 David Lean film *Ryan's Daughter* in which a young, Irish woman, Rosy Ryan (Sarah Miles), pursues her former teacher, Charles Shaughnessy (Robert Mitchum) with complicated consequences for both of them after she has an affair with a British officer that coincides with the 1916 Easter Rising. I saw the film first as a young girl without any context for the politics of the story, but even then the cinematic beauty of the film and nuanced interpersonal dynamics of the characters were inescapable. And, there can be no doubt, that Shaughnessy fits The Hollywood Model of the good teacher.

3. Of course, it wasn't always this way. In an earlier era, the dominant stereotype of the professor was as an "egghead" who functioned fine so long as he was locked up in an ivory tower but not so comfortable in the "real world" guided by a different sort of masculinity. See *The Dancing Co-Ed* (1939), *The Male Animal* (1942), and *The Affairs of Dobie Gillis* (1952) as three examples. *The Male Animal* is remarkably topical in its examination of how the mission of universities is undermined by the focus on "revenue sports" and the willingness of administrators to sacrifice the free exchange of ideas for avoiding controversy.

· 8 ·

WHEN THE PODIUM BECOMES
A PEDESTAL

Race, Ethnicity, and Social Class in the Classroom

As I finish writing this chapter, it is only days after the tragic shootings in Orlando, Baton Rouge, St. Paul, and Dallas. In Florida, a shooter killed 49 people at a gay nightclub; the gunman, an American Muslim, claimed allegiance to ISIS, and many of the victims were Latino. Two black men were killed by white police officers in Louisiana and Minnesota. Five white officers in Texas were gunned down by a black Army veteran while they were protecting peaceful demonstrators protesting the shootings in Baton Rouge and St. Paul. I frame these events in terms of identity because that is important to understanding that we are all linked to multiple identities and to one another. These events don't occur in a cultural vacuum, but finding the connections is not always easy to do, especially when our perspectives – each informed intertextually by our lived experience, the media we consume, and the ideologies that resonate and shape our beliefs – seem marked more by our divisions than by what connects us. How do we make sense of the senseless? We must interrogate ourselves, understand the implications of our cultural narratives, and engage with others in difficult conversations to find a better way forward. Intersectionality has been a buzzword in academic circles for some time and has recently begun to creep into mainstream discourse. The term was originally coined by Kimberlé Creshaw in a law article in 1989, but the idea of exploring multiple vectors of oppression based on overlapping identities is not new in and of itself. Many public intellectuals and scholars and artists have explored the idea in various contexts with compelling results, and I am incapable of thinking about my own life or about the artifacts of media without applying multiple lenses simultaneously and grappling with layers of meaning and competing truths.

Narratives link all of us because it is the stories of our lives and the stories we encounter in our lives that inform our perceptions of others and, even more fundamentally, lead us to construct our own identities. It may sound like a cliché for me to say that at age 13 my life was forever changed when I read *I Know Why the Caged Bird Sings*, but it is nonetheless true. Integration came to my suburban elementary school in North Carolina when I was in the third grade. I don't recollect my parents saying anything to me about it beforehand, but there were two new children in my class that fall. In the years since, I have thought a lot about who they were and how they felt and why I didn't do more to welcome them. That year, like most others in school, I mostly sat at my desk and read books after finishing my work, and I rushed through my work as quickly as I could to get to those books. Then and throughout my schooling, reading was my escape from the tedium of the classroom, my way to explore the larger world. Sometimes, that world was challenging. With the turning of each page of Maya Angelou's classic autobiography, I began to attend to the issues of race, gender, and social class and to feel the seeds of a challenge that would go unanswered for some years. As a middle-class, white girl in the South, I did not have to attend to race or class except when I chose to do so. Such is the condition of white privilege, a term I would not encounter for a couple of decades. There have been many experiences and many texts that prodded my emerging consciousness, but I will share two here, one story linked to my identity as a teacher and the other to my identity as a student.

For 30 years, I have taught at my undergraduate *alma mater* and by this time have had thousands of students enrolled in my classes. Some of them, even from the earliest years, are indelibly etched into my memory. In particular, I remember a conversation with a talented student from my television production class, a football player with an innate talent for directing. He missed class one day, which was uncharacteristic, and wanted to explain why. The telling of the story was painful for him. He was with a group of friends from home and – in a now familiar phrase that did not exist in the vernacular then – was pulled over for "driving while black." They all ended up being taken to jail, though my student was not ultimately charged with any crime. Sitting in the control room of our little studio listening to his story after the other students had left the classroom, I was flooded with a sense of empathy that I had not felt so palpably before. Suddenly, I looked at this person I cared about, whose talent I nurtured, and I put myself in his place. What was it like to walk around in his shoes and see others feel visibly threatened by his size, his strength, and his race? How often had I felt unreasonably afraid at the sight of men who resembled him? Now, I felt afraid *for* him. The depth of my feelings in that moment, which has not abated, started me on a path of working for social justice through my teaching, scholarship, filmmaking, and political action. I have read many things that stay with me today, but maybe the first time I really "got" white privilege was the same as for many other people – by reading something provocative in graduate school. Peggy McIntosh's simple, powerful, and now classic essay "White Privilege and Male Privilege: A Personal Account of Coming to See Correspondences Through Work in Women's Studies," which is often known as "Unpacking the Invisible Knapsack," rocked my world. Once you know something, it cannot be unknown. Once you feel something and know it, the only path to take leads forward.

Minimizing Difference: Race, Ethnicity, and Social Class

We can't avoid the brutal game of tug-a-war being waged over schooling, especially when it comes to providing a quality education to the students who need it most because they lack other resources outside of school. Debates over unequal funding because of budgets tied to property taxes are longstanding, and the work of Jonathan Kozol among others has made these stories personal and indelible.[1] Poor zip codes have less money allocated to schools, which languish in disrepair, while wealthy areas have public schools with resources that rival private schools. Instead of addressing the inequality, conservative forces have intensified efforts to undermine public instruction by adopting policies that favor privatizing schools and adopting inflammatory rhetoric to damage public schools, such as replacing the term public schools with government schools. Because many of the schools that suffer the most under this system enroll students of color in disproportionate numbers, the problem is one of race, ethnicity, and social class. What does Hollywood say about these identities and schooling? Less than you would think when films are examined holistically. The bias of Hollywood has always been – though I hope it may not always remain – toward the individual. As noted throughout this book, the dominant narrative structure of mainstream films favors individual solutions to personal problems and avoids showcasing collective action to resolve systemic injustices. The most popular of these films follow The Hollywood Model of the good teacher (educator) regardless of the other identities and educational context depicted on screen.

Take this sample of ten films from the 1980s as evidence: *Educating Rita* (1983), a burned-out university professor is assigned to an adult, working-class student, contrasting their mismatched privilege and passion for learning then reinvigorating him; *Teachers* (1984), a burned-out public school teacher works mainly with middle-class students and is renewed by helping them get the education they deserve; *The Karate Kid* (1984), a mysterious maintenance man trains a high school student from New Jersey in martial arts after the boy moves to Hawaii with his single mom; *Children of a Lesser God* (1986), a speech pathologist with innovative pedagogical practices works with deaf students in a residential school and challenges the status quo; *Hoosiers* (1986), inspired by a true story, a coach with a checkered past leads a rural, Indiana team to win the state basketball championship; *The Principal* (1987), a rogue teacher is assigned to be the principal of a troubled, urban high school and turns it around; *Summer School* (1987), a gym teacher is blackmailed into teaching remedial English to mostly white, middle-class students in summer school and learns some things about himself; *Stand and Deliver* (1988), based on the true story of Jaime Escalante, a Latino math teacher inspires his students to high levels of achievement on the AP calculus test after other teachers have under-estimated them; *Dead Poets Society* (1989), a teacher uses poetry to inspire his students at an elite, single-sex boarding school to think beyond the staid cur-riculum; and, *Lean on Me* (1989), based on a true story, a progressive teacher becomes an authoritarian administrator after the white, middle-class school where he taught becomes a largely black school with discipline problems. The main characters are mostly men, as they tend to be in films featuring educa-tors and in most Hollywood films, but the broad patterns of the narratives are the same whether they are teaching poor students or middle-class students or wealthy students *and* whether the students are white, black, or Latino *and* whether the students are male or female *and* whether the students are disabled or able-bodied.[2]

Movies reveal schools to be places of multiple fissures where people are placed into groups and separated by different needs in the scheme of things – needs that go largely unmet – with the largest rupture separating students from adults except, of course, for the idealized teacher who bridges the gap. This pattern holds true whether the school is an elite private school, a stereo-typical inner-city school, or a middle-class suburban school. These Hollywood schools may feature a good teacher who works hard to form connections with troubled students and smooth their transition into the implied "dominant culture" waiting outside the cinematic frame, but even these iconic teachers do not mount serious threats to the status quo, which is represented in these films by administrators and the institution of education. In other words, when the credits roll at the end of the motion picture, there may have been some personal transformations along the way and a symbolic challenge to the uncaring system by a good teacher or a group of resistant students, but ultimately the status quo has been protected, and the dominant ideology of maintaining the existing class structure (and as a byproduct maintaining segregation) is intact. I find the similarities among these narratives – the maintenance of the status quo in mainstream, commercial films – as a dominant overarching theme, a theme that minimizes the effect of race, ethnicity, and social class on schooling. Films are rife with competing messages. We are diverted by the actions of the caring educator and engaged in the teacher's success in "reaching" a "difficult" student or even a whole class of them, but this is a superficial engagement, a sparkling veneer on what is a more troubling story beneath the surface.

Yes, films do depict schools that are distinctly lower-class, middle-class, and upper-class. As Jacqueline Bach discovered in her research on cinematic approaches to teaching Shakespeare, "there were clear connections between socioeconomic setting and the ways that pedagogical strategies positioned students' social class and racial identities" (330).[3] Just as Jean Anyon's groundbreaking work on "the hidden curriculum" demonstrated in the late 1970s, schools prepare students for jobs that correspond to their social strata. Robert C. Bulman splits the difference a bit in his sociological study of 177 films featuring schools, *Hollywood Goes to High School: Cinema, Schools, and American Culture*. He surveys 37 poor or working-class schools, mostly in urban areas where the teacher and principal heroes are altruistic outsiders who save students. There are 104 films considered featuring middle-class students in mostly suburban schools where the hero is a student who overcomes conformity. And, there are 36 films in the study that feature a mixture of rich and upper-middle-class students in private schools where the hero is a working-class or middle-class outsider, an interloper who challenges the culture of privilege at the school. While Bulman looks at schools as sociological sites in films than more broadly at films as cultural texts including both cultural truths over time and competing messages, some general patterns inform both approaches:

> Individualism is the dominant theme in most of the films. Adolescents in these films are expected to transcend the limitations of their communities, the narrow-mindedness of their families, the expectations of their parents, the conformity of their peers, the ineffectiveness of their schools, their poverty or wealth, and the insidious effects of racism or sexism in order to express themselves as individuals apart from social constraints. The source of their academic success and/or personal fulfillment is to be found within the heart and mind of each individual regardless of social context. (9)

Clearly, social class is a defining element of American culture, but popular culture dictates (as it has since the earliest days of our country's history) that social class is not defining or definitive because anyone can succeed in America if she, ze, or he tries hard enough.

Both film and television tend to minimize the influence of race and social class on success in favor of stories of individual triumph. Even with the inspiring personal narratives, however, the overarching theme in conventional Hollywood cinema is the maintenance of the status quo. In other words, despite the competing messages within the texts and the apparent differences according to race and social class, good teacher movies follow similar patterns that transcend (and minimize) difference. Granted, there are exceptions (and we are grateful for those films – and television shows like *The Wire* (2002–08) and *Friday Night Lights* (2006–11) – that expand on and complicate the conventions of the genre), but the dominant patterns of representation have become so familiar and entrenched, as I have maintained, that we have enough identifiable characteristics, or conventions, to call these good teacher movies a genre. And, aside from the more narrowly defined good teacher movies, these conventions spill over into films that more broadly represent teachers, students, and schools. Because the patterns are so recognizable, it is intriguing to take a look at a couple of movies released within a two-week period in 2012: *Won't Back Down* (logline: "Two determined mothers, one a teacher, look to transform their children's failing inner city school. Facing a powerful and entrenched bureaucracy, they risk everything to make a difference in the education and future of their children.") and *Here Comes the Boom* (logline: "A high school biology teacher looks to become a successful mixed-martial arts fighter in an effort to raise money to prevent extra-curricular activities from being axed at his cash-strapped school.") Sounds familiar, doesn't it? The format for these films is so deeply entrenched into popular culture that the 1996 parody *High School High*, to be discussed in detail later in this chapter, riffs mercilessly on such staples of the genre as *Blackboard Jungle* (1955), *Dead Poets Society*, and *Dangerous Minds* (1995). The parody is silly but still a testament to the enduring popularity of movies featuring dedicated teachers as heroes, and it provides evidence that these depictions resonate with viewers.

Remember the paradigm outlined in Chapter 2: good teachers are outsiders who are not liked by other teachers; they care about students and become involved with them on a personal level; they learn from students in what becomes a reciprocal process; they personalize the curriculum to meet everyday needs in students' lives; and, they do not get along with administrators. No one is surprised that the biology teacher played by Scott Voss in *Here Comes the Boom* meets the criteria laid out in The Hollywood Model whether or not you've seen the film because the preview trailers provide all of the necessary clues. Curiously, the film *Won't Back Down* engages in a similar set of narrative devices employed in good teacher movies but manipulates some of them in service of a readily transparent political agenda. Specifically, for a burned-out teacher to regain her good teacher status by re-engaging in the classroom, she needs to free herself from the educational bureaucracy at her school and separate from the teacher's union. The implications of all film depictions affect teachers, students, parents, and policymakers. Idealized good teacher characters are both heroic and ineffective because they can transform the lives of individual students but are not able to challenge the status quo and make change on an institutional level. Movies and television encourage viewers to categorize real teachers into camps of "good" and "bad" in ways that are not only simplistic but that also foster a lack of trust in teachers, their training, and their professionalism. *Won't Back Down* employs superb actors and an aesthetic sleight of hand to elevate a melodramatic script, one that claims to be inspired by actual events though the details about what that means are sketchy. It is common to base such films on "true stories" as a means of enhancing credibility, and memoirs have been the basis for popular films like *Up The Down Staircase* (1967), *Conrack* (1974), *Dangerous Minds*, and *Freedom Writers* (2007) while *Stand and Deliver*, *Music of the Heart* (1999), and *The Ron Clark Story* (2006), which are not derived from autobiographies but are also based on actual people.

In *Won't Back Down*, a frustrated mom (played by Maggie Gyllenhaal) and a burned-out teacher (played by Viola Davis) join forces to enact a law that lets parents and teachers take over failing public schools. What ensues is a lot of rhetoric about doing what is best for students, cinematography that begins with a muted range of colors that gets brighter and bolder as the women make progress toward their goal, a lot of clichéd scenarios and lines of dialogue, and a lot more attention to taking over Adams Elementary School than to what happens next.[4] The fact of the matter is that charter schools transfer public funds into the private sector without delivering better results in the aggregate in terms of measurable outcomes, such as standardized tests. This is not one of the main points addressed in the film, just as the fact that public schools out-perform charter schools overall is glossed over in *Waiting for Superman* (2010), a documentary that mounted a spirited but little-seen defense of charter schools as the answer to everything that ails public education.[5] It is not coincidental that Walden Media, the company that released *Waiting for Superman* (along with Paramount Pictures and Participant Media) produced *Won't Back Down*. If the idea was to create more mainstream awareness of the educational movement presented in *Waiting for Superman* and to generate more widespread support, those goals were not accomplished. The documentary earned just over $6,400,000 at the box office domestically while the narrative feature earned a bit over $5,300,000 and less-favorable reviews. The implication in both films is that privatizing education is the only way to give poor students (and perhaps even middle-class students) access to the type of education more economically (and often racially) privileged students take for granted.

Educational policies that focus on accountability and outcomes measured solely by standardized testing may be the linchpin that keeps public discourse spinning right now, but there is a curious inverse in good teacher movies where caring teachers are more important than curriculum and desired educational outcomes extend beyond test scores. Maggie Gyllenhaal's character is moved to take over the school because her dyslexic daughter has a cruel teacher who torments rather than teaches the little girl. But, it is poor test scores that designate the school as failing and give her the opening to take action, however implausible that course of action may be, and the most impassioned elements of *Won't Back Down* seem directed at discrediting and dismantling teachers' unions. This is troubling when considering the film situated as it is in an economic landscape that includes ever-widening disparities in personal wealth at the same time the balance of power has tilted against organized labor. How does *Won't Back Down* compare to *Here Comes the Boom*? In terms of critical and public opinion, the conventional story of the latter, a comedy starring Kevin James as the disengaged biology teacher who becomes so incensed when budget cuts threaten a music program that he starts fighting in mixed martial arts matches to raise money to save the music teacher's job, fares a bit better critically than the drama does. *Here Comes the Boom* scores 35% positive in an aggregate of critical reviews while

Figure 8.1. Kevin James as Scott Voss in *Here Comes the Boom*, 2012. Somehow I doubt that teachers entering mixed martial arts competitions will catch on as a way to fund school arts programs.

Won't Back Down scores 33% positive overall according to the Rotten Tomatoes website. Audiences share similar reactions to the films, too, with a 65% positive rating for *Here Comes the Boom* and a 61% positive rating for *Won't Back Down*. Of course, *Here Comes the Boom* did earn nearly $45,300,000 at the box office, over eight and a half times what *Won't Back Down* earned domestically. I don't believe the movies are very good at giving us specific answers about how to improve education. Different types of movies could be useful in helping viewers identify important issues and engaging the public emotionally in those issues. As it stands now, with popular movies mainly repeating conventional themes or unconventional and challenging revisionist films not typically being seen broadly, the movies seem most effective at identifying our preconceptions and biases.

What are those biases? Not surprisingly, some of them are the same as what we find in the larger culture. There is a tension in most films between the value of the test score and vocational training and learning for its own sake. While this does break down in expected ways with economically disadvantaged students of color – remember the problems Pat Conroy encounters in *Conrack* when he wants to bring culture to his isolated, rural black students – it is not always so neatly delineated – as when Mr. Keating wants his students at the most elite of male boarding schools to appreciate poetry for its own sake

62

and pursue the arts if they choose in *Dead Poets Society*. In real life, too, the bias toward STEM and professional training at most colleges and universities is analogous to the preparation of students at lower levels for jobs dictated by the needs of business and industry. This is shortsighted at best. I have taught at a selective, private university my entire career and have witnessed the decline of the humanities and the arts alongside the ever-increasing tuition bills that squeeze the middle-class most of all and prompt parents to think more about the return on investment in practical terms than personal terms. As William Deresiewicz writes in *Excellent Sheep: The Miseducation of the American Elite and the Way to a Meaningful Life*:

> The things that are most worth doing are worth doing for their own sake. Anyone who tells you that the sole purpose of education is the acquisition of negotiable skills is attempting to reduce you to a productive employee at work, a gullible consumer in the market, and a docile subject of the state. What's at stake, when we ask what college is for, is nothing less than our ability to remain fully human. (79)

Deresiewicz may be writing about college students, particularly those at the elite institutions like Yale University where he taught while formulating some of these ideas, but the larger point about the value and purpose of education takes us back to earlier conceptions when universal public instruction was less about training workers than about educating citizens who would be fully engaged in public life and capable of self-actualization. This type of education is surely helpful in becoming and remaining fully human. Not only is schooling falling short, but movies are missing an opportunity to advance that cause.

Just as films minimize the role of social class in favor of a broad "you can succeed if you work hard enough and have a good teacher" ideology, movies also minimize race as a critical identity. While there are a few films that address race and ethnicity in direct and meaningful ways with regard to education – in *Conrack*, teaching children to swim for their survival; in *Stand and Deliver*, teaching students that math is "in their blood" and is "the great equalizer"; in *Half Nelson* (2006), equating whiteness with "the man"; and, in *The Man Who Knew Infinity* (2015), exploring the discriminatory practices of English colonialism in India – for the most part, its effects are minimized. Perhaps this is not surprising since in life "every use of 'race' has always been loose, whether applied to black, white, yellow, brown, red, or other. No consensus has ever formed on the number of human races or even on the number of white races. Criteria constantly shift according to individual taste and political need" (Painter 383). It is a slippery slope, and long-term interests worth critiquing, narrative and otherwise, are served by sidestepping neat categories in favor of something that seems more universal.

Until very recently, a commonly held idea has been the invisibility of whiteness, the very thing that allowed me as a young girl not to think very much about race and, as a young woman, to decide when and how I would attend to it. Fortunately, that cultural myopia is beginning to change. As Nell Irvin Painter explains:

> Whiteness studies hold white race, ordinarily invisible in the black/white dichotomy, up to the light. In them it appears as social, not biological, a powerful social construct letting whites think of themselves first and foremost as individuals. Although white people may exempt themselves from race, white privilege comes into view as a crucial facet of white race identity. At the same time, many other characteristics – class, region, gender, age, able-bodiedness, and sexual orientation – all affect the manifestation of this privilege. (388)

Dismantling white privilege, a project mostly unexamined in film although celebrated in *Half Nelson*, is undermined by films that uncritically valorize the white savior teacher, an analysis that has been published widely as it relates to *Dangerous Minds* (for example, Applegate 139–44; Barlowe and Cook 34–35; Boyd 161–62; Bulman 33–34; Chennault 103, 117–18, 127; Giroux, 1996; Leopard 16; Lewis and Renga 70–72; Parton 150–51; Perlstein and Faw 135; Squire 173–75) and many related critiques have arisen about similar films, including *Freedom Writers*, though there are differences in style and scope between the films (for example, Applegate 139–44; Barlow and Cook 35–37; Boyd 161–62; Bulman 42, 46, 60; Long and Pope 31; Parton 150–51; Perlstein and Faw 135; Renga 42–54; Searcy 143–48; Squire 172–73; Whitney 42). Since there is a lot of published work on these films, I won't address them in detail here.

I do want to address two points made by Ta-Nehisi Coates in *Between the World and Me*. Written as a letter to his 15-year-old son (structured after James Baldwin's 1963 book *The Fire Next Time*), Coates talks about race in America, his own life, and his fears for his son. A good portion of the book deals with education – both popular and formal. Using his own lived experience, Coates makes clear connections between the popular and the personal and describes with uncommon eloquence how one informs the other. Writing about his life as a boy in Baltimore, he remembers how he knew the world:

> Somewhere out there beyond the firmament, past the asteroid belt, there were other worlds where children did not regularly fear for their bodies. I knew this because there

was a large television resting in my living room. In the evenings I would sit before this television bearing witness to the dispatches from this other world. There were little white boys with complete collections of football cards, and their only want was a popular girlfriend and their only worry was poison oak. (20)

Coates writes that he knew his portion of the "American galaxy, where bodies were enslaved by a tenacious gravity, was black and the other, liberated portion was not" but "did not yet understand the relation between that other world and me" (20–21). Though he felt the injustice of it, before Coates could escape, he had to survive. Unfortunately, schools were not the salvation promised in popular narratives. "Schools did not reveal truths, they concealed them," Coates writes (27). He came to see schools and the streets as "arms of the same beast" using fear and violence as a common set of weapons to dictate outcomes (33). And, he might have been writing a critique of the teacher as savior narrative in place of systemic reform in this passage:

It does not matter that the "intentions" of individual educators were noble. Forget about intentions. What any institution, or its agents, "intend" for you is secondary. Our world is physical.... No one directly proclaimed that schools were designed to sanctify failure and destruction. But a great number of educators spoke of "personal responsibility" in a country authored and sustained by criminal irresponsibility. The point of this language of "intention" and "personal responsibility" is a broad exoneration. (33)

A complex examination of the criminal irresponsibility of the past and the present is not likely to take place in films, certainly not in mainstream, Hollywood fare, but that is not to say that there are not competing texts and competing messages within texts, pockets of resistance, and ways to read popular texts against the grain for more nuanced understandings of the narratives. Don't underestimate the value of context and perspective.

Hidden Truths in *High School High*

Writing about contemporary black sitcoms, Robin Means Coleman et al. begin an essay with the sentence: "Playwright/literary critic George Bernard Shaw once advised, 'When a thing is funny, search it carefully for a hidden truth'" (279). Some of the truths in the good teacher parody film *High School High* are not surprising because the role of parody is to take commonly agreed upon conventions and poke fun at them. It is tempting for some people to dismiss this film without giving it serious consideration. After all, it only has a 13% positive rating from the Rotten Tomatoes aggregate of reviews by critics, a 37% positive rating by viewers, and its domestic gross at the box office was a little over $21,300,000. By most standards of evaluation, it is a bad movie. There are hidden truths to be found by digging deeper into the film that say more about how race, ethnicity, and social class are coded than the casual viewer will expect to find. *High School High* is promoted with the line "There's a new teacha in the Hood!" and includes direct references to films like *Dead Poets Society*, *Blackboard Jungle*, *Dangerous Minds*, *Music of the Heart*, *Stand and Deliver*, and *Lean on Me*.[6] While the good teachers sent into these "diverse" schools are often white, like Richard Clark (Jon Lovitz), there is an amazing lack of attention to racial politics in the conventional Hollywood films. Interestingly, because the character he plays is connected to a WASPy world – students colleagues, and father – Lovitz carries an ethnic identity fitting into a long tradition of Jewish teachers working for social change.[7] *High School High* satirizes the racial/socioeconomic politics of other films in a two-step process.

First, elite private schools are lampooned in the opening sequence of the film. This model is familiar in mainstream films such as *Dead Poets Society*, *The Emperor's Club* (2002), *Finding Forrester* (2001), *Goodbye Mr. Chips* (1939), *The Prime of Miss Jean Brodie* (1969), and *School Ties* (1992). The particular target is Welton Academy, a prestigious northeastern prep school featured in *Dead Poets Society*. *High School High* opens with a shot of the manicured lawns and stately brick buildings of Wellington Academy. The interior of the school is equally well-appointed and teeming with students in uniforms consisting of jackets and ties, students who look like future titans of industry and government leaders but murmur annoying and even cruel remarks to one another and to their history teacher, Mr. Clark. The interior shot tracks over to the reception desk where a voice answers the phone, "Wellington Academy. Are you white? I'll put you right through." There's no pretense or omission here; Wellington Academy is clear on its racial politics because fostering elitism and an endorsement of meritocracy is what sustains such an institution.[8] The opening sequence is very brief: the establishing exterior shot of Wellington Academy and the shots of Clark hurrying through the foyer area past the reception desk and into a meeting room. There is a long table of old, white teachers, mostly men, who all smoke identical pipes to denote their self-satisfaction and presumed intellectualism. Clark's father fits right in with the traditions of legacy and nepotism that permeate such institutions. John Neville, who plays the senior Clark, codes as an uptight WASP whose stereotypical elitism, slimness, and chiseled features contrast with Lovitz, who – meant in the kindest way possible – portrays Clark as a bit of a schlub. When the elder Clark tells his son that the meeting has been called in his honor to celebrate his promotion to "Assistant Vice Chairman of the History Department," the younger man announces that he has taken a job at Barry High School. His obvious rejection of their standards and values stuns the other faculty members. It is a very brief but effective set up for the main narrative thread: the good (white) teacher comes to the blighted inner-city ("diverse") school to save the students from themselves and from jaded, disengaged, or corrupt administrators.

The remainder of the film develops that central storyline. As Clark drives his rust-bucket heap of a Chrysler through leafy suburbs, the radio plays the Carpenters's 1974 hit song "Top of the World." The song stops abruptly when he passes a sign on the road that reads "Inner City." When Clark changes the setting from station to station, all he can tune in is an identical rap song. Above his California license plate, there is a sign with a heart symbol followed by "2 Teach." It becomes clear as sight gags outside his car window indicate the deterioration of the neighborhood approaching the school that Clark will need a passion for teaching to sustain him in this particular 'hood. The school itself looks like a burned-out war zone, and there is an explosion from a second-story window as he pulls into the parking lot. The lot features signs for "Student," "SWAT," "National Guard," and "Johnnie Cochran" parking, and Clark's clunker is stolen as soon as he turns his back upon exiting the vehicle. It's obvious that Clark is a long way from Wellington Academy now. Other symbols of the degeneration of the school abound. This is Marion Barry High School, and students dismantle a statue of the former Washington DC mayor. They replace the flag Barry is holding with a bong pipe. There is darkness and chaos inside the school. Massive metal detectors are buzzing as students disarm (significantly, many will later exit the school with undetected weapons), a guy selling watches out of a case tries to interest Clark who declines only to discover that his own watch is missing, the halls are crowded and dimly lit, and graffiti defaces every available surface. There is almost immediately a stand-off between a cool dude, Griff McReynolds (Mekhi Phifer), and a menacing guy surrounded by his gang, Paco Rodriguez (Guillermo Diaz), that Clark effectively and (intentionally) unconvincingly diffuses by getting them to shake hands and make nice.

Like so many of these films, there is a challenge presented early on – in the case of *High School High*, it's the Academic Proficiency Test that students must

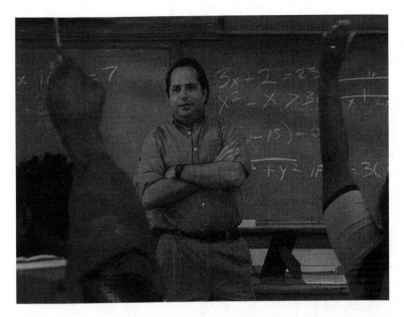

Figure 8.2. Jon Lovitz as Richard Clark in *High School High*, 1996. There are many truths hidden amid the silly situations and corny lines that constitute this parody.

take and pass to go to college – that is both concrete and reductive in terms of what it can do to improve students' lives at a point so late in the academic game. There is a subplot involving Clark's romance with the principal's secretary (in one scene that is a direct parody of *Blackboard Jungle*, Clark tries to thwart her attempted rape by Paco in the school library, but she doesn't need his "help," and he injures her and endangers himself instead of coming to her rescue), another subplot involving Clark's attempt to reach Griff and turn his life around, and yet another subplot about gang activity and drug dealing in the school. As the students fall under Clark's influence, which is achieved by design in a manner that is both pat and unconvincing, they begin studying for the Academic Proficiency Test to learn in 12 weeks what has gone unlearned for 12 years. Simultaneously, they take over the school and paint, plant, and generally beautify so that Barry High School looks like a Hollywood near incarnation of Wellington Academy. If Barry is faux Wellington, it is clear that the veneer is just that because these students have been given no meaningful purpose beyond passing a particular test, and a coat of paint inside and some planted shrubs and blossoms outside are not enough to level this playing field.

In the end, *High School High* is a film that reveals the flaws beneath the veneer. At first, it appears that none of the students passed the Academic

Proficiency Test, which sends morale through the floor, and the immediate decay of the school beautification project begins to mirror the students' loss of confidence. The principal uses this opportunity to fire Clark without just cause for getting the students' hopes up then letting them down. Clark won't give up, however, and he learns that the tests were stolen in a convoluted plot twist that links the principal to Paco in a scheme to keep the students demoralized and on drugs – drugs that she supplies. In fact, when order is restored, the principal and Paco are carted off to jail, and Griff is averted from returning to the gang, it turns out that some of them did pass the test after all. The film ends as Principal Pro Tem Richard C. Clark presents diplomas to the six students who comprise the graduating class, including Griff McReynolds, the valedictorian with a 2.35 grade point average. Clark makes the grade, gets the girl, and – in the end – even gets the approval of his father, who arrives on the scene just in time to tell his son that he's proud of him. His mother, played by Lovitz in drag, a character reduced to a random sight gag, beams proudly, too.

What are the most compelling readings of *High School High* that we can use to broaden our understanding of mainstream Hollywood good teacher movies? *High School High* directly addresses class and race in ways the films it parodies do not and reveals in direct contrast the disparity between Wellington Academy and Barry High School. Even after the locally initiated school beautification project, there are no computers, or even extra books, in the classroom, and it is clear that the big clean-up has been mere windowdressing. By presenting the Academic Proficiency Test as a sham, *High School High* reveals a common sentiment that such standardized tests are suspect and a poor measurement of meaningful learning and achievement. The test is dictated and constructed by some unseen administrative force, and its implications in the real lives of these students seem nebulous, much murkier than the practical implications of the military recruiters who deploy to the Barry High School campus with regularity (and with the support of the principal). The recruiters' sanctioned presence would be unimaginable at Wellington Academy. There is no common purpose that unites teachers or students at Barry High School in a way that rings true (even the way "Academic Proficiency Test" is articulated on screen seems tongue in cheek, an effect amplified by the inane facts that are reviewed in preparation for students to take the examination), just as there is nothing that seems particular to link students to one another or to link school faculty aside from a couple of subplots involving romantic couplings. There really aren't any teachers included who engage the students pedagogically other than Clark, and the only administrator who is woven into the storyline in a significant way is the villainous principal, who is presented in dramatic conflict with the good teacher rather than in some coalition in keeping with the conventional roles of good teachers and administrators in Hollywood films. In short, the parody makes clear the lies of the films it parodies, which is another way of saying this movie reveals hidden truths.

Are there other important readings of *High School High*? One of the storylines of the film that deserves further consideration is given short shrift if we think of this only as a parody of the good teacher movie. The plotline that emerges after the Academic Proficiency Tests are stolen can be read as a commentary on films where gangs and the drug trade – often represented by characters "otherized" as black (*The Principal*, 2002), Latino (*The Substitute*, 1996), or punkers (*Class of 1984*, 1982) – intersect with school. In *High School High*, the drug kingpin turns out to be Principal Evelyn Doyle (Louise Fletcher), who carries with her the villainous iconography of her Nurse Ratched character in *One Flew Over the Cuckoo's Nest* (1975). While she gets caught and ends the film in handcuffs, I can't help but think of the men beneath her in the organization – layers and layers of men of color who also end up behind bars – and make a link unforeseen by the director and writers of the film. Perhaps this particular hidden truth is prescient. Michelle Alexander's book *The New Jim Crow: Mass Incarceration in the Age of Colorblindness*, published 14 years after *High School High* was released, is part of a major reconsideration of drug policies that developed in the United States over the last several decades. Alexander compares the war on drugs to slavery in terms of its effect in controlling black men through unequal arrest rates and prosecutions. Launched under the administration of Richard Nixon and intensified under Ronald Reagan (who can forget Nancy Reagan's trite "Just Say No" campaign?), Alexander sees the war on drugs and its contingent mass incarceration of men of color as a backlash against the civil rights movement that has resulted in a devastating effect on black America. The convergence of the school and the street with dire, unforeseen consequences for most and a "happy ending" that is tacked on to celebrate the six students who actually graduate from Barry High School suggests that films celebrating the heroic teacher without addressing the institution and the systems that intersect with it are simplistic and deceitful.

Conclusion

Race, ethnicity, and social class matter in America, and schools in films provide a space that reveals but minimizes the disparity between those with various types of privilege and those without it. After all, our myth of meritocracy depends on believing that structural conditions and collective identity are not barriers to success for hard-working individuals who play by the rules to achieve the American Dream of prosperity and upward mobility. Films also depict schools as spaces that reveal the disconnect between students and the adults hired to teach and manage them. Unfortunately, those elements are presented more directly in the parody *High School High* and in revisionist films like *Half Nelson* than in most good teacher movies in the classical mode, which do show all or most of the educators in schools as disengaged, but these depictions are set as a contrast to and are vastly outweighed by the celebrated good teacher. Just look at the difference one good teacher makes in *Freedom Writers* despite the daunting obstacles she faces. The individual solution supplied by movies like *Freedom Writers*, *Music of the Heart*, *Dangerous Minds*, and *Stand and Deliver* (all biopics so they are considered "true") suggests that if the teachers are good enough and dedicated enough then race, ethnicity, and social class do not matter. These movies, because they are so inspiring and entertaining, successfully minimize the roles race and class play in education. But, there is another thing to consider that *High School High*, perhaps unwittingly, reveals about the larger culture. The link that Coates makes about the streets and the schools operating as "arms of the same beast" is made manifest in this parody as an example of hidden truths. What happens to all of the students who do not graduate at the end of *High School High* and in daily life? They fall under the weight of the other arm of the beast: the street. As Coates puts it, "Fail in the schools and you would be suspended and sent back to those same streets, where they would take your body" (33). There are two likely places for those bodies to go: jail or death.

The question arises that if media reflects culture and culture reflects media and all of us are learning "scripts" about the possibilities and limitations we face based on the narrative texts we encounter (both popular texts and lived experience), then how can we expand the possibilities presented to include a different type of narrative? How can we challenge the dominant discourse and work on issues of social justice instead of perpetuating the status quo? How can we repair or at least bridge the rupture between students' needs and adults' policies and curricular imperatives? How can we take idealized teachers down from their pedestals while retaining the trust and respect of the podium (even as a metaphorical platform)? One answer is suggested by the fleeting scene in *Elephant* (2003) of the black teacher talking with students about their lives – open, honest discourse. Another film, *American History X* (1998), speaks to the power of discourse to join a black teacher (turned administrator) in healing friendship with a former student who ultimately renounces his past as a white supremacist to become a confidential informant spying on the group. The stakes are high and the sacrifices great when serious issues are at stake. Open discourse among all invested parties should be used as a tool for identifying common values – like social justice and democratic engagement and rights of citizenship – and integrating those values into a curriculum that recognizes the worth of the political, of the aesthetic, and of the creative as well as instilling conventional skills designed to create a supply of competent workers. There can be no lasting connection among disparate parties in the hallways and classrooms of our schools – onscreen or offscreen – without the voluntary investment of all parties in open discourse to try to create the tie that binds. When connection fails, sometimes the results are extreme, as the group of films depicting student resistance demonstrates in Chapter 10.

On the other hand, maybe acknowledging difference is a first step to finding common ground beyond identity. Social class is also a malleable concept in what is otherwise a more stratified role, the governess. In real life, the movie star makes headlines when he (the examples that come to mind are male) beds or weds the nanny. In the movies, the governess is also the teacher, but I have not heretofore considered them as a category, though I've read *Jane Eyre* more than once and have seen more versions of the movie than I can recollect off the top of my head. It is Elizabeth Currin's essay on *The Sound of Music* that motivates me to think about the governess as teacher.

Though *The Sound of Music* has heretofore escaped recognition as a teacher film, Maria's fluid identity and practical temperament hold valuable lessons for educators. Ironically enriching the wealthy von Trapps, Maria gains purpose and insight by interacting with the children and ultimately acknowledging her feelings for their father. Maria solves the problem of the Captain's rigidity while her own problematic flightiness undergoes moderation. Maria's social class – as perplexing as her personality – facilitates this shift: unaccustomed to an aristocratic lifestyle, she brings a critical outsider's perspective and a certain amount of provincial pluck, nurtured in part by her ecclesiastical education. Initially jarring and discordant, Maria's interactions with her employer harmoniously soften as the socioeconomic gulf between them fades. (201)

While the nuns wrestle with the options in trying to solve a problem like Maria, it turns out that Maria, like Jane before her, is the one who solves all the problems posed in iconic narratives while crossing boundaries that suggest social class is no barrier to the greater power of education and, yes, of love. I will leave a more systematic and exhaustive study of the governess as teacher to another scholar and would be curious to read what that work would yield.

I am drawn to two particular essays in the anthology *Screen Lessons: What We Have Learned from Teachers on Television and in the Movies* as examples of teachers putting themselves in the place of others to increase understanding beyond traditional boundaries. In "Race *Up the Down Staircase*: Teacher as Savior and Other Identities," Chad E. Harris poses important questions that make the 1967 biopic (still) topical:

> But, what type of person would become a teacher in an environment where her race, ethnicity, appearance, and education are not the norm? Who is willing to deal with the constant barrage that seems intent to impede teaching? What type of person would want to be a teacher in an inner-city school? In a suburban school? The lessons from *Up the Down Staircase* are startlingly, but not surprisingly, still pertinent. As an African-American, male teacher who teaches in a large, suburban school, I, despite differences in race, gender, and environment, have experiences similar to Sylvia Barrett when it comes to identity in our respective contexts. We bring similar philosophies and skill sets to our profession. Consequently, I feel validated when watching Miss Barrett. (forthcoming)

Harris connects with the character Sylvia Barrett (Sandy Dennis) despite their contrasting markers of identity and because of their shared status as "other" as well as their shared commitment to empowering students, maintaining their individuality as educators, and holding students to high standards in the classroom.

In her essay "*Unexpected* Opportunities: Teaching and Learning While Pregnant," Abigail Kindelsperger writes about a provocative, independent film from 2015 that parallels her own experience as a teacher in Chicago and her familiarity with the "two Chicagos" juxtaposed in the film. Like Samantha Abbott (Cobie Smulders) in *Unexpected*, Kindelsperger discovered that her pregnancy was a shared experience that helped her understand her students in ways she had not been able to before:

> While the lessons my students taught me were many, it was specifically when I was pregnant that I stopped just saying I learned from them and instead started truly listening and asking questions. More than one-third of my students were parents. Being a pregnant teacher of school-age parents was transformative to my teaching. I certainly learned a lot of practical information along with some misinformation about pregnancy, childbirth, and the early weeks of parenting. One of my students and I regularly compared what size our fetuses were, using fruit-based analogies from an app we both had on our phones. I listened to my students with a newfound urgency,

seeking practical information about a topic they knew more about than I did. In a larger sense, the reciprocal relationship between teaching and learning, student and teacher, became more central to my approach. The tone of my classroom shifted, as my students and I saw each other as more fully human and respected each other as people with lives and valuable knowledge that is often untapped in the classroom. Our discussions were deeper as I slowed down, asked more authentic questions, and actually listened to their responses. I realized how often I glossed over students' comments in service of reaching my objectives. (forthcoming)

Without seeing *Unexpected*, one might think a film about a pregnant teacher connecting with her pregnant student would be filled with dramatic – or even melodramatic – classical narrative conventions, but the film, though flawed, is surprisingly understated. Kindelsperger writes about the realism of the representation of this teacher and how it is this depiction of a teacher as a whole person that resonates with her (129–33). Overcoming difference to find common ground doesn't always have to be based on a shared experience, as I learned so many years ago from my student who told me about his experience with the police in a television studio control room after class, but it does depend on sharing experiences, on listening to one another, on caring for one another, and on learning from one another.

I don't mean to suggest that change is easy, but it is essential for us to imagine a way forward from a time and a place when things feel so very fractured. In *White Rage: The Unspoken Truth of Our Racial Divide*, Carol Anderson writes about how 150 years of "anger and fear have undermined American democracy, trampled on the Constitution, and treated some citizens as chattel and others as collateral damage" while calling on us to rethink America and choose a different future (161). What does that future look like? Anderson provides a starting point:

Imagine the education prowess our populations might now boast had *Brown* [*v Board of Education*] actually been implemented. What a very different nation we would be if all the enormous legal and political efforts that went into the subverting and undermining the right to education had actually been used to uphold and ensure that right. If all those hundreds upon hundreds of millions of federal dollars poured into science education had actually rained down on those hungry for education, regardless of race, ethnicity, or income. Think about what a different national conversation we might be having, even as the economy turns ever more surely to knowledge-based, rather than watching our share of the world's scientists and engineers dwindle. (163)

Whatever the future becomes, it will be the result of priorities we set and choices we make collectively. Unlike the movies where conventional narratives of individual success perpetuate the status quo and dominate screens large and small, we need to locate and pay attention to stories that reveal hidden truths about ourselves, about the limitations we have imposed, and about the possibilities we have foreclosed. Sometimes the painful truths about the lies we've been told – lies that minimize the effect of race, ethnicity, and social class in determining our destiny – are delivered in a silly-seeming film like *High School High*. The personal may be political, but it takes collective action to make change. We must recognize difference and its enforcement by the systems at work before we can find common ground and purpose.

Notes

1. It is hard to believe that *Savage Inequalities: Children in America's Schools* was written in 1991, but the stories Kozol tells remain powerful.
2. It is worth noting here that casting black actors as principals has become somewhat commonplace (the recent examples are *Music of the Heart*, *Mean Girls* and *The Duff*), but it is still unusual to see an Asian-American actor playing an educator. Mr. Arthur (Ken Jeong) is a striking exception in *The Duff*. Unfortunately, the advisor to the school newspaper who encourages and challenges the female student at the center of the film is reduced to a stereotype, which takes on outsized importance when there are no competing depictions. When assigning a story about homecoming, he shares with the class, "I never went to a dance as a kid. I was a nerd." Mr. Arthur believes that he has overcome nerd status, but the students (and viewers) are presented with a different view.
3. Jacqueline Bach uses the following films in her analysis: *10 Things I Hate About You*, *American Pie*, *Blackboard Jungle*, *Clueless*, *Crazy/Beautiful*, *Dead Poets Society*, *Fame*, *Freedom Writers*, *High School High*, *Jawbreaker*, *Mean Girls*, *Orange County*, *Outside Providence*, *Renaissance Man*, *The Princess Diaries*, and *Up The Down Staircase*.
4. In her chapter "Deconstructing a New Teacher Savior: Paladins and Politics in *Won't Back Down*," Ashley Boyd writes about the construction of a new type of teacher savior. "I argue that this more recent version of the teacher savior is a figure who impacts education broadly, as opposed to more individualistic heroes in films of the past" (160–61). Her analysis of the film and how she uses it teacher education to help students plan "for their future selves" and realistically and to be able to "articulate a response to the political agenda set forth in popular media regarding education" is valuable (168).
5. For a detailed examination of non-fiction depictions of teachers, see Jacqueline Bach's *Reel Education: Documentaries, Biopics and Reality Television about Education*.
6. Other films are memorably parodied, too, including *Rebel without a Cause* (1956) and *The Deer Hunter* (1978).
7. See Kathleen Casey's book *I Answer with My Life: Life Histories of Women Teachers Working for Social Change*.
8. In her book *Tales Out of School: Gender, Longing, and the Teacher in Fiction and Film*, Jo Keroes writes primarily about sexuality, but she also notes in Chapter 4, "Race and

Representation in *To Sir, with Love, Conrack*, and *A Lesson Before Dying*," that "teacher narratives have trouble with race" (71). Keroes does an excellent job detailing two of the common problems:

> When the teacher belongs to a minority group, he must, despite his "difference," uphold conventional mainstream values; when the students are members of minorities, they appear to represent the liberal vision of an oppressed group waiting to be rescued, usually by a white teacher-knight, while they remind us of the fears such groups engender. They must be tamed. (71)

· 9 ·

DRAMA IS CONFLICT

The Roles of Administrators in Hollywood Movies

Introduction

While guidance counselors are generally presented as marginal characters who are out of touch[1] and school board members and union representatives are routinely characterized as uncaring or even corrupt, the school principal – and sometimes the assistant principal as surrogate – stands alone in Hollywood movies as the force most vested in establishing or maintaining control in the school. Sometimes that control is related to raising standards, a euphemism for improving standardized test scores; more often, the principal is charged with maintaining order by exercising disciplinary action on an unruly student population. Of course, once order is established, raising test scores will not be far behind as the primary goal for celluloid constructions, or, for that matter, in today's culture for administrators made of flesh and blood. Chapter 1 discussed the cultural importance of Hollywood representations of teachers and the "leaky boundaries" between popular culture narratives and actual lived experience. It follows that the same is true of mass media portrayals of principals: our perceptions of real principals are informed by our experiences with their fictive counterparts in movies.

Standards and Practices

If we regard the school as a factory, an assembly line model leading to credentialing that is common in the movies, then some of the problems that confront both real and movie administrators become apparent. As Linda M. McNeil points out:

> A school that is designed like a factory has a built-in contradiction: running a factory is tightly organized, highly routinized, and geared for the production of uniform products; educating children is complex, inefficient, idiosyncratic, uncertain, and open-ended. Historically, the two purposes of schooling, that is, educating children and running large-scale educational institutions, have been seen as separate domains. The one is aimed at nurturing individual children and equipping them with new knowledge and skills; the other focuses on processing aggregates of student through regularized requirements of the credentialing process. (2000, 11)

This dichotomy is the source of the central conflict between teachers and administrators in the movies: teachers educate the children, and administrators run the institution.

When the two functions of education are at odds, it falls to teachers to battle administrators on behalf of their students, and the administrators try to exert control over both. McNeil argues that there is a vicious cycle in schools because the more administrators try to control teachers and students, the more teachers and students disengage from enthusiastic, involved learning then the more they disengage from learning, the more administrators try to manage and control them (1986, xviii). This pattern of control and disengagement is very similar to the prevailing dynamic presented in Hollywood movies where the role of principals and their surrogates is to follow, whether implicitly or explicitly stated, the conservative philosophy of school boards, superintendents, and other supervising administrators while "do gooder" teachers try to intercede on behalf of their students. The narrative is familiar through repetition, but it also resonates with viewers on other levels.

Alfie Kohn has advanced a cogent and compelling argument against the damaging overemphasis on standardized testing that is running rampant and largely unchallenged in American schools. While establishing order in celluloid schools may be the top priority for movie principals, raising standardized test scores is often their other major goal. Both of these goals emphasize the principals' need to be in control. In either case, it is clear that in Hollywood schools, just as in real schools across the country, the traditional, or conservative, philosophy is dominant while nontraditional, or progressive, classroom practices are largely unrepresented. In the first case, the classroom is centered on the teacher, who imparts knowledge to students according to an established curriculum. Kohn describes the "Old School" model as one in which academic areas are taught separately with concepts broken into bits and taught in a very specific sequence and including "traditional grades, plenty of tests and quizzes, strict (punitive) discipline, competition, and lots of homework" (3). The progressive classroom, suggested as a temporary oasis created by good teachers for a limited time in perennially popular films such as *To Sir, With Love* (1967), *Stand and Deliver* (1988), *Dead Poets Society* (1989), *Dangerous Minds* (1995), and *Freedom Writers* (2007) is one in which students and their needs are taken seriously.

Kohn articulates the difference between this nontraditional philosophy of education and the conventional model:

> Because learning is regarded as an active process, learners are given an active role. Their questions help to shape the curriculum, and their capacity for thinking critically is honored even as it is honed. In such classrooms, facts and skills are important but not ends in themselves. Rather, they are more likely to be organized around broad themes connected to real issues, and seen as part of the process of coming to understand ideas from the inside out. A classroom is a place where a community of learners – as opposed to a collection of discrete individuals – engages in discovery and invention, reflection and problem solving. (3)

Clearly, progressive education with its shared responsibilities and openness is a threat to the control administrators are expected to exert over teachers and students. In the movies, it is precisely this need to control that often provides part of the dramatic conflict that drives the screen narrative forward and generally casts principals as adversaries of teachers and students.

Administrator Archetypes

In his survey of 35 television programs and films from 1950 to 1996, Jeffrey Glanz identifies three distinct depictions of the principal as prototypical. First, he identifies the authoritarian principal as one who uses autocratic administrative practices. "Ruling by fiat and relying on intimidation, principals of this type, mostly male, legitimize their methods based on hierarchical and patriarchal sources of authority" (4–5). Second, the principal-as-bureaucrat is "characterized by the principal who is overly concerned with administrative reports, scheduling exigencies, and logistical procedures. Adhering to organizational mandates at the expense of individual needs is of primary concern" (5). Third, principal-as-numskull is a character developed through caricature and exaggeration and "these images imply that principals are dimwitted dolts who haven't the foggiest notion of what is transpiring in the school" (5). Glanz allows that the images are related but distinct and consistent (4). In "Looking at the Man in the Principal's Office," Kate Rousmaniere takes a more expansive view of the position than mine in this volume by considering radio programs, comic strips, and television programs as well as films, but her conclusion, when distilled to a fine point, confirms that principals have tended to be depicted as buffoons or bullies in artifacts of mass culture over the last 70 years (212).

Another paradigm is advanced by Harold J. Burbach and Margo A. Figgins, who sample only seven films – *Teachers* (1984), *Ferris Bueller's Day Off* (1986), *The Principal* (2015), *The Chocolate War* (1988), *Stand And Deliver*, and *Pump Up The Volume* (1990) – and use those films to identify the same number of screen images of principals: The Principal as a Figure of Authority; The Principal as Simple-Minded Foil; The Principal as Hero; The Principal as Villain; The Principal as Faceless Bureaucrat; and, The Principal as Social and Emotional Isolate. Their proposed categories are not distinct because surveyed films are included in more than one of the categories. Burbach and Figgins seem to be advancing an argument that most of the screen images of principals are inaccurate and negative, that these images influence public perception of actual principals, and that more positive portrayals of principals who administer authority based on mutual trust and respect between them and teachers and them and students would be useful (57–58).

From of my survey of films featuring teachers, I have encountered many principals and other administrative characters. From the analysis of those characters, I have identified four categories of Hollywood principals that seem to represent the depiction of these characters more accurately. The principal as buffoon is analogous to Glanz's principal-as-numskull and Burbach and Figgins's Simple-Minded Foil; this character is played for laughs and cannot be taken seriously by students or teachers. The principal as bureaucrat and as autocrat are categories advanced by Glanz as well as by Burback and Figgins. Finally, the caring pragmatist is a category, though small, that is important in several of the films analyzed, a category that is not present in any form in the work of other researchers.

Principal as Buffoon

The examples of foolish, bumbling principals are pervasive in popular culture and notable. Glanz calls the type principal-as-numskull and offers several examples from long-running sitcoms as well as Edward R. Rooney (Jeffrey Jones), from *Ferris Bueller's Day Off*, the same example chosen by Burbach and Figgins and labeled The Principal as Simple-Minded Foil. Rooney, who suffers one mishap after another as he chases a privileged, high school student playing hooky from school, is certainly a memorable, if unfortunate, character. There are, however, many other examples of movie principals who fit this category.

In *Forrest Gump*, it is hard to forget the principal of Greenbow County Central School where young Forrest attends classes. Forrest's mama tells her son that he's just like everyone else, but Mr. Hancock (Sam Anderson) shows Mrs. Gump (Sally Field) an IQ chart. Mr. Hancock indicates that the cut off for students attending public school is an IQ of 80 while Forrest has an IQ of 75. Mrs. Gump is an attractive woman, which is not incidental to the principal.

Mr. Hancock:	We're a progressive school system. We don't want to see anyone left behind. Is there a Mr. Gump, Mrs. Gump?
Mrs. Gump:	He's on vacation.

So far as we can tell, Mr. Gump is on permanent vacation. The next thing we know, there are peculiar, sexual sounds coming from the Gump's large, white house. A little later, the principal emerges from the house where Forrest waits out front.

Mr. Hancock:	Your mama sure does care about your schooling, son.

Sweaty, and with his tie undone, Mr. Hancock walks into the humid, Southern night. Young Forrest (Michael Conner Humphreys) may be "slow," but he knows a buffoon when he sees one and later mimics the sounds emitted by the principal during sex.

Other examples are less evocative but just as relevant. Most of the clueless principal characters are male, but the benign and hopelessly out-of-touch principal in *House Party* (1990), played by Edith Fields, is one of the few white faces in this film and the only woman principal in this category. In *Scary Movie* (2000), the principal is little more than an in-joke: his name is Principal Squiggman, and he is played by the same actor, David Lander, who played Squiggy in the popular situation comedy *Laverne & Shirley* (1976–83). Squiggman does not have an active role in the film; he merely sits behind the desk garnering laughs from viewers who have seen the television show and know Squiggy as a dolt. In *Orange County* (2002), *Saturday Night Live* (1975–)

alumnus Chevy Chase plays Principal Harbert. This particular incarnation of the buffoon may also be suffering from a stereotypical midlife crisis. In his only scene in the film, the principal of this Southern California high school wants to bring in Britney Spears instead of Toni Morrison as the graduation speaker. These are small parts, but they are memorable and create vivid, unflattering impressions of school principals.

It might be argued that most of the characters of *Billy Madison* (1995) are buffoons, and it is beyond the scope of this work conduct a reception study and assess the audience, but the principal character merits special attention. Adam Sandler plays the eponymous role in this film about a rich guy who must successfully complete grades one through twelve in two weeks in order to take over his father's hotel empire. The film is about as ridiculous as that logline suggests, though it has enjoyed remarkable success with young audiences. Principal Anderson (Josh Mostel) is a nerdy, soft-spoken, middle-aged man who sends Billy a valentine that reads "I'm horny." The principal takes a $5,000 bribe to charge Billy with cheating then recants when confronted by the children. It turns out that this strange principal is in disguise: he's actually a professional wrestler named "Revolting Blob." The wrestler was forced to alter his identity after accidentally killing someone in the ring. Revolting Blob's signature move was to sit on an opponent's face, and in this instance the technique suffocated his opponent. What better masquerade for a blob than as a buffoon?

Principal as Bureaucrat

Although he is actually an assistant principal, Roger Rubell of *Teachers* is named as the prime example of the principal as bureaucrat by Glanz and by Burbach and Figgins. As Glanz puts it, this portrayal "is indicative of the penchant for administrators to maintain, at all costs, bureaucratic mandates, even above ethical and moral imperatives related to teaching and learning" (5). Since Rubell's character is discussed in some detail in Chapter 3, other characters will be presented as examples of this type of Hollywood principal. When good teacher William Hundert catches a prominent student cheating at an academic competition in *The Emperor's Club*, Headmaster Woodbridge (Edward Herrmann) tells the teacher to let it go in the interest of not ruffling feathers and threatening the financial stability of the elite prep school. In *Pump Up The Volume*, which will be discussed extensively in Chapter 10, Principal Crestwood (Annie Ross) wants to enhance her own reputation by following the mandate from her supervisors to raise test scores; she accomplishes this goal for a while by ridding her school of students who perform poorly on standardized tests. Principal Gowan

(John Ingle) is interested only in avoiding scandal and keeping on schedule when students apparently begin committing serial suicide in *Heathers* (1988). In an administrative role that bears some narrative correlation to the filmic principal, Winchester University Dean Fairbanks (Dennis Haysbert) wants to keep order at the school, avoid racial unrest, and keep his own son – who is a student there – on a very tight leash in *Dear White People* (2014).[2] These are relatively small parts, because the principal as bureaucrat is not, by nature, a compelling character. Still, one example is worth considering in more detail.

Abraham Lincoln High School is populated with babes wearing big hair and bold make-up, punks, drug dealers, and a few band geeks in *Class of 1984* (1982). When the film opens, Andrew Norris (Perry King) is the new band teacher entering the school on his first day. Norris sees biology teacher Terry Corrigan, played indelibly by Roddy McDowell, and cannot miss the gun that the older teacher is carrying in his briefcase. The school entryway is marked by metal detectors and security guards, but Norris sees two students pass a straight razor openly. Principal Morganthau (David Gardner) is as colorless as the other middle-aged, white actors playing the principal bureaucrats, but the bifocals he continuously peers over almost assume the magnitude of a supporting player. When Norris is ushered into his office, Morganthau can barely take his eyes off the banks of surveillance monitors lining one wall. Unfortunately, the cameras are not positioned so that they can detect the worst of what the school bully/drug dealer/pimp and his gang are up to in the classrooms, bathrooms, and corridors. Time and time again the principal refuses to support his teachers and come down on the thugs. These students vandalize faculty automobiles, torture and kill Corrigan's rabbits in his classroom, gang rape then kidnap Norris's pregnant wife, and this does not begin to cover what they do to other students. Finally, Corrigan pulls a gun on the worst of the lot so that he can get their attention long enough to "teach" them, but he later dies in a fiery crash trying to run some of the worst offenders down outside a club where they hang out. The film comes to a climax when Norris kills the gang members one by one during the band concert as he tries to rescue his wife from the ringleader. What is the principal doing? Enjoying the concert, of course. After all, it is the appearance of efficiency that counts to these administrators.

Principal as Autocrat

Of the many films surveyed in this book, only two star principals as the protagonist of the narrative, *Lean on Me* (1989) and *The Principal* (1987).[3]

Glanz cites Joe Clark as a classic example of the "authoritarian, almost dictatorial-type principal" (5). Burbach and Figgins choose another label, The Principal as Hero, but describe both of these films in ways that note parallels between the two characters, one based on a real person and the other fictive, and that acknowledge their autocracy:

> The main characters are both default choices to take over failing and tension-ridden urban schools. Both are characterized as strong-willed, but caring, adults, both have their authority challenged by a violent element of the student body, and both establish their right to govern the school through a countervailing show of force. (54)

Since Joe Clark's character in Lean on Me has been examined in some detail in Chapters 2 and 5, this section will take a closer look at Rick Lattimer (James Belushi), who becomes a principal in the film of the same title.

Rick Lattimer's wife has left him when the film opens. He drinks too much. He chain smokes. He has a violent temper. He ogles female students through binoculars while they take a test. He's a teacher. To save his job after assaulting a man who is on a date with Lattimer's former wife, he must, ironically, be promoted to principal of a tough school no one else wants. He wears a black leather jacket, sports a black helmet, and gets on a black motorcycle

Figure 9.1. Morgan Freeman as Principal Joe Clark in Lean on Me, 1989. Joe Clark epitomizes the autocratic principal in this biopic.

to commute to work the first day. The drive takes Lattimer from the suburbs to industrial decay, and the farther he rides, the more white faces along the route are replaced by faces of color. When he arrives at the school, it looks like a deserted prison compound with tall fences and graffiti. It is not surprising moments later when a gang fight breaks out, but it is surprising, and perhaps implausible, when the older guy on the motorcycle breaks it up.[4]

At first, Lattimer is planning to put in his hours until he can find something better. The head of school security Jake Phillips, played by Louis Gossett, Jr., has seen this type before and confirms his suspicions after giving the new principal a tour of the school.

Phillips:	Hey, do you mind if I ask you a question I ask all imported principals?
Lattimer:	Sure.
Phillips:	What is a fine, white bread boy like you doing in a place like this?
Lattimer:	Keepin' my warm ass planted in this chair.
Phillips:	Right.

Phillips picks up a newspaper from the desk and sees the want ads Lattimer has circled.

Phillips:	Looking for something better comin' up, right?
Lattimer:	Right.
Phillips:	Didn't know why I should think it would be something different.

This is the end of scene but not the end of the story.

In short order, Lattimer begins to live up to his responsibility and stand up to the school gang leader and major thug. At first, he does this to impress his former wife. Later, he is operating from a sincere interest in some of the students and teachers and out of his developing friendship with Phillips. He saves a pretty teacher from being raped – and they share some tender moments together – but he cannot save a former gang member, Emile, from retaliation when he tries to break away from the group.

Lattimer:	Hey, Emile. You look like shit. Oh, God, I'm sorry. I'm so fuckin' sorry. I though I was doing something good, you know. Something right. (Sigh.) You know, Emile, I fucked up with my old man. I fucked up my marriage. I fucked up at Willoughby. I run a school of fuckups, and I even fuck that up. Ah, Jesus. I'm sorry, man. You know, I didn't mean for you to get hurt. I didn't want that to happen. I don't know why I thought I could change things there. I can't. (He begins to cry.) I just can't man. (Sigh.)
Emile:	(Whispering.) Wuss.

Lattimer leans in to hear him.

| Emile: | Wuss. You don't mean I got my ass kicked for nuthin', Ricky. |

That is all it takes to put the badass principal back in charge.

There is a major confrontation with the gang leader, of course, but the outcome is never really in doubt. When Lattimer and Phillips have subdued the gang members with help from one of the students, Auturo, the gang leader is taken away in a police cruiser. They stand around outside the school as a crowd gathers.

Lattimer:	Am I gonna see you here tomorrow?
Phillips:	Yeah, I'll be here.
Lattimer:	We are very stupid men.
Phillips:	Yeah, I know, but what do you do?

Someone from the crowd calls out to Lattimer.

Voice:	Hey, man, who do you think you are?
Arturo:	He's the principal, man.
Lattimer:	Yeah, I'm the principal, man.

Lattimer tears off from the school on his macho motorcycle. This time, the school is photographed from a more flattering angle than when the principal first arrived on the premises. He has exerted control over this institution.

There are many examples of the principal as autocrat in the movies, from Mr. Warneke (John Hoyt) in *Blackboard Jungle* (1955) to Dr. Edgar Caldicott (Bruce Greenwood) in *Disturbing Behavior* (1998)[5] to Miss Trunchbull (Pam Ferris) in *Matilda* (1996). Some are tough. Some are sinister. Some are evil. A very few are heroic. There are traits that delineate these autocratic principals, and that is worth noting, but it is more important that there is one fundamental characteristic that links them inextricably: all of these celluloid principals do whatever is called for to establish and maintain control.

Principal as Caring Pragmatist

Finally, there is an emerging set of positive images of principals in the movies. The caring pragmatist is a principal who gets the job done but feels the tension between the dictates of budgets and administrative supervisors and the very real concerns and needs of teachers and students. This principal tries to accommodate both or, when that level of detail is not presented in the movie, presents a persona that is competent but kind. In the smaller roles, consider the principals in *Kindergarten Cop* (1990) and *Mr. Holland's Opus* (1995). Recall Miss Drake (Bebe Neuwirth) in *The Faculty* (1998). Before an alien being takes over her body, this principal appears in a faculty meeting lamenting budget cuts and the need to cancel the field trip, to cancel the school musical, and to pass on buying new computers. She has to make the hard choices, but she does not feel good about those choices. As Miss Drake puts it, "I'm sorry. I'm frustrated. My hands are tied." In *American History X* (1998), a black history teacher, who has been promoted to principal, goes out of his way to help at risk students. Avery Brooks plays Principal Bob Sweeney, and the story reveals that Sweeney has been visiting a former student, a white supremacist in jail for murdering two black men, and teaching him a different set of lessons about survival, tolerance, and forgiveness. Sweeney reaches out to the imprisoned man's younger brother, but he also expects the older brother to keep repaying his debt to society when he is released from jail. Sweeney is tough and practical, but his capacity for caring seems limitless.

The best example of the principal as caring pragmatist that I have seen is Janet Williams (Angela Bassett) in *Music of the Heart* (1999). When Roberta Guaspari, a middle-class, white woman without teaching experience, comes to talk with Williams, the black principal knows that Guaspari does not have the proper qualifications for a permanent position and that there is no infrastructure in the school to support the type of program the music teacher is suggesting. When the teacher is persistent on a return visit and announces that she brings fifty violins to the table, Williams hires Guaspari as a substitute teacher and helps the less-experienced woman as much as she can. Ten years pass, and Guaspari has developed a program so successful that it spans three schools and students must apply through a lottery system for the chance to be accepted. Even successful programs can be "excessed," however, and this is exactly what happens when a "back to basics" school board cuts music and art classes from the public schools.

Guaspari:	There must be some way we can fight this.
Williams:	Fight it with what? I don't have any other extra programs I can give them instead.
Guaspari:	(Scoffing.) I see. I see. After ten years, after 1,400 kids have learned the violin, this is just an "extra program."
Williams:	You know I don't feel that way, and you know *damn well* I've been standing by you for all these years! You think I haven't noticed what you've done for these kids?

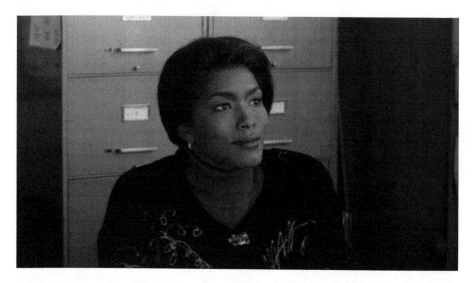

Figure 9.2. Angela Bassett as Principal Janet Williams in *Music of the Heart*, 1999. Janet Williams is pragmatic, but she is also caring, which is a potent combination too little seen in depictions of education administrators.

Guaspari:	Well, then do something!
Williams:	I have been on this phone for the past three days trying to *do* something! They're sick of hearing my voice! Believe me, there are other people around here I would much rather get rid of, but as far as the board is concerned, violin classes are not a priority! I don't have the power here, Roberta! I am so sorry. (Her voice breaks.)

Williams does not stop with three days of phone calls and heartfelt sympathy.

She shows up at a meeting to organize parents at Guaspari's home. The principal comes armed with lots of food because, as she puts it to the teacher, food helps get people involved.

Guaspari:	I didn't expect you to be here at all.
Williams:	Why not? We gotta figure out a way to fight this. And after ten years, I don't know, I just can't imagine walking down those hallways and not hearing that ... off-key, nails-on-blackboard violin music.
Guaspari:	Thank you.

There is a benefit concert, the program is spared – for the time being – and these two strong women, one black and one white, work together to save a program that is good for students. The outcome may seem all Hollywood, but this film (like so many iconic good teacher movies) is based on a true story. This portrayal of a principal offers the type of vision of an engaged, caring, competent, and politically active administrator that will serve us equally well in cinema and in real schools.

Conclusion

In the Harry Potter movies, Headmaster Albus Dumbledore (played with regal kindness by Richard Harris and, later, Michael Gambon) leads Hogwarts School of Witchcraft and Wizardry with unerring judgment founded on an omniscience that is unavailable to mere muggles. Hollywood principals, like their real counterparts, must operate despite their personal limitations and the obstacles imposed on one end by their administrative supervisors and on the other by teachers and students under their supervision. Kohn argues that there are basically two ways to change what happens in schools: the support model and the demand model. In the first case, the support model begins with the premise that "the role of teachers, administrators, parents, public officials, and the community at large is to help students act on their desire to make sense of the world" (93). Students are not expected to assume responsibility for their own learning but are assisted by schools in guiding their interests, developing competence at "playing with words and numbers and ideas" (93). In the second case, the demand model is pretty much the system in place now. Decisions about curriculum and assessment are imposed from outside (above) the classroom, and the idea is that classrooms should be increasingly tougher and more competitive. If the goal is exerting control over students and all activity in the classroom, then the demand model is clearly superior and its dominance in actual classrooms is understood.

This goal should be contested. There must be the desire for change and an understanding that life-long learners, citizens engaged in democratic practice, and people who prioritize an ethic of care for others are not as likely to emerge from the traditional classroom as from a progressive classroom we have yet to construct in any systematic way. For Hollywood principals, competence is mostly measured by the degree of control the administrator can exert over teachers and students, and the result is schools in which teachers and students feel more fear than freedom. There are much better ways of schooling. In recent years the public discourse on education has been heavily tilted toward "raising standards" and "accountability." Politicians and administrators have preached efficiency and promoted standardized tests with little attention to just what these tests measure and less concern for what damage the culture of testing inflicts on our children. There has been some backlash recently, mostly from parents but also from some teachers, against the huge increase in homework, especially for young children, and against the use of testing for punitive rather than diagnostic purposes. Several weeks before writing the initial draft of this chapter for the second edition of the book, my then 10-year-old son – who was in the fifth grade, a "good" student, and the recipient of several "citizenship" awards at his school – sat at my parents' kitchen table looking at the homework assignments, many of them rote tasks repeating class work from earlier in the day or week. He had already been working on these assignments for an hour. He said, "I'd rather blow up the school than do my homework." Of course, he did not mean this literally. I patiently explained to him why it would not be prudent to say something like that at school, but on some level I understood the sentiment. Clearly, as Chapter 10 will reveal, this desire for change in the institutions of education is widespread among students featured in Hollywood films.

Notes

1. I would be remiss not to mention Mrs. Griffith (Lisa Kudrow) from Easy A, a duplicitous counselor who has an affair with a 21-year-old high school student (much is made of the fact that the high school student is over 18), gives him Chlamydia, and lets another student take the blame for spreading the infection.
2. Good portrayal of a media studies professor in Dear White People by the way; Professor Bodkin (Terry Hempleman) motivates and encourages students while exacting tough standards. This is an important film to see for its depiction of campus climate prevalent at many campuses in the mid-2010s as conflicts are beginning to be discussed openly.
3. For a detailed examination of the conservative ideology of Lean on Me, see Ronald E. Chennault's Hollywood Films About Schools: Where Race, Politics, and Education Intersect (47–63).
4. Chennault also discusses how crime and poverty as associated with characters of color in The Principal (43).
5. Actually, Dr. Caldicott is a "resident faculty fellow," but he is calling the shots at Cradle Bay High (with the blessing of the actual principal) and implanting microchips in nonconformist students to create a Blue Ribbon Club academic and athletic overachievers.

· 1 0 ·

SCHOOLS, SCHOOLING, AND STUDENT VOICES

Summary

Throughout earlier chapters, I have tried to make connections between a group of Hollywood films about teachers and teaching and Huebner's value frameworks of curriculum and also to inject various, more fluid, theories of popular culture and social critique into that discussion. I have established a generic representation of the good teacher in these Hollywood movies that is presented as a radical model when, in fact, the good teacher in the movies may tug a little at the cornerstone of the institutional hierarchy, but this structure is never shaken. Similarly, I have identified equally vivid representations in these films of the bad teacher and the gendered teacher. These celluloid images influence our individual and collective constructions about teaching and what it means to be a teacher. As Michael Ryan and Douglas Kellner write in *Camera Politica: The Politics and Ideology of Contemporary Hollywood Film*:

> Films transcode the discourses (the forms, figures, and representations) of social life into cinematic narrative. Rather than reflect a reality external to the film medium, films execute a transfer from one discursive field to another. As a result, films themselves become part of that broader cultural system of representations that construct social reality. That construction occurs in part through the internalization of representations. (12–13)

Recognizing the role popular culture plays in our everyday lives and asking questions about how we can use the intersection between the popular and the personal as a space for creating new incarnations of teachers is crucial, as is empowering ourselves to openly challenge the very limited construction of curriculum and radical teaching in popular culture.

In Chapter 2, I laid out The Hollywood Model as a means of outlining the shared characteristics of the stock character presented in the movies as the good teacher. The good teacher is generally an outsider who is usually not well-liked by other teachers or by administrators. The good teacher gets involved with students on a personal level and, by inviting a reciprocal relationship, learns from those students. These teachers frequently personalize the curriculum to meet everyday needs in their students' lives. Nevertheless, these teachers, who are ostensibly "radical" or "progressive," serve, in the tradition of Hollywood film, to legitimatize dominant institutions and reinforce traditional values identified by Ryan and Kellner as individualism, capitalism, patriarchy, and racism, and they use the formal conventions of film to imply neutrality as they do so. Ryan and Kellner write:

> The conventions habituate the audience to accept the basic premises of social order, and to ignore their irrationality and injustice. The mapping of personal life stories over structural social issues like war and crime makes the existing order seem moral and good. And personal identification with representations of public order creates the psychological disposition for inducement into voluntary participation in a system of exploitation and domination. (1)

Ryan and Kellner are writing generally about various genres of films released between 1967 and 1987 to argue that Hollywood films are not "monolithically ideological" because analysis, such as I have undertaken of teachers and teaching in the movies, can take films into a "plural social and political terrain" (2). These films draw on the dramatic possibilities presented by the tension that exists between the forces of resistance and those of social conformity to present undercurrents of radical opportunity, and the excitement those themes possess, in a context of entrenched institutions and dominant ideology, which carries with it the weight of stability.

In Chapters 3 and 4, I developed connections between Dwayne Huebner's value frameworks of curriculum and the Hollywood curriculum. In both chapters, my discussion expanded on Huebner's clearly delineated value frameworks to discuss the concept of curriculum in film more broadly by looking at embedded themes and patterns and making connections between various films and theories of popular culture, particularly the Critical Theorists' "dialectics of culture" and Fiske's notion of intertextuality. Intertextuality became increasingly significant in Chapters 5–8 when I looked at the role individual and intersecting identities play in movies about teachers, and Chapter 9 expanded the focus to look specifically at film depictions of education administrators. It becomes my task now to ask more pointed questions about the movies and make new connections between images projected in these motion pictures and the notion of critical pedagogy while raising additional questions about the role of race and social class in these films. I also introduce interpretations of several films that may be termed radical. These films, which openly attack oppressive educational institutions, rely on students to voice their discontent and try to tear down the infrastructure of their schools. In several cases, these students literally blow up their schools when the issues they raise are not substantively addressed.

We have talked about films where there is some evidence of student resistance, but by and large, Hollywood films repeatedly present codes that constitute schools as sites of limited resistance staged by students and, sometimes, by a progressive teacher or two. As I have written in "The Hollywood View: Protecting the Status Quo in Schools Onscreen," schools are constructed as spaces where the disconnect between what matters to students and what matters to faculty is a profound rupture that is not bridged in any convincing way by the final frames of most of the films. In the Hollywood view, schools are sites where dramas are played out in hallways and classrooms, but the personal dramas of students and teachers are secondary, ultimately to the dominant discourse, that calls for the maintenance or restoration of the status quo.[1] Most films that focus on what matters to teens use high school cliques as the organizing principle for the narrative as well as the school, perhaps none so memorably as the iconic John Hughes film *The Breakfast Club* (1985). Will the brain, the athlete, the basket case, the princess, and the criminal socialize outside of Saturday detention? Probably not in the long-run, but they did form a bond that developed by breaking down barriers, making themselves vulnerable, and engaging in open conversation. The theme is one I articulated regarding race, ethnicity, and social class in Chapter 8: we must recognize and acknowledge difference before we can locate common ground. This is more difficult than it appears because it requires authenticity and trust, which is not a bountiful commodity in the movies.

Considering how high school cliques are depicted in films, it seems there are three typical narrative patterns that emerge: they are perpetual (*Not*

Another Teen Movie, 2001), they can be ameliorated (*Mean Girls*, 2004), or they can be subverted (*Me and Earl and the Dying Girl*, 2015). The categories may shift a bit over time, but the vast majority of films present cliques as a given, and there is no better way to demonstrate this than by referencing a parody because this type of film, as noted regarding *High School High*, is a commentary on a whole category of films and, for it to work, requires a consensus about the conventions that constitute that genre or subgenre. *Not Just Another Teen Movie* opens with a tour guide at the appropriately named John Hughes High School telling prospective students and parents, "This is not your typical high school. Here at John Hughes, there are no cliques, no exclusive social clubs. You're accepted for who you are, not for who you hang out with." Then, he promptly divides them into jocks, slutty girls, and losers before saying that the kids standing beside them will be their only friends for the next four years. The remainder of the film involves an improbable romance between two students from different cliques (a not particularly funny send up of *Sixteen Candles* [1984], *Pretty in Pink* [1986], *Can't Buy Me Love* [1987], *Some Kind of Wonderful* [1987], and my personal favorite *Say Anything* [1989] among others). All bridges among cliques are individual and, probably, temporary.[2] *Mean Girls*, which suggests cliques can be ameliorated, has been touted for a math teacher's success in changing school culture by helping

Figure 10.1. Tina Fey as Ms. Norbury in *Mean Girls*, 2004. This sensible and empathetic math teacher is able to lead the students at her school into kinder and more authentic interactions with one another.

students see that all cliques have problems and getting students to talk openly with one another. Ms. Norbrey (Tina Fey) starts a series of team-building exercises with a pep talk. "Everybody close your eyes. I want you to raise your hand if you have ever had a girl say something bad about you behind your back. (All hands are raised.) Open your eyes. Now, close your eyes again, and this time, I want you to raise your hand if you have ever said anything about a friend behind her back. (Most hands are raised.) Open. There's been some girl-on-girl crime here." And, so there is in ways that should be recognizable to anyone who has ever been a teenager.

Acknowledging the system and accepting it are two different things. *Me and Earl and the Dying Girl* opens with a sequence in which Greg (Thomas Mann) walks through the spaces of his high school demonstrating how he has managed to be accepted by every clique so long as he doesn't let his classmates know that he is friendly with all of them, which subverts the system. Of course, as the story unfolds and he becomes closer to Rachel (Olivia Cook), a girl who has cancer, he sees that the layers of social construction – from high school cliques to getting into the "right" college – are based on expectations and obligations that that divert us but do not keep the crucial events in our lives at bay unless we choose to avoid them. In the end, this is the type of high school narrative we need more of because it addresses serious issues in an emotionally authentic way, presents caring teachers who are real people, and affirms the strength, frailty, dignity, and creativity of human spirit. The point should be made that if students are wrapped up in the social world of high school hierarchies based around ingroups and outgroups, then there are other issues inside and outside of the school that will receive no attention and, just as with good teachers operating in a culture of individualism, there will be no meaningful collective action to improve the system that depends on their participation and of which they are major stakeholders. This is true even in wonderful, understated films like *The Edge of Seventeen* in which the seemingly detached history teacher Mr. Bruner (Woody Harrelson) turns out to be the only friend troubled teen Nadine (Hailee Steinfeld) has for large portions of the story.

If race and social class are glaring examples of cultural disconnects in inner-city schools and elite prep schools, as discussed in Chapter 8, the divide between students and adults in predominately white, suburban public schools is equally glaring. While the gap is mostly employed to celebrate youth culture in films like *Clueless* (1995), *Dazed and Confused* (1993), *Election*, *Fast Times at Ridgemont High* (1992), *Ferris Bueller's Day Off* (1986), *Heathers* (1998), *Mean Girls*, *Orange County* (2002), *Pretty in Pink*, *Pump Up the Volume* (1990),

Rock "n" Roll High School, Saved! (2004), *Summer School* (1987), *Teaching Mrs. Tingle* (1999), and *Varsity Blues* (1999), some films made in the wake of the Columbine school shootings and those that have followed seek to explore how the anomie of students assigned to schools where there is a divide between the stated goals of administrators and the centralized curriculum on the one hand and what is meaningful in students' daily lives on the other hand is a recipe for disaster.[3] While *Thirteen* (2003) is a riveting and rather harrowing look at how a 13-year-old girl with little guidance at school or at home falls under the unstable influence of a slightly older girl at her school, the problems of middle-class teens are more directly linked to schools in another movie, one also worth watching.

Gus Van Sant's *Elephant* is an elliptical and apocalyptic film that promises to be a slice of life drama inspired by the Columbine shootings. Where the parody must be predictable to be true to form, a form that circumscribes the events and representations in *High School High*, *Elephant* raises more questions than it answers. Although Van Sant's two earlier variations on good teacher movies, *Good Will Hunting* (1998) and *Finding Forrester* (2000), begin to broach the territory by looking at social class and race in the context of education, those films are each more conventional stories than *Elephant*. The earlier films raise less troubling questions as they explore individual narratives of academic achievement "despite the odds." Gus Van Sant's film *Elephant* that takes us inside a Portland, Oregon high school that could double as a movie set for most of the schools in the films listed above, but Van Sant's view of the school and the people in it is markedly different from the narratives of mainstream Hollywood cinema. His film may be fragmented and flawed, but this elliptical narrative follows several students around the school on what starts out as an average day and ends up as tragically as the April 20, 1999 attack on Columbine High School. The value of such a work, when examined from the perspective of critics looking at popular culture and schools, is that *Elephant* includes many of the same dramatic elements found in the other films – students with crushes, those with family problems or self-esteem issues or eating disorders, those who are bullied alongside those who are exalted among their peers, and those who seem well-adjusted alongside those who are gay and struggling with their sexuality – and presents a series of vignettes about them in a non-judgmental, documentary style that intentionally avoids contextualizing the relationships and events of the day to draw connections and reveal themes in a way that a conventional narrative would.

Elephant is a students' eye view of an average school day; at least, the day is average until it turns tragic. What does the camera record? There's a turbulent gray sky punctuated by power cords and lots of lush, autumn foliage. The school itself is non-descript, modern and clean, large and a bit institutional. It is an average suburban high school. The students appear mostly middle-class to upper-middle-class and are predominately white. The students group together, talking about mundane events – especially those related to their social lives – or walk alone and don't interact with others, but there are noticeably few interactions with faculty, administrators, and staff. There is one notable scene in which an African-American teacher is engaged in what seems more like a consciousness raising session on gay teenagers than a class session, but our view of this episode is truncated, which suggests that honest exchanges between adults and students about issues that might be relevant to their lives are peripheral and fleeting. Notably, the students who seem to need this sort of intervention the most are not present to receive it. This scene is significant for its content and for the fact that it is eclipsed by much more mundane social encounters in school hallways, the cafeteria, the ball field, and even the library. This is where the real action seems to be rather than in classrooms, which are largely unexplored territory in the film.

In *Elephant*, the narrative unfolds from a camera that seems to follow students like a silent observer, but this camera knows neither temporal nor spatial bounds. The apparent randomness of its recording follows one student for awhile then another student before returning to a previous scene to record the perspective of yet a different student. The camera seems also to transcend time with the inclusion of flashbacks that are not clearly marked. The only students who are presented extensively at home rather than at school are Eric and Alex, boys who are bullied and largely ignored by the adults who might have intervened. These two boys are linked together by common interests, they are linked to one another sexually, and they are linked indelibly by their plan to destroy their school and as many of the people in it as they can. How could they have been so alienated and yet so invisible to others? Van Sant's fragmented film depicts widespread anomie among students, but he offers no insight into why two of the disaffected youth plot and plan and return to their school clothed as mercenaries toting big bags of weapons and bombs bent on the destruction of as many of their peers, teachers, administrators, and staff as they can claim. Even to the end, it seems a game to Eric and Alex, and it is more than we can ask of a film director to put that scenario into a context that renders it understandable.

Figure 10.2. Eric Deulen as Eric and Alex Frost as Alex in *Elephant*, 2003. The high school students are reviewing plans for a murderous rampage at their high school.

Prophetic Voice and Critical Pedagogy

Part of what's missing in these films is a prophetic voice for teachers as the concept is explored by David E. Purpel in *The Moral and Spiritual Crisis in Education: A Curriculum for Justice and Compassion in Education*. Purpel suggests that the prophetic tradition could provide a mechanism for addressing cultural problems:

> The educator as prophet does more than re-mind, re-answer, and re-invigorate – the prophet-educator conducts re-search and joins students in continually developing skills and knowledge that enhance the possibility of justice, community, and joy ... In order to encourage "prophecy," educators themselves need to be "prophets" and speak in the prophetic voice that celebrates joy, love, justice, and abundance and cries out in anguish in the presence of oppression and misery. (105)

Such "prophecy" cannot be generated on behalf of students; it must arise in tandem with the students' own visions. It is impossible for a liberator to maintain a position over those to be liberated without remaining a part of the oppressive hierarchy, without, in effect, remaining an oppressor. Following the model of liberation theology, the cure for poverty is for everyone to embrace poverty, not to raise the poor into affluence (see Boff; Gutiérrez; Lebacqz; Pieris). Similarly, Paulo Freire says the following in *Pedagogy of the Oppressed*, "This, then, is the great humanistic and historical task of the oppressed: to liberate themselves and their oppressors as well. The oppressors, who oppress, exploit, and rape by virtue of their power, cannot find in this power the strength to liberate either the oppressed or themselves. Only power that springs from the weakness of the oppressed will be sufficiently strong to free both" (105). Teachers must join with students to affect liberation. For teachers, Freire argues, transformation brought about by liberation must come from dialogue, which he defines as "the encounter between men [sic], mediated by the world, in order to name the world."

Teachers in the movies wade into these waters, but they do not jump in and swim. Many of the Hollywood teachers jeopardize their jobs by tossing aside, if not openly defying, school policies. Most try to transform their school's stated curriculum into a curriculum that better meets the needs of their students. Many take risks of one sort or another to try to connect with students on a personal level. Still, these Hollywood teachers are working on easing transitions for their students between school and the world outside the classroom walls instead of participating in transformations that could radically recreate schools and other societal institutions as agencies invested in creating justice. Are we likely to see many of the teachers projected on the big screen or transmitted to the smaller screens in our own homes engage in praxis? No. Just as real teachers feel the tug of their personal compassion for and obligation to students being countered by the need to maintain their positions of authority in the school hierarchy, real movie writers and directors are torn between realizing their artistic or political vision and producing a product that studios know how to market and audiences find familiar enough to buy. That's precisely why the persistent incarnation of Hollywood's good teacher is a staple in films of all genres and time periods – the teacher in the movies is idealized enough to inspire viewers and manageable enough to leave the status quo intact.

Henry A. Giroux is one of the most vocal advocates of critical pedagogy as a tool for revitalizing democratic public life, but he is certainly not the first. Giroux is quick to point out that John Dewey wrote about the role of education in securing the democratic process as early as 1916 in *Democracy and Education*. This theme is articulated convincingly by Giroux in his discourse on critical pedagogy (1989, 1991, 1992, 1994). He begins his essay "Resisting Difference: Cultural Studies and the Discourse of Critical Pedagogy" with a rallying cry that has been repeated so often its ring has become a little hollow:

"American public education is in crisis. … At stake here is the refusal to grant public schooling a significant role in the ongoing process of educating people to be active and critical citizens capable of fighting for and reconstructing democratic public life" (1992, 199). Giroux, writing here with Freire, calls for teachers to practice their craft as "transformative public intellectuals" in schools configured as cultural sites for teachers and students to work together to produce knowledge that is "both relevant and emancipatory" from sources including popular culture (1989, ix).

Part of this argument for critical pedagogy means meeting students where they are by valuing the knowledge they already have. Clearly, students construct meaning before they enter the classroom. Giroux and Simon write: "By ignoring the cultural and social forms that are authorized by youth and simultaneously empower and disempower them, educators risk complicity in silencing and negating their students" (3). Kellner argues for an expansion of the concept of literacy with attention to fostering competencies that he considers important to students' everyday lives. He says that modern pedagogy organized around acquiring the skills of reading and writing are focused on a narrow conception of literacy that is particularly applicable to print culture.[4] Instead of merely expanding the range of desirable competencies to combine "great books" with, say, balancing a checkbook and analyzing a popular film, Kellner builds his theory of critical media literacy on Giroux's program of critical literacy, which is based on "a discourse of emancipation, possibility, hope, and struggle."[5] Particularly, Kellner is discussing the need for competencies in reading images critically, and he chooses print advertisements as his examples:

> These examples pose in a provocative way the need to expand literacy and cognitive competencies in order to survive the onslaught of media images, messages, and spectacles which are inundating our culture. The goal will be to teach a critical media literacy which will empower individuals to become more autonomous agents, able to emancipate themselves from contemporary forms of domination and able to become more active citizens, eager and competent to engage in processes of social transformation. (63)

All of which are competencies necessary for those same individuals to engage in fully participatory democracy as it is envisioned by Giroux.

Giroux and Freire write in the introduction of *Popular Culture, Schooling, and Everyday Life* that commitment to a democratic society through the ideals of freedom, equality, and justice provides the unifying elements in a curriculum that should otherwise celebrate "diverse voices, experiences, histories, and community traditions that increasingly characterize many countries" (x).

Their notion of critical pedagogy is neither a repudiation of "great books" nor an uncritical embrace of popular culture, but instead arises from a "need to reclaim a cultural literacy for each and every person as part of a democratic idea of citizenship that dignifies and critically engages the different voices of students from both dominant and subordinate groups in ways that help them to redefine schools as part of the communities and neighborhoods they serve" (x–xi). They recognize that multiple perspectives must be acknowledged and interrogated for students to become critical citizens rather than merely good citizens.

Pedagogy does not fall solely under the purview of schools. Giroux and Simon point out that there is the possibility for pedagogy at any site where a practice "intentionally tries to influence the production of meaning" (230). There are many of those sites visited by students during the hours they are out of school and others that compete with the stated curriculum during the school day. All of these sites may be connected to what Giroux calls the "pedagogy of representation." In *Disturbing Pleasures: Learning Popular Culture*, Giroux says that it is important for viewers to identify the ways in which representations are constructed to help us understand the past through the present while also sanctioning a particular vision of the future:

> … a pedagogy of representation is not wedded to the process of narrating an authentic history, but to the dynamics of cultural recovery, which involves rewriting the relationship between identity and difference through a retelling of the historical past. Such a pedagogy is rooted in making the political more pedagogical by addressing how a critical politics can be developed between a struggle over access to regimes of representation and using them to re-present different identities as part of the reconstruction of democratic public life. (89)

For teachers, there are very specific challenges and opportunities in giving students the tools they need to make sense of their lives in a postmodern image culture. To do so requires dialogue. One place to begin that dialogue is through an exploration of the meaning(s) of artifacts of popular culture.

Through looking at these films critically and using them in the classroom, we locate a starting point for discussing issues related to curriculum (power), gender roles, racial identity, sexual identity, social class, politics, and a variety of other topics relevant to students' lives. These films, as is possible with any number of other artifacts of popular culture, provide a meeting place for experiences from students' everyday lives and the theories of meaning that they illustrate. It requires student and teacher working in concert to create opportunities for this sort of critical pedagogy to ignite a classroom. When students begin to realize their own value as human beings and realize that they possess the power to make meaning(s) and create change, a democratic vision may be realized. It's an argument made well by Giroux and Freire in *Popular Culture, Schooling, and Everyday Life*:

> At its best, the language of educational theory should embody a public philosophy dedicated to returning schools to their primary task: to be places of critical education in the service of creating a public sphere of citizens who are able to exercise power over their own lives, and especially over the conditions of knowledge production and acquisition. This is a language linked to the imperatives of a practical hope, one that views the relationship between leadership and schooling as part of a wider struggle to create the lived experiences of empowerment for the vast majority. (viii)

There is an opportunity for teachers to assume leadership in this process, but the opportunity carries enormous risk. In the closing paragraph of his essay on teachers and teaching in the movies, Ayers articulates the tension that exists between the ideal teacher in films working to save students and his own notion of outstanding teachers finding salvation for all.

> Outstanding teachers need to question the common sense-to break the rules, to become political and activist in concert with the kids. This is true heroism, an authentic act of courage. We need to take seriously the experiences of youngsters, their sense-making, their knowledge, and their dreams; and in particular we must question the structures that kids are rejecting. In other words, we must assume an intelligence in youngsters, assume that they are acting sensibly and are deriving meaning from situations that are difficult and often dreadful-and certainly, not of their own making. In finding common cause with youngsters, we may also find there our own salvation as teachers. (156)

For teachers, this means they must choose students over schools and other societal institutions and, in doing so, explore radical alternatives to the status quo. It is an obvious choice but not an easy one to make.

Alternative Visions of Schools and Schooling in the Movies

Often, in films that feature teenagers as the central characters, school is little more than a locus at which students' lives converge and might be interchangeable with any number of other locations, such as a mall or another "hangout." There are, however, a few films that depict the school as an overt terrain of struggle where students form a collective group of opposition and begin resistance activities against the educational hierarchy and, by implication, the larger societal institutions of control represented by their school and school personnel. Unlike the good teacher who goes up against "the system" and unleashes a bit of temporary chaos without really affecting lasting change, these students dismantle the system that oppresses them. Another system of oppression will undoubtedly rise in its place, but it is equally certain that these students will continue their rebellion.

Here are five examples of such films: *Class of 1999*; *Class of Nuke 'Em High*; *Pump Up the Volume*; *Disturbing Behavior*; and *Rock "n" Roll High School*. *Class of 1999* has already been referenced in some detail during a discussion of the bad teacher in Chapter 4, but it is important, I believe, to elaborate on the final minutes of the film. After the battledroid "teachers" have orchestrated a gang war between the Razorhawks and the Blackhearts to try to kill the students, the leaders of the two gangs instead join forces to wipe out the battledroids. Cody, the main character in the film, who has recognized early in the movie that something is wrong with the new teachers, calls them "Three inhuman teaching monsters" and calls out to his rival, "You've gotta know who your real enemies are. I'm going in there to waste some teachers. Now, are you with me?" The others join up, realizing that their "real enemies" are not teachers in any traditional sense, but the system that puts killing machines in schools to eradicate insurgence. The electronic sign in the hallway reads "Welcome to Night School," and the audience is certain that lessons taught this evening will be different than ever before. The leaders ride motorcycles through the hallways, a theme repeated in several of these films, and fight the battledroids whose various attachments include a flame-thrower device from the "female's" head, a machine gun mounted on the gym teacher's arm, and a giant claw on the third droid's arm that decapitates a student as the droid gleefully intones, "I love to mold young minds." This school has been transformed from prison to battlefield, and finally the students begin to win. Losses have been heavy, but Cody and his girlfriend Christy finally walk out of the school at dawn. The school is burning behind them, conveying the message that the only way to change the system is to destroy it.

As with *Class of 1999*, it may at first seem difficult to take *Disturbing Behavior*, *Class of Nuke 'Em High*, or *Rock "n" Roll High School* seriously. The latter two, especially, are low-budget films with low production values, unsatisfactory scripts, and generally poor direction and acting. In comparison, these two films elevate *Class of 1999* and *Disturbing Behavior* to near classic status. But, there is an interesting theme that cuts across all four pictures. In each film, students are the victims of large-scale conspiracies that endanger their health, curtail their freedom, or both. In *Class of 1999*, the battledroids dressed up as teachers and, at the behest of school officials, hurt and murder students as a matter of course. In *Disturbing Behavior*, a "resident faculty fellow" implants a microchip in students to help them "leave mediocrity behind" and become over-achieving, conformist clones. In *Class of Nuke 'Em High*, students at Tromaville High School[6] have been exposed to nuclear contaminants. The Tromaville Nuclear Facility, which is located next door to the school, failed to report an underground leak. The typical school and teacher clichés appear throughout the film—a crotchety teacher with her hair in a gray bun, thick glasses, and a shrieking voice—joined by new plot points arising from the "atomic high" students get after smoking marijuana grown at the nuclear power plant. Finally, some students begin to recognize their plight and protest the conspiracy that covered it up, a protest that loosely links the school and the plant. When a timely nuclear blast blows up the school, the students cheer. A voice announces over a public address system (from where?) that Tromaville High will be temporarily closed for remodeling.

At Vince Lombardi High School, also known as *Rock "n" Roll High School*, the scene is similar, even if the issue is different. Here Riff Randall, played by P. J. Soles, is a self-proclaimed rock "n" roller with "more detentions than anyone in the school's history." The film pivots on Randall's altercations with Ms. Togar, played Mary Woronow, the new principal who arrives after her predecessor has been carried out in a straitjacket. We learn very quickly that Togar hates rock "n" roll even more than she detests Randall and the other students she cannot control. Their interplay goes something like this: Randall blasts rock music from the school public-address system; Togar sets out to get her; Randall skips school to get tickets to see her favorite band, the Ramones; Togar burns Ramones' records in a bonfire. And, so it goes until the Ramones show up at the school just as a banner flies from the upper story of the school proclaiming it "Rock 'n' Roll High School." The students take over the school and again blast rock music – the Ramones, of course – over the public-address system. Even Mr. McGree, the one teacher featured regularly in the film, exchanges his dry, pedantic lecture on Beethoven for a brisk dance with Riff Randall. When he rips off his clothes, he has underneath a Ramones tee-shirt and jeans. Outside, Ms. Togar stands behind her bullhorn and is backed up by police reinforcements. Finally, she forces Randall to come out of the building.

Togar: And just what do you have to say for yourself, young lady?

Riff: I've seen the error of my ways. I'd first like to say to all students everywhere that you may think the school is yours for awhile, but it is always run by the principal and her administration.

Togar:	Oh, that's nice.
Riff:	Vince Lombardi High is your school, Miss Togar.
	So, you can have it.
Togar:	Well, I'm very happy to see that you've come to your senses. And, what would you have done with the school anyway?
Riff:	Rock the roof off it. Hit it Marky ...

She cues the Ramones to begin the song "Rock 'n' Roll High School." The students begin to dance madly as the adults grimace at the sound and at the appearance of the Ramones. The adults have cooperated with Togar throughout to rid the school and the teenagers' lives of the evil influence of rock music, and the students respond to their conspiracy by literally blowing up the school. The film ends as it began with a principal being carried away in a straitjacket – this time it is Ms. Togar. And so, the cycle continues. Despite the relatively low production values of the film, it tells a story about students operating collectively as a force of resistance against the opposing forces that try to control them; this is a storyline that is clearly attractive to the audience it targets, an audience mainly of students.[7]

While the four films just discussed might be described as fantastic tales that greatly amplify the circumstances surrounding the students' sense of angst and oppression and offer greatly exaggerated resolutions, there is one film in the group that seems to resonate more directly with the high school experience. In *Pump Up the Volume*, Christian Slater plays Mark Hunter, a high school student whose radio alterego is variously known as "Hard Harry" and "Happy Harry Hard-on." Mark, whose dad is a school administrator, is new in town and has not made any friends at his new school, Hubert H. Humphrey High School. Unknown to his classmates, he is the guy they begin listening to at night when they tune in the low-power radio station that he sets up illegally in the basement of his home. While Mark speaks openly about sexual frustration and the alienation and oppression of youth, students gather at the school's darkened baseball field where the reception is good. Soon students are passing around audiotapes of various broadcasts and calling or writing the mysterious voice – a voice that seems to speak for all of them – for advice. There is a good teacher in the film, Jan Emerson (Ellen Green), who tries to get Mark to share his feelings about a composition he has written for her writing class; she also asks him to write for a school publication she advises. Emerson's good intentions are not enough to deal with the depth of despair that the students at the school feel, and the school publication, *The Clarion*, is not a forum that will allow Mark to address the issues he is able to address over the airwaves.

The illegal radio show and the tapes circulating in the school do not go unnoticed. In a scene that could have been scripted from virtually any student's imagination, the principal, Miss Crestwood (Annie Ross), ruminates in the teacher's lounge.

Crestwood: This school is judged on one category only, academic scores. The lesson of modern education is nothing good comes easy. No pain, no gain.

Murdock: Excuse me, everyone. Miss Crestwood, would you want to listen to this? It's the third tape this week. Unbelievable!

They listen to a bit of the tape the shop teacher has confiscated, and the younger teachers, including Jan Emerson, begin to laugh.

Crestwood: Jan, it's no laughing matter.

And, in a way, Crestwood is right. As "Harry," Mark begins to address issues that the school administration and more directly the school counselor are unaware of or prefer to ignore, including teen pregnancy, being gay in a straight world, and suicide. "Harry" gets a letter from a student that reads:

Hello Hard Harry-
            Do you think I should kill myself?
                I'm Serious

"Harry" calls the letter writer and asks him why he is considering suicide.

Student: I'm all alone.
Harry: Oh, hey, look ... maybe it's okay to be alone sometimes. I mean, uh, everybody's alone.
Student: You're not.
Harry: I didn't talk to one person today, not counting teachers.

The student, whom we learn is named Malcolm Kiser, does take his own life. "Harry" allows that "being young is sometimes less fun than being dead," and his character's popularity continues to grow with the students just as most of the adults feel increasingly threatened by his broadcasts. His trademark "So be it!" appears on the school wall in spray paint, and there is a thriving black market in old tapes. Listening to "Harry" seems to be the one thread that really unifies diverse groups of students. At school, they dissolve into stratified cliques, but at night, they are unified while "Harry" voices their universal discontent as well as their passion.

Finally, the guidance counselor, who has been a particular target of "Harry's," calls in federal investigators and the Federal Communications Commission (FCC) at the same time he and Crestwood have scheduled an emergency meeting for parents. Ironically, Mark's father is one of the school administrators scheduled to speak. There is a very heated atmosphere at the school. The parents are talking in no uncertain terms about going after "Harry." An honor student who has been portrayed throughout the film as a "super-overachiever" walks to the front of the room.

Page:	My name is Page Woodward, and I have something to say to you people. People are saying that Harry is introducing bad things and encouraging bad things ... well, it seems to me that these things were already here.
Crestwood:	Please go and sit.
Page:	My god. Why won't you people listen? He's trying to tell you that there's something wrong with this school. Half the people that are here are on probation of some kind.
Crestwood:	Page!
Page:	And we're all really scared to be who we really are. I am not perfect. I've just been going through the motions of being perfect. And, inside, I am screaming.
Crestwood:	Page, you were a model student.
Page:	Why won't you listen?

As the girl leaves the stage a few people mutter that they should listen to her and a few others call her back. Instead, Page makes faces at the mass of news reporters outside the school and implores "Harry" not to listen to them. With the feds in pursuit, Mark and his friend Nora ride around the suburban neighborhoods and the desert canyons broadcasting on the road. As "Harry" makes his final broadcast, students gather at the baseball field outside the school, and inside the building his dad learns that the principal weeded out students with low SAT scores but kept them on the rosters to get the money allocated for them. Just as the FCC officials and police close in on Mark and Nora, the jeep they are driving roars onto the baseball field, and they merge with the crowd gathered there. The film ends with the promise that many more teenagers will follow in the path "Harry" blazed. Against a dark screen, we see electronic flashes of light and hear voice after voice illegally sign-on.

Even though *Pump Up the Volume* offers viewers an alternative voice, the scenes preceding the final moments of the film, scenes that contribute to the "resolution," fall back on a device that has become numbingly familiar in other films – demonizing and ousting the principal, ostensibly in an amelioration of schools. In this case, getting rid of the "mean" principal to make schools more humane offers a forced resolution, and a false one at that, while avoiding the more profound issue of the teenagers' alienation, an issue that cannot be resolved easily if at all. Mark and the kids listening to "Harry" are concerned about issues of life and death from their own personal perspectives and in a larger cultural context. Critical pedagogy may not be able to remove the overlay of existential angst that the students long to overcome, but deconstructing images that exacerbate that angst and finding personal empowerment in the process of deconstruction can teach them that their alienation is, in fact, shared.

Although the focus is different in the films introduced in this chapter, they all echo the themes identified in almost all of the other movies. Good teachers mean well but are either too deeply connected with the dominant ideology to change it or are unwilling to launch the sort of direct challenge that is necessary to break the bonds of an oppressive system. Jan Emerson, like many of the other good teachers, merely provides a buffer to ease some of the pain students feel and to help them through their transition into the world of work outside the school. There is no prophetic voice in Hollywood's teachers. There are no groups of teachers in the movies who address moral, cultural, and aesthetic issues in a sense that is consciously political, and no schools that promote social change instead of individual change. There is no commitment to struggle against the dominant ideology in their teaching and certainly no recognition that the dominant ideology goes far beyond bad or mean teachers. The films fail to make the fundamental connection that politics is everywhere and schools are cultural sites teeming with possibility for direct political action.[8] There is pleasure but no praxis in these films. And, it is the students who see this more clearly than anyone else. Ferris Bueller knows that school is boring, and he won't miss anything important or fun by staying away. Mark Hunter knows that school personnel are not addressing the issues that really matter to students, the matters of life and death. And, students know that the system under which all of this operates is inherently corrupt.

In the film *School Ties* (1992), for example, a wealthy, northeastern prep school has recruited a working-class, Jewish quarterback as a scholarship student to help their football team. The film is set around 1960. David Green (Brendan Fraser) and Charlie Dillon (Matt Damon) become friends then competitors, rivals over a girl, over the quarterback position, and over grades. Dillon cheats on a test and, instead of taking the blame, tries to blame Green. Because Green is the outsider, everyone initially believes Dillon. Finally,

Dillon's roommate, who has known the truth from the start, tells what he knows and Green is cleared. As Green walks out of the headmaster's office, he sees a black limousine picking up Dillon in the cold hours near dawn. Dillon rolls down the window.

Dillon:	You know something, I'm still gonna get into Harvard. And, in ten years, nobody's gonna remember any of this. But, you'll still be a goddamn Jew.
Green:	And you'll still be a prick.

With that, the limousine drives away, and David Green is left alone to suffer through the rigors of St. Matthews and further trials as he attempts to enter an Ivy League college. He knows that instead of individually breaking through the system, he may be validating it, but, in the absence of a collective resistance movement, he has few ready options.

From their position on the underside of the educational hierarchy, students see the oppressiveness of the system quite clearly. And, as the movies so vividly tell us, the good teachers at least partially share that view. Because of the intertextuality that exists between our lived experiences and the movies that become part of those experiences, it is difficult, if not impossible, to say how the one form influences the other. Some time back, I sat in a theater lobby munching popcorn and waiting for a friend who was supposed to meet me for a movie. Two high school students lounged behind the counter waiting to sell tickets and snacks. It was a lazy Sunday afternoon, and business was slow. Unaware that I could hear them, the young man said, "School is so pointless. I spend most of my time there just daydreaming. I mean, it is so pointless." The young girl said, "Yeah?" He replied, "Pointless." She thought a moment. "You know, every time I take a test, like, the next week I don't remember a thing. ... I know what you mean." Soon they moved on to other topics, but it struck me that their dialogue could easily have been excised from any number of movies about high school students and their experiences in school.

Students in the movies find schooling largely meaningless, and the good teachers who attempt to help them find meaning in the experience come up against an institutional hierarchy that discourages or forbids that type of interchange between teachers and students. The Hollywood curriculum allows teenage wish fulfillment in the form of schools being blown up or burned down and allows us to pretend, if only for a couple of hours, that a good teacher working alone can fix the damaged system if he or she is committed enough. These films dichotomize teachers and teaching into the "good" and the "bad" and present a reductionist view that being "good" enough is, in fact, good enough. The undercurrent of resistance that runs through the films is enough to satisfy audiences by giving them hope that something better, an alternate vision, is possible without ever threatening the comfort they take in the dominance of the status quo. These dreams, conjured by a distant light projected on the screen, reassure us with their powerful resolutions that things aren't really so bad despite newspaper headlines and nightly newscasts and conversations with our friends and neighbors to the contrary. In the movies, children are not hungry and sick, poverty is not a trap, only "certain" students use drugs and alcohol, teenage sex is usually played for laughs, and violence is neither random nor widespread. These themes, if they appear at all, are orchestrated into traditional narrative structures in such a way that lets us believe these problems do not affect us. These problems are real, however, just as the films that contradict them are real. To turn the films into something useful, even instructive, means to claim the images for ourselves through discourse and divest the good teacher and bad teacher of their respective pretensions. To think about and talk about these films is to give our experience with the movies meaning. And, perhaps, from this discourse will come change.

Notes

1. Daniel Perlstein and Leah Faw's chapter "Students Without A Cause: *Blackboard Jungle*, High School Movies, and High School Life" offers a compelling reading of this film as a hallmark of the bifurcated experience in schools as one narrative thread (the social problem film) favors adults, policy, and attempts at pragmatic problem solving while the other (the teenpic) focuses on youth culture.
2. Of course, Diane Court (Ione Skye) and Lloyd Dobler (John Cusack) get together after graduation in *Say Anything*, so maybe they will survive. We can attribute this note to the fact that I'm listening to the *Pretty in Pink Soundtrack* while writing this paragraph.
3. One film with a swath of destruction at a high school was scheduled for release soon after Columbine but delayed. *O* is an upated version of Shakespeare's *Othello* set at an elite school with a young cast.
4. The debate over the primacy of written or oral competencies is not a new one. Ironically, the oral tradition, which is in many ways more closely related through storytelling traditions to the dominant forms of popular culture, is revered in ancient civilizations. The notion of the spoken word as an integrated whole, and of the written word as an inferior counterfeit of it, goes all the way back to Plato. In the *Phaedrus*, Socrates recounts the story of the Egyptian King Thamus, who is offered the gift of writing by a deity named Theuth. Thamus declines the gift saying, "This discovery of yours will create forgetfulness in the learners souls, because they will not use their memories ... They will be hearers of many things and will have learned nothing; they will appear to be omniscient and will generally

know nothing; they will be tiresome company, having the show of wisdom without the reality" (278–79). Socrates goes on to comment," ... when [words] have been once written down they are tumbled about anywhere among those who may or may not understand them, and know not to whom they should reply, to whom not: and, if they are maltreated or abused they have no parent to protect them; and they cannot protect or defend themselves ... Is there not another kind of word or speech far better than this, and having far greater power? ... I mean an intelligent word graven in the soul of the learner, which can defend itself, and knows when to speak and when to be silent" (278–79). Plato recounts Socrates in *The Dialogues of Plato*. Trans. Benjamin Jowett, 1892; Oxford University Press, 1920. Now the debate seems more focused on the value and dominance of print as opposed to moving image forms.

5. Kellner is writing in "Reading Images Critically" from *Postmodernism, Feminism, and Cultural Politics: Redrawing Educational Boundaries* and he cites Giroux in *Schooling and the Struggle for Public Life*, 1988.

6. Troma is the name of the production and distribution company responsible for this film.

7. Jason Dean, played by Christian Slater, plans to blow up the school in *Heathers*, but his is a generalized, psychotic acting out in which the school is more a ready target than a specific one. As JD says when he thinks his plan will work, "People are going to look at the ashes of Westerbrook and say 'Now there is a school that self-destructed not because society didn't care but because the school was society.' Pretty deep, huh?" His girlfriend Veronica Sawyer, played by Winona Ryder, thwarts his plan to blow up the school and the students, faculty, and staff in it, but he has other bombs strapped to his body underneath a trenchcoat; when he succeeds in blowing himself up, she is singed.

8. I want to point out that this glaring absence in Hollywood films cannot be directly connected to "real" teachers teaching in "real" classrooms. As Kathleen Casey's work so ably demonstrates, there are many teachers who are political activists, whether or not they so identify themselves.

FILMOGRAPHY

The Affairs of Dobie Gillis. Dir. Don Weis. 1952.

Akellah and The Bee. Dir. Doug Atchison. 2006.

All Over The Guy. Dir. Julie Davis. 2001.

American History X. Dir. Tony Kaye. 1998.

American Pie. Dirs. Paul Weitz and Chris Weitz. 1999.

An Education. Dir. Lone Scherfig. 2009.

Animal House. Dir. John Landis. 1978.

Anna and The King. Dir. Andy Tennant. 1999.

Anna and The King of Siam. Dir. John Cromwell. 1946.

Annie Hall. Dir. Woody Allen. 1977.

Any Given Sunday. Dir. Oliver Stone. 1999.

Arlington Road. Dir. Mark Pellington. 1999.

Arrival. Dir. Denis Villeneuve. 2016.

Art School Confidential. Dir. Terry Zwigoff. 2006.

A Single Man. Dir. Tom Ford. 2009.

Bad News Bears. Dir. Michael Ritchie. 1976.

Bad News Bears. Dir. Richard Linklater. 2005.

Bad Teacher. Dir. Jake Kasdan. 2011.

Back to School. Dir. Alan Metter. 1986.

A Beautiful Mind. Dir. Ron Howard. 2001.

Bend It Like Beckham. Dir. Gurinder Chadha. 2002.

Billy Elliot. Dir. Stephen Daldry. 2000.

Billy Madison. Dir. Tamra Davis. 1995.

Blackboard Jungle. Dir. Richard Brooks. 1955.

The Blue Angel. Dir. Josef von Sternberg. 1930.

Blue Car. Dir. Karen Moncrieff. 2002.

Blue Chips. Dir. William Friedkin. 1994.

Boston Public. Creator David E. Kelley. 2000–2004.

Bound. Dirs. Lana Wachowski and Lilly Wachowski. 1996.

Boyhood. Dir. Richard Linklater. 2014.

The Boy Next Door. Dir. Rob Cohen. 2015.

The Boys in The Band. Dir. William Friedkin. 1970.

Boyz n the Hood. Dir. John Singleton. 1991.

The Breakfast Club. Dir. John Hughes. 1985.

Bright Road. Dir. Gerald Mayer. 1953.

Bull Durham. Dir. Ron Shelton. 1988.

Carrie. Dir. Brian De Palma. 1976.

Chalk. Dir. Mike Akel. 2006.

Cheaters. Dir. John Stockwell. 2000.

Children of a Lesser God. Dir. Randa Haines. 1986.

The Children's Hour. Dir. William Wyler. 1962.

Class of 1984. Dir. Mark L. Lester. 1982.

Class of 1999. Dir. Mark L. Lester. 1990.

Class of 1999 II: The Substitute. Dir. Spiro Ratazos. 1994.

Class of Nuke 'Em High. Dirs. Richard W. Haines and Samuel Weil. 1986.

Clueless. Dir. Amy Heckerling. 1995.

Coach Carter. Dir. Thomas Carter. 2005.

Conrack. Dir. Martin Ritt. 1974.

Cooley High. Dir. Michael Schultz. 1975.

The Corn Is Green. Dir. Irving Rapper. 1945.

Crazy/Beautiful. Dir. John Stockwell. 2001.

The Dancing Co-Ed. Dir. S. Sylvan Simon. 1939.

Dangerous Minds. Dir. John N. Smith. 1995.

Dazed and Confused. Dir. Richard Linklater. 1993.

Dead Poets Society. Dir. Peter Weir. 1989.

Dear White People. Dir. Justin Simien. 2014.

The Deer Hunter. Dir. Michael Cimino. 1978.

Detachment. Dir. Tony Kaye. 2011.

Disturbing Behavior. Dir. David Nutter. 1998.

Doubt. Dir. John Patrick Shanley. 2008.

The Duff. Dir. Ari Sandel. 2015.

Easy A. Dir. Will Gluck. 2010.

The Edge of Seventeen. Dir. Kelly Fremon Craig. 2016.

Educating Rita. Dir. Lewis Gilbert. 1983.

Election. Dir. Alexander Payne. 1999.

Elegy. Dir. Isabel Coixet. 2008.

Elephant. Dir. Gus Van Sant. 2003.

The Emperor's Club. Dir. Michael Hoffman. 2002.

The English Teacher. Dir. Craig Zisk. 2013.

The Faculty. Dir. Robert Rodriquez. 1998.

Fame. Dir. Alan Parker. 1980.

Fast Times at Ridgemont High. Dir. Amy Heckerling. 1982.

Ferris Bueller's Day Off. Dir. John Hughes. 1986.

Finding Forrester. Dir. Gus Van Sant. 2001.

Forrest Gump. Dir. Robert Zemeckis. 1994.

Freedom Writers. Dir. Richard LaGravenese. 2007.

Friday Night Lights. Dirs. Peter Berg and Josh Pate. 2004.

Friday Night Lights. Creator Peter Berg. 2006–2011.

Girls. Creator Lena Dunham. 2012–.

The Giver. Dir. Phillip Noyce. 2014.

Glory Road. Dir. James Gartner. 2006.

Goodbye, Mr. Chips. Dir. Sam Wood. 1939.

Good Morning, Miss Dove. Dir. Henry Koster. 1955.

Good Will Hunting. Dir. Gus Van Sant. 1997.

Grease. Dir. Randal Kleiser. 1978.

Grease 2. Dir. Patricia Birch. 1982.

The Great Debaters. Dir. Denzel Washington. 2007

Half Nelson. Dir. Ryan Fleck. 2006.

Hamlet 2. Dir. Andrew Fleming. 2008.

Harry Potter and The Sorcerer's Stone. Dir. Chris Columbus. 2001.

Harry Potter and The Chamber of Secrets. Dir. Chris Columbus. 2002.

Harry Potter and The Prisoner of Azkaban. Dir. Alfonso Cuaron. 2004.

Harry Potter and The Goblet of Fire. Dir. Mike Newell. 2005.

Harry Potter and The Order of The Phoenix. Dir. David Yates. 2007.

Harry Potter and The Half-Blood Prince. Dir. David Yates. 2009.

Happy-Go-Lucky. Dir. Mike Leigh. 2009.

Heathers. Dir. Michael Lehmann. 1988.

Here Comes The Boom. Dir. Frank Coraci. 2012.

High School High. Dir. Hart Bochner. 1996.

The History Boys. Dir. Nicholas Hytner. 2006.

Hoosiers. Dir. David Anspaugh. 1986.

House Party. Dir. Reginald Hudlin. 1990.

The Imitation Game. Dir. Morten Tyldum. 2014.

In & Out. Dir. Frank Oz. 1997.

Irrational Man. Dir. Woody Allen. 2015.

Jawbreaker. Dir. Darren Stein. 1999.

The Karate Kid. Dir. John G. Avildsen. 1984.

The Karate Kid, Part II. Dir. John G. Avildsen. 1986.

The Karate Kid, Part III. Dir. John G. Avildsen. 1989.

Kicking and Screaming. Dir. Jesse Dylan. 2005.

Kindergarten Cop. Dir. Ivan Reitman. 1990.

The King and I. Dir. Walter Lang. 1956.

Kinsey. Dir. Bill Condon. 2004.

Knute Rockne All American. Dir. Lloyd Bacon. 1940.

Lean on Me. Dir. John G. Avildsen. 1989.

Learning to Dive. Dir. Isabel Coixet. 2014.

Legally Blonde. Dir. Robert Luketic. 2001.

The Legend af Bagger Vance. Dir. Robert Redford. 2000.

The Life of David Gale. Dir. Alan Parker. 2003.

Little Man Tate. Dir. Jodie Foster. 1991.

Little Miss Sunshine. Dirs. Jonathan Dayton and Valerie Faris. 2006.

The Longest Yard. Dir. Robert Aldrich. 1974.

The Longest Yard. Dir. Peter Segal. 2005.

Looking for Mr. Goodbar. Dir. Richard Brooks. 1977.

Major Payne. Dir. Nick Castle. 1995.

Malcolm X. Dir. Spike Lee. 1992.

The Male Animal. Dir. Elliott Nugent. 1942.

The Man Who Knew Infinity. Dir. Matt Brown. 2015.

McFarland, USA. Dir. Niki Caro. 2015.

The Man Without a Face. Dir. Mel Gibson. 1993.

Matilda. Dir. Danny DeVito. 1996.

Me and Earl and the Dying Girl. Dir. Alfonso Gomez-Rejon. 2015.

Mean Girls. Dir. Mark Waters. 2004.

Meet The Parents. Dir. Jay Roach. 2000.

Menace II Society. Dirs. Albert Hughes and Allan Hughes. 1993.

The Mighty Ducks. Dir. Stephen Herek. 1992.

Million Dollar Baby. Dir. Clint Eastwood. 2004.

Miracle. Dir. Gavin O'Connor. 2004.

The Miracle Worker. Dir. Arthur Penn. 1962.

The Mirror Has Two Faces. Dir. Barbra Streisand. 1996.

Mona Lisa Smile. Dir. Mike Newell. 2003.

Mr. Holland's Opus. Dir. Stephen Herek. 1995.

Music of The Heart. Dir. Wes Craven. 1999.

My Girl. Dir. Howard Ziff. 1991.

My So-Called Life. Creator Winnie Holzman. 1994–1995.

Never Been Kissed. Dir. Raja Rosnell. 1999.

Not Another Teen Movie. Dir. Joel Gallen. 2001.

Notes on A Scandal. Dir. Richard Eyre. 2006.

The Nutty Professor. Dir. Jerry Lewis. 1963.

The Nutty Professor. Dir. Tom Shadyac. 1996.

O. Dir. Tim Blake Nelson. 2001.

The Object of My Affection. Dir. Nicholas Hynter. 1998.

October Sky. Dir. Joe Johnston. 1999.

Oleanna. Dir. David Mamet. 1994.

187. Dir. Kevin Reynolds. 1997.

One True Thing. Dir. Carl Franklin. 1998.

Only The Strong. Dir. Sheldon Lettich. 1993.

The Opposite of Sex. Dir. Don Roos. 1998.

Orange County. Dir. Jake Kasdan. 2002.

Outside Providence. Dir. Michael Corrente. 1999.

Palo Alto. Dir. Gia Coppola. 2013.

Pay It Forward. Dir. Mimi Leder. 2000.

Phoebe in Wonderland. Dir. Daniel Barnz. 2008.

Porky's. Dir. Bob Clark. 1981.

Powder. Dir. Victor Salva. 1995.

Precious. Dir. Lee Daniels. 2009.

Pretty in Pink. Dir. John Hughes. 1984.

The Princess Diaries. Dir. Garry Marshall. 2001.

The Principal. Dir. Christopher Cain. 1987.

Pump Up the Volume. Dir. Allan Moyle. 1990.

The Prime of Miss Jean Brodie. Dir. Ronald Neame. 1969.

Rachel, Rachel. Dir. Paul Newman. 1968.

Radio. Dir. Michael Tollin. 2003.

Raiders of the Lost Ark. Dir. Steven Spielberg. 1981.

Ray Donovan. Creator Ann Biderman. 2013–.

Real Genius. Dir. Martha Coolidge. 1985.

Rebel Without A Cause. Dir. Nicholas Ray. 1955.

Remember The Titans. Dir. Boaz Yakin. 2000.

Renaissance Man. Dir. Penny Marshall. 1994.

Rock "n" Roll High School. Dir. Allan Arkush. 1979.

The Ron Clark Story. Dir. Randa Haines. 2006.

The Rookie. Dir. John Lee Hancock. 2002.

Rope. Dir. Alfred Hitchcock. 1948.

Rudy. Dir. David Anspaugh. 1993.

Rushmore. Dir. Wes Anderson. 1998.

Ryan's Daughter. Dir. David Lean. 1970.

Sarafina! Dir. Darrell James Roodt. 1992.

Saved! Dir. Brian Dannelly. 2004.

Say Anything. Dir. Cameron Crowe. 1989.

Scary Movie. Dir. Keenan Ivory Wayans. 2000.

School of Life. Dir. William Dear. 2005.

School of Rock. Dir. Richard Linklater. 2003.

School Ties. Dir. Robert Mandel. 1992.

Searching for Bobby Fischer. Dir. Steven Zaillian. 1993.

Shameless. Creators John Wells and Paul Abbott. 2011–.

Sister Act. Dir. Emile Ardolino. 1992.

The Skeleton Twins. Dir. Craig Johnson. 2014.

Sleepers. Dir. Barry Levinson. 1996.

Songcatcher. Dir. Maggie Greenwald. 2000.

The Sound of Music. Dir. Robert Wise. 1965.

South Park: Bigger, Longer, & Uncut. Dir. Trey Parker. 1999.

The Squid and The Whale. Dir. Noah Baumbach. 2005.

Stand and Deliver. Dir. Ramon Menendez. 1987.

Starship Troopers. Dir. Paul Verhoeven. 1997.

Still Alice. Dirs. Richard Glatzer and Wash Westmoreland. 2014.

The Substitute. Dir. Robert Mandel. 1996.

Summer School. Dir. Carl Reiner. 1987.

Surviving Desire. Dir. Hal Hartley. 1993.

Take The Lead. Dir. Liz Friedlander. 2006.

Tea and Sympathy. Dir. Vincente Minnelli. 1956.

The Teacher. Dir. Hikmet Avedis. 1974.

Teacher's Pet. Dir. George Seaton. 1958.

Teachers. Dir. Arthur Hiller. 1984.

Teaching Mrs. Tingle. Dir. Kevin Williamson. 1999.

10 Things I Hate About You. Dir. Gil Junger. 1999.

Terms of Endearment. Dir. James L. Brooks. 1983.

Then She Found Me. Dir. Helen Hunt. 2007.

These Three. Dir. William Wyler. 1936.

Thirteen. Dir. Catherine Hardwicke. 2003.

To Sir, with Love. Dir. James Clavell. 1967.

Top Gun. Dir. Tony Scott. 1986.

Transparent. Creator Jill Soloway. 2014–.

Unexpected. Dir. Kris Swanberg. 2015.

Up The Down Staircase. Dir. Robert Mulligan. 1967.

Varsity Blues. Dir. Brian Robbins. 1999.

Waiting for Superman. Dir. Davis Guggenheim. 2010.

Waterland. Dir. Stephen Gyllenhaal. 1992.

We Are Marshall. Dir. McG. 2006.

We Don't Live Here Anymore. Dir. John Curran. 2004.

Whiplash. Dir. Damien Chazelle. 2014.

Wit. Dir. Mike Nichols. 2001.

The Wire. Creator David Simon. 2002–2008.

Words and Pictures. Dir. Fred Schepisi. 2013.

Wonder Boys. Dir. Curtis Hanson. 2000.

Won't Back Down. Dir. Daniel Barnz. 2012.

X-Men. Dir. Bryan Singer. 2000.

WORKS CITED

AAUW Report. "How Schools Shortchange Girls." 1992.

Abbott, Terry. "More Teachers Are Having Sex With Their Students. Here's How Schools Can Stop Them." *The Washington Post*, 20 Jan. 2015.

Acker, Sandra, editor. *Teachers, Gender and Careers*. New York: Falmer Press, 1989.

Alexander, Michelle. *The New Jim Crow: Mass Incarceration in the Age of Colorblindness*. New York: The New Press, 2012.

Anderson, Carol. *White Rage: The Unspoken Truth of Our Racial Divide*. New York: Bloomsbury USA, 2016.

Anyon, Jean. "Social Class and the Hidden Curriculum of Work." *Journal of Education*, vol. 162, no. 1, 1980, pp. 67–92.

Apple, Michael W. "'Hey Man, I'm Good': The Aesthetics and Ethics of Making Films in Schools." *Reflections from the Heart of Educational Inquiry*, edited by George Willis and William H. Schubert, Albany, NY: State University of New York Press, 1991, pp. 213–221.

Applegate, Carey. "Moving Beyond the Teacher Savior: Education Films, Teacher Identity and Public Discourse." *Exploring Teachers in Fiction and Film: Saviors, Scapegoats and School-marms*, edited by Melanie Shoffner, New York: Routledge, 2016.

Aronowitz, Stanley. "Working-Class Identity and Celluloid Fantasies in the Electronic Age." *Popular Culture: Schooling & Everyday Life*, edited by Henry A. Giroux and Roger I. Simon, New York: Bergin & Garvey, 1989, pp. 197–217.

Atchison, R. Jarrod. "*The Great Debaters*: The Inspiring Story of Melvin B. Tolson." *Screen Lessons: What We Have Learned from Teachers on Television and in the Movies*, edited by Mary M. Dalton and Laura R. Linder, New York: Peter Lang, 2017, pp. 153–157.

Ayers, William. "A Teacher Ain't Nothin' But a Hero." *Images of Schoolteachers in Twentieth-Century America: Paragons, Polarities, Complexities*, edited by Pamela Bolotin Joseph and Gail E. Burnaford, New York: St. Martin's Press, 1993, pp. 147–156.

Bach, Jacqueline. "On Size Does Not Fit All: Cinematic Approaches to the Teaching of Shakespeare." *Changing English*, vol. 16, no. 3, 2009, pp. 323–331.

——. *Reel Education: Documentaries, Biopics and Reality*. New York: Peter Lang Publishers, 2016.

Barlowe, Avram, and Ann Cook. "From Blackboard to Smartboard: Hollywood's Perennially Misleading Teacher Heroes." *Teaching, Learning, and Schooling in Film*, edited by Daniel P. Liston and Ian Parker Renga, New York: Routledge, 2015.

Bauer, Dale M. "Indecent Proposals: Teachers in the Movies." *College English*, vol. 60, no. 3, 1998, pp. 301–317.

Benatar, David. "Two Views of Sexual Ethics: Promiscuity, Pedophilia, and Rape." *Public Affairs Quarterly*, vol. 16, no. 3, 2002, pp. 191–201.

Berger, John. *Ways of Seeing*. New York: Penguin Books, 1972.

Boff, Leonardo. *Saint Francis: A Model for Human Liberation*. Translated by John W. Diercksmeier, New York: Crossroad, 1982.

Boyd, Ashley. "Deconstructing a New Teacher Savior: Paladins and Politics *Won't Back Down*." *Exploring Teachers in Fiction and Film: Saviors, Scapegoats and Schoolmarms*, edited by Melanie Shoffner. New York: Routledge, 2016, pp. 160–70

Bulman, Robert C. *Hollywood Goes to High School: Cinema, Schools, and American Culture*. New York: Worth Publishers, 2015.

Burbach, Harold J. and Margo A. Figgins. "Screen Images of Principals: A New Vision is Needed." NASSP Bulletin. Volume 75, Number 539, December 1991, 52–58.

Casey, Kathleen. "Teacher as Mother: Curriculum Theorizing in the Life Histories of Contemporary Women Teachers." *Cambridge Journal of Education*, vol. 20, no. 3, 1990, pp. 301–320.

——. "Why Do Progressive Women Activists Leave Teaching? Theory, Methodology and Politics in Life-History Research." *Studying Teachers' Lives*, edited by Ivor Goodson, New York: Teachers College Press, 1992, pp. 187–208.

——. *I Answer With My Life: Life Histories of Women Teachers Working for Social Change*. New York: Routledge, 1993.

Casey, Kathleen, and Michael Apple. "Gender and the Conditions of Teachers' Work: The Development of Understanding in America." *Teachers, Gender and Careers*, edited by Sandra Acker, New York: Falmer Press, 1989, pp. 171–186.

Chennault, Ronald E. *Hollywood Films About Schools: Where Race, Politics, and Education Intersect*. New York: Palgrave Macmillan, 2006.

Chodorow, Nancy. *The Reproduction of Mothering: Psychoanalysis and the Sociology of Gender*. Berkeley, CA: University of California Press, 1978.

Coates, Ta-Nehisi. *Between the World and Me*. New York: Spiegel & Grau, 2015.

Crenshaw, Kimberlé. "Mapping the Margins: Intersectionality, Identity Politics, and Violence Against Women of Color." *Stanford Law Review*, vol. 43, no. 9, 1991, pp. 1241–1299.

Currin, Elizabeth. "Solving Problems Like Maria: Governess Guidance in *The Sound of Music*." *Screen Lessons: What We Have Learned from Teachers on Television and in the Movies*, edited by Mary M. Dalton and Laura R. Linder, New York: Peter Lang, 2017, pp. 201–207.

Dalton, Mary M. "The Hollywood Curriculum: Who is the 'Good' Teacher?" *Curriculum Studies*, vol. 3, no. 1, 1995, pp. 23–44.

——. "Revising the Hollywood Curriculum." *Journal of Curriculum and Pedagogy*, vol. 3, no. 2, 2006, pp. 29–34.

——. "The Hollywood View: Protecting the Status Quo in Schools Onscreen." *Mirror Images: Popular Culture and Education*, edited by Diana Silberman Keller, Zvi Bekerman, Henry A. Giroux, and Nicholas C. Burbules, New York: Peter Lang Publishing, 2008, pp. 9–22.

——. "Bad Teacher is Bad for Teachers." *Journal of Popular Film and Television* theme issue "Teaching Popular Film & Television: Critical Media Literacy & Narratives in (Teacher) Education," vol. 41, no. 2, 2013, pp. 78–87.

Dalton, Mary M., and Laura R. Linder. *Teacher TV: Sixty Years of Teachers on Television*. New York: Peter Lang Publishing, 2008.

——. Editors. *Screen Lessons: What We Have Learned From Teachers on Television and in the Movies*. New York: Peter Lang Publishing, 2017.

Dean, Jennifer S. "Teacher as Object in Wes Anderson's *Rushmore*." *Screen Lessons: What We Have Learned from Teachers on Television and in the Movies*, edited by Mary M. Dalton and Laura R. Linder, New York: Peter Lang, 2017, pp. 109–114.

de Lauretis, Teresa. *Alice Doesn't: Feminism, Semiotics, Cinema*. Bloomington, IN: Indiana University Press, 1984.

Denzin, Norman. *Interpretive Biography*, Qualitative Research Series 17. Newbury Park, CA: Sage Publications, 1989.

Deresiewicz, William. "Love on Campus: Why We Should Understand, and Even Encourage, a Certain Sort of Erotic Intensity Between Student and Professor." *The American Scholar*, Summer 2007, pp. 36–46.

——. *Excellent Sheep: The Miseducation of the American Elite and the Way to a Meaningful Life*. New York: Free Press, 2014.

Dewey, John. *Democracy and Education*. New York: The Free Press, 1944.

Doty, Alexander. *Making Things Perfectly Queer*. Minneapolis, MN and London: University of Minnesota Press, 1993.

Dovico, Adam. "Ron Clark: The Real 'Good' Teacher." *Screen Lessons: What We Have Learned from Teachers in Television and the Movies*, edited by Mary M. Dalton and Laura R. Linder, 2017, pp. 3–10.

Duncan, Charles A., Joe Nolan, and Ralph Wood. "See You in the Movies? We Hope Not!" *Journal of Physical Education, Recreation & Dance*, vol. 73, no. 8, 2002, pp. 38–44.

Dyer, Richard, editor. *Gays and Film*. London: British Film Institute, 1977.

Edelman, Rob. "Teachers in the Movies." *American Educator: The Professional Journal of the American Federation of Teachers*, vol. 7, no. 3, 1990, pp. 26–31.

Ehman, Robert. "What Really Is Wrong with Pedophilia." *Public Affairs Quarterly*, vol. 14, no. 2, 2000, pp. 129–140.

Eidsvik, Charles. *Cineliteracy: Film among the Arts*. New York: Random House, 1978.

Eisner, Elliot, and Elizabeth Vallance, editors. "Five Conceptions of Curriculum: Their Roots and Implications for Curriculum Planning." *Conflicting Conceptions of Curriculum*. Berkeley, CA: McCutchan, 1974, pp. 1–18.

Fish, Stanley. "Literature in the Reader: Affective Stylistics." *New Literary History*, vol. 2, no. 1, 1970, pp. 123–162.

———. *Is There a Text in This Class? The Authority of Interpretive Communities.* Cambridge, MA: Harvard University Press, 1980.

Fisher, Roy, Ann Harris, and Christine Jarvis. *Education in Popular Culture: Tell Tales on Teachers and Learners.* Abingdon, England: Routledge, 2008.

Fiske, John. *Understanding Popular Culture.* Boston, MA: Unwin Hyman, 1989.

———. "Cultural Studies and the Culture of Everyday Life." *Cultural Studies*, edited by Lawrence Grossberg, Cary Nelson, and Paula A. Treichler, New York: Routledge, 1992, pp. 154–173.

Flax, Jane. *Thinking Fragments: Psychoanalysis, Feminism, and Postmodernism in the Contemporary West.* Berkeley, CA: University of California Press, 1990.

Freire, Paulo. *Pedagogy of the Oppressed.* Translated by Myra Bergman Ramos. New York: Herder & Herder, 1970.

Gilligan, Carol. *In a Different Voice: Psychological Theory and Women's Development.* Cambridge, MA: Harvard University Press, 1982.

Giroux, Henry A., editor. *Postmodernism, Feminism, and Cultural Politics: Redrawing Educational Boundaries.* Albany, NY: State University of New York Press, 1991.

———. "Resisting Difference: Cultural Studies and the Discourse of Critical Pedagogy." *Cultural Studies*, edited by Lawrence Grossberg, Cary Nelson, and Paula A. Treichler, New York: Routledge, 1992, pp. 199–212.

———. *Disturbing Pleasures: Learning Popular Culture.* New York: Routledge, 1994.

———. "Race, Pedagogy, and Whiteness in *Dangerous Minds.*" *Cineaste*, vol. 22, no. 4, 1996, pp. 46–49.

Giroux, Henry A., and Paulo Freire. "Foreword." *Popular Culture: Schooling & Everyday Life*, edited by Henry A. Giroux and Roger I. Simon, New York: Bergin & Garvey, 1989.

Giroux, Henry A., and Roger I. Simon. "Popular Culture as Pedagogy of Pleasure and Meaning" and "Conclusion: Schooling, Popular Culture, and a Pedagogy of Possibility." *Popular Culture: Schooling & Everyday Life*, edited by Henry A. Giroux and Roger I. Simon, New York: Bergin & Garvey, 1989, pp. 1–29, 219–35.

Glanz, Jeffrey. "From Mr. Wameke to Mr. Rivelle to Mr. Woodman: Images of Principals in Film and Television." American Educational Research Association. Chicago, Illinois, 25, March, 1997, 1–29.

Goering, Christian Z., and Shelbie Witte. "'Good' Teacher as Predator: Crossing the Double Yellow Lines in *Blue Car.*" *Screen Lessons: What We Have Learned from Teachers on Television and in the Movies*, edited by Mary M. Dalton and Laura R. Linder, New York: Peter Lang, 2017, pp. 115–121.

Goodson, Ivor, editor. *Studying Teachers' Lives.* New York: Teachers College Press, 1992.

Gramsci, Antonio. *Selections from the Prison Notebooks of Antonio Gramsci.* Edited and translated by Q. Hoare and G. N. Smith. New York: International, 1980.

Gravells, Jonathan, and Susan Wallace. *Dial M for Mentor: Reflections on Mentoring in Film, Television and Literature.* Charlotte, NC: Information Age Publishing, 2011.

Greene, Maxine. "The Art of Being Present; Educating for Aesthetic Encounters." *Journal of Education*, vol. 166, no. 2, 1985, pp. 123–135.

Gross, Larry, and James D. Woods, editors. *The Columbia Reader on Lesbians and Gay Men in Media, Society, and Politics.* New York: Columbia University Press, 1999.

Grossberg, Lawrence, Cary Nelson, and Paula A. Treichler. *Cultural Studies.* New York: Routledge, 1992.

Grumet, Madeleine R. *Bitter Milk: Women and Teaching.* Amherst, MA: The University of Massachusetts Press, 1988.

Gutiérrez, Gustavo. *A Theology of Liberation.* Maryknoll, NY: Orbis Books, 1973.

Hall, Stuart. "Cultural Studies and its Theoretical Legacies." *Cultural Studies,* edited by Lawrence Grossberg, Cary Nelson, and Paula A. Treichler, New York: Routledge, 1992.

Hanson, Ellis, editor. *Out Takes: Essays on Queer Theory and Film.* Durham, NC: Duke University Press, 1999.

Harris, Chad E. "Race *Up the Down Staircase*: Teacher as Savior and Other Identities." *Screen Lessons: What We Have Learned from Teachers on Television and in the Movies,* edited by Mary M. Dalton and Laura R. Linder, New York: Peter Lang, 2017, pp. 137–142.

hooks, bell. *Teaching to Transgress: Education as the Practice of Freedom.* New York: Routledge, 1994.

Huebner, Dwayne. "Curricular Language and Classroom Meanings." *Curriculum Theorizing: The Reconceptualists,* edited by William Pinar, Berkeley, CA: McCutchan, 1975, pp. 217–236.

Kellner, Douglas. *Critical Theory, Marxism, and Modernity.* Baltimore, MD: Johns Hopkins University Press, 1989.

———. *Media Culture: Cultural Studies, Identity, and Politics between the Modern and the Postmodern.* London: Routledge, 1994.

———. *Cinema Wars: Hollywood Film and Politics in the Bush-Cheney Era.* West Sussex, England: Wiley-Blackwell, 2010.

Keroes, Jo. *Tales Out of School: Gender, Longing, and the Teacher in Fiction and Film.* Carbondale and Edwardsville, IL: Southern Illinois University Press, 1999.

Kindelsperger, Abigail. "*Unexpected* Opportunities: Teaching and Learning While Pregnant." *Screen Lessons: What We Have Learned from Teachers on Television and in the Movies,* edited by Mary M. Dalton and Laura R. Linder, New York: Peter Lang, 2017, pp. 129–133.

Kliebard, Herbert. "Metaphorical Roots of Curriculum Design." *Curriculum Theorizing: The Reconceptualists,* edited by William Pinar, Berkeley, CA: McCutchan, 1975, pp. 84–85.

Kohn, Alfie. *The Schools Our Children Deserve: Moving Beyond Traditional Classrooms and "Tougher Standards."* Boston: Houghton Mifflin Co., 1999.

Kozol, Jonathan. *Savage Inequalities: Children in America's Schools.* New York: Harper Perennial, 1991.

Lebacqz, Karen. *Justice in an Unjust World: Foundations for a Christian Approach to Justice.* Minneapolis, MN: Augsburg Publishing House, 1987.

Lewis, Mark A., and Ian Parker Renga. "(Re)Imagining Life in the Classroom: Inciting Dialogue Through an Examination of Teacher-Student Relationships in Film." *Exploring Teachers in Fiction and Film: Saviors, Scapegoats and Schoolmarms,* edited by Melanie Shoffner, New York: Routledge, 2016, pp. 65–75.

Leopard, Dan. *Teaching with the Screen: Pedagogy, Agency, and Media Culture.* New York: Routledge, 2013.

Long, Sheryl, and Carol A. Pope. "Playing the Role of Teacher: Using Film to Explore Teacher Identities." *Exploring Teachers in Fiction and Film: Saviors, Scapegoats and Schoolmarms*, edited by Melanie Shoffner, New York: Routledge, 2016.

Lyotard, Jean-François. *The Postmodern Condition: A Report on Knowledge. Theory and History of Literature*, vol. 10. Minneapolis, MN: University of Minnesota Press, 1984.

MacKinnon, Catharine. *Toward a Feminist Theory of the State*. Boston, MA: Harvard University Press, 1991.

Mallozzi, Christine. "When Worlds Collide: Van Halen's 'Hot for Teacher' and Gender in the Classroom." *Screen Lessons: What We Have Learned from Teachers on Television and in the Movies*, edited by Mary M. Dalton and Laura R. Linder, New York: Peter Lang, 2017, pp. 101–107.

Marcus, Alan S., editor. *Celluloid Blackboard: Teacher History with Film*. Charlotte, NC: Information Age Publishing, 2007.

McCluskey, Raymond, and Stephen J. McKinney. *How 'The Teacher' is Presented in Literature, History, Religion, and the Arts*. Lewiston, NY: The Edwin Mellon Press, 2013.

McIntosh, Peggy. *White Privilege and Male Privilege: A Personal Account of Coming to See Correspondences Through Work in Women's Studies*. Wellesley, MA: Wellesley College, Center for Research on Women, 1988.

McNeil, Linda M. *Contradictions of Control: School Structure and School Knowledge*. New York: Routledge & Kegan Paul, 1986.

———. *Contradictions of School Reform: Educational Costs of Standardized Testing*. New York: Routledge, 2000.

Means Coleman, Robin Means, Charlton D. McIlwain, and Jessica Moore Matthews. "The Hidden Truths in Contemporary Black Sitcoms." *The Sitcom Reader: America Re-viewed, Still Skewed*, edited by Mary M. Dalton and Laura R. Linder, Albany, New York: State University of New York Press, 2016, pp. 279–294.

Morrison, Toni. *Beloved*. New York: Knopf, 1990.

Mulvey, Laura. *Visual and Other Pleasures*. Bloomington, IN: Indiana University Press, 1989.

Nelson, Margaret. "Using Oral Case Histories to Reconstruct the Experiences of Women Teachers in Vermont, 1900–50." *Studying Teachers' Lives*, edited by Ivor Goodson, New York: Teachers College Press, 1992, pp. 167–186.

Painter, Nell Irvin. *The History of White People*. New York: W. W. Norton & Company, 2010.

Parton, Chea. "Revisionist Films: Detaching From Teacher as Hero/Savior." *Exploring Teachers in Fiction and Film: Saviors, Scapegoats and Schoolmarms*, edited by Melanie Shoffner, New York: Routledge, 2016, pp. 149–159.

Paul, Dierdre Glenn. "The Blackboard Jungle: Critically Interrogating Hollywood's Vision of the Urban Classroom." *Multicultural Review*, vol. 10, no. 1, 2001, pp. 20–27, 58–60.

Perlstein, Daniel, and Leah Faw. "Students without a Cause: *Blackboard Jungle*, High School Movies, and High School Life." *American Popular Culture and Media: From the Blackboard to the Silver Screen*, edited by Sevan G. Terzian and Patrick A. Ryan, New York: Palgrave Macmillan, 2015.

Pieris, Aloysius, S. J. *An Asian Theology of Liberation*. Maryknoll, NY: Orbis Books, 1988.

Primoratz, Igor. "Pedophilia." *Public Affairs Quarterly*, vol. 13, no. 1, 1999, pp. 99–110.

Purpel, David E. *The Moral and Spiritual Crisis in Education: A Curriculum for Justice and Compassion in Education.* New York: Bergin & Garvey, 1989.

Regan, Suzanne. "Bad Teacher: Bad Judgment, Bad Intentions, or Abuse?" *Screen Lessons: What We Have Learned from Teachers on Television and in the Movies,* edited by Mary M. Dalton and Laura R. Linder, New York: Peter Lang, 2017, pp. 123–128.

Renga, Ian Parker. "Exploring the Heroic Teacher Narrative with Help from the Trickster." *Teaching, Learning, and Schooling in Film,* edited by Daniel P. Liston and Ian Parker Renga, New York: Routledge, 2015, pp. 41–55.

Rosenblatt, Louise. *The Reader, The Text, The Poem: The Transactional Theory of the Literary Work.* Carbondale, IL: Southern Illinois Press, 1978.

Rousmaniere, Kate. "Looking at the Man in the Principal's Office." *American Popular Culture and Media: From the Blackboard to the Silver Screen,* edited by Sevan G. Terzian and Patrick A. Ryan, New York: Palgrave Macmillan, 2015, pp. 195–217.

Rubin, Gayle. *Deviations: A Gayle Rubin Reader.* Durham, NC: Duke University Press, 2011.

Ryan, Michael, and Douglas Kellner. *Camera Politica: The Politics and Ideology of Contemporary Hollywood Film.* Bloomington, IN: Indiana University Press, 1988.

Ryan, Patrick A. "Chalk It Up To Experience: The Sacrificial Image of the Teacher in Popular Media, 1945–1959." *American Popular Culture and Media: From the Blackboard to the Silver Screen,* edited by Sevan G. Terzian and Patrick A. Ryan, New York: Palgrave Macmillan, 2015, pp. 85–105.

San Filippo, Maria. "*Transparent* Family Values: Unmasking Sitcom Myths of Gender, Sex(uality), and Money." *The Sitcom Reader: American Re-viewed, Still Skewed,* edited by Mary M. Dalton and Laura R. Linder, SUNY Press, 2016, pp. 305–318.

Searcy, Lara. "*Freedom Writers* as a Narrative for Teaching Social Justice." *Screen Lessons: What We Have Learned from Teachers on Television and in the Movies,* edited by Mary M. Dalton and Laura R. Linder, New York: Peter Lang, 2017, pp. 143–148.

Smith, Carol A. "I Teach Jim and Jane; I Don't Teach Gym." *Exploring Teachers in Fiction and Film: Saviors, Scapegoats and Schoolmarms,* edited by Melanie Shoffner, New York: Routledge, 2016, pp. 103–107.

Soetaert, Ronald, Andrew Mottart, and Ive Verdoodt. "Culture and Pedagogy in Teacher Education." *The Review of Education, Pedagogy, and Cultural Studies,* vol. 26, 2004, pp. 155–174.

Squire, Walter E. "*Chalk*: Overwriting the Savior Narrative." *Exploring Teachers in Fiction and Film: Saviors, Scapegoats and Schoolmarms,* edited by Melanie Shoffner, New York: Routledge, 2016, pp. 171–180.

Stanhope, Kate. "Peak TV: Scripted Series Surpass 400 in 2015." *The Hollywood Reporter,* 16 Dec. 2015.

Stillwaggon, James, and David Jelinek. *Filmed School: Desire, Transgression and the Filmic Fantasy of Pedagogy.* New York: Routledge, 2016.

Trier, James. "Inquiring into 'Techniques of Power' with Preservice Teachers through the 'School Film' *The Paper Chase.*" *Teaching and Teacher Education,* vol. 19, 2003, pp. 543–557.

——. "'Sordid Fantasies': Reading Popular 'Inner-city' School Films as Racialized Texts with Pre-service Teachers." *Race Ethnicity and Education,* vol. 8, no. 2, 2005, pp. 171–189.

———. "Reconceptualizing Literacy Through a Discourse Perspective by Analyzing Literacy Events Represented in Films About Schools." *Journal of Adolescent & Adult Literacy*, vol. 49, no. 8, 2008, pp. 510–523.

Tropiano, Stephen. "Out (and Proud) in America's Classrooms: Gay and Lesbian Teachers on 1970s Television." *Screen Lessons: What We Have Learned from Teachers on Television and in the Movies*, edited by Mary M. Dalton and Laura R. Linder, 2017, pp. 93–99.

Tyack, D. B., and M. H. Strober. "Jobs and Gender: A History of the Structuring of Educational Employment by Sex." *Educational Policy and Management: Sex Differentials*, edited by P. A. Schumuck, W. W. Charters, Jr., and R. O. Carlson, New York: Academic Press, 1981, pp. 131–152.

Waugh, Patricia. *Feminine Fictions: Revisiting the Postmodern*. London: Routledge, 1989.

Weaver, Heather. "Beyond Apples and Ice Cream: The Teacher-Student Relationship as Cinematic Romance, 1919–1939." *Film & History*, vol. 39, no. 1, 2009, pp. 9–20.

Weems, Lisa. "Representations of Substitute Teachers and the Paradoxes of Professionalism." *Journal of Teacher Education*, vol. 54, 2003, pp. 254–265.

Whitney, Jason. "The Role of the Teacher, Real and Imagined." *Exploring Teachers in Fiction and Film: Saviors, Scapegoats and Schoolmarms*, edited by Melanie Shoffner, New York: Routledge, 2016.

Witherell, Carol, and Nel Noddings, editors. *Stories Lives Tell: Narrative and Dialogue in Education*. New York: Teachers College Press, 1991.

INDEX

N

O

P

X

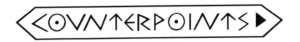

Studies in Criticality

General Editor
Shirley R. Steinberg

Counterpoints publishes the most compelling and imaginative books being written in education today. Grounded on the theoretical advances in criticalism, feminism, and postmodernism in the last two decades of the twentieth century, Counterpoints engages the meaning of these innovations in various forms of educational expression. Committed to the proposition that theoretical literature should be accessible to a variety of audiences, the series insists that its authors avoid esoteric and jargonistic languages that transform educational scholarship into an elite discourse for the initiated. Scholarly work matters only to the degree it affects consciousness and practice at multiple sites. Counterpoints' editorial policy is based on these principles and the ability of scholars to break new ground, to open new conversations, to go where educators have never gone before.

For additional information about this series or for the submission of manuscripts, please contact:

Shirley R. Steinberg
c/o Peter Lang Publishing, Inc.
29 Broadway, 18th floor
New York, New York 10006

To order other books in this series, please contact our Customer Service Department:

(800) 770-LANG (within the U.S.)
(212) 647-7706 (outside the U.S.)
(212) 647-7707 FAX

Or browse online by series:
www.peterlang.com